Reinscribing Moses

Reinscribing Moses

HEINE, KAFKA, FREUD, AND SCHOENBERG IN A EUROPEAN WILDERNESS

Bluma Goldstein

HARVARD UNIVERSITY PRESS
Cambridge, Massachusetts, and London, England 1992

This book is printed on acid-free paper, and its binding materials
have been chosen for strength and durability.

Library of Congress Cataloging-in-Publication Data

Goldstein, Bluma.
  Reinscribing Moses: Heine, Kafka, Freud, and Schoenberg in a
European wilderness / Bluma Goldstein.
    p. cm.
  Includes bibliograpghical references and index
  ISBN 0-674-75406-9 (alk. paper)
  1. Jews—Germany—Cultural assimilation. 2. German literature—Jewish
authors—History and criticism. 3. Moses (Biblical leader) in literature.
  4. Germany—Ethnic relations. I. Title.
DS135.G33G58 1992
943'.004924—dc20
92-3918
CIP

Contents

1

Moses in a European Wilderness: Nineteenth- and Twentieth-Century Germany and Austria

And she bore him a son, and he called his name Gershom:
for he said I have been an alien in a foreign land.

EXODUS 2:22

But the stranger that dwelleth with you shall be unto you
as one born among you, and thou shalt love him as thyself;
for ye were strangers in the land of Egypt . . .

LEVITICUS 19:33–34

For some time I have been interested in problems of Jewish-German (and Jewish-Austrian) identity in the age of emancipation.[1] But the impetus for this inquiry into representations of Moses grew out of a curiosity about the incisive, yet subtle, ways in which literary and cultural texts may communicate attitudes and values about social conditions. Heinrich Heine, Franz Kafka, Sigmund Freud, and Arnold Schoenberg, German and Austrian writers who were Jewish by birth, have all written significantly about Moses. In their works Moses figures seem to wander between bondage and liberation in an urban European desert; and though it may be merely the illusions that an unfamiliar desert landscape can conjure, there are moments when their Moses figures more closely resemble Europeans than traditional images of the biblical prophet. It may not be difficult to understand why a ghettoized Jewish community, before emancipation, would hope for a Moses to liberate it, but what use could these modern, acculturated Jews have for a biblical desert wanderer who had never even entered the promised land? It seems to me that this strange group of Moses figures wandering through European texts offers a small but illuminating insight into the peculiar and passionate struggle with Jewish identity among German and Austrian Jews during the period of emancipation.

In a 1983 symposium on Jews in German literature the literary scholar and critic Hans Mayer indicated that his attempt "to situate the beginnings of a Jewish-German literary history" goes back to what he had once learned in his Bar Mitzvah lessons. "At that time," he noted, "we learned, in the year 1920, that there were in Jewish intellectual history three great epochs, always connected with the name Moses. First the lawgiver and prophet; then Moses ben Maimon; finally Moses ben Mendel."[2] Thus, when a young German Jew was about to be accepted into the adult Jewish community, he was taught a memorable lesson: while the modern era began with Moses Mendelssohn, the foremost Jewish representative of the German Enlightenment, all Jewish history and tradition was grounded in the continuous legacy of the biblical Moses. Although the persistent presence of Moses clearly emphasizes the overriding importance of biblical history, the tripartite division seems to lend to the modern period and to Mendelssohn, a proponent of emancipation, an importance equal to that of the biblical Moses. In any case, the Enlightenment figure has apparently inherited the liberator's mantle from the prophet.

This dual conception of Jewish history—a continuously interpreted biblical legacy and the record of historical changes in Jewish life, particularly in the diaspora—has, however, posed significant difficulties for European Jews. The problematic nature of this twofold commitment was identified by Joseph Roth in March 1933, a few months after the National Socialists had come to power. Roth, who had fled to France from Germany, discussed the issue in a letter to Stefan Zweig who was, like himself, an Austrian, a Jew, and a writer. "The six thousand year old Jewish heritage," he wrote, "cannot be disavowed; but just as little can the two thousand year old *non-Jewish* one. After all we come out of the 'Emancipation,' out of *Humanitas,* out of 'the humane,' rather than out of Egypt. Our ancestors are no less Goethe, Lessing, Herder than Abraham, Isaac, and Jacob."[3] Here the two traditions are presented, namely, the six-thousand-year-old Jewish tradition and the two-thousand-year-old Christian one: the former as ancient, originating in the most distant Patriarchal period of the Bible; the latter as modern, reflected in the relatively recent secular humanism of the eighteenth and nineteenth centuries that still informs cultural and political ideas of the West. For Roth, these traditions have equal value and significance. However, by depicting the Jewish heritage as archaic (after all, the Patriarchs precede the history of the Jewish people as a nation) and socially undeveloped (what is exodus without the legislation of Sinai) and by ignoring four or five millennia of Jewish history, Roth presents a heritage that is hardly relevant for contemporary Europeans. Both the diminished substance of Jewish tradition and the impressive accomplishments of the German one—"Emancipation," "*Humanitas,*" and "the humane," in contrast to the achievements of biblical personages before the advent at Sinai—contribute to a view of society and culture that is for Roth, as for the Jewish German intelligentsia of the past two centuries, synonymous with German or Austrian nationality and European culture.

Though Roth thought that as a people Jews were "in the process of dissolution . . . and will no longer exist in fifty to a hundred years,"[4] he did not renounce Jewish tradition for European history; after all, Abraham, Isaac, and Jacob continue to inform his identity. From the time that emancipation became a possibility European Jews struggled seriously with a dual conception of history, and it is this struggle that characterizes the work of the four major European figures with which this study is concerned.

THE LEVITICAN ADMONITION quoted in the epigraph is a reminder that recurs repeatedly in the Pentateuch. The advice that Jews, because of their painful history as foreigners in Egypt, treat strangers as peers may have provided an appropriate lesson for those about to inhabit a permanent homeland, but one wonders whether it would be equally useful for a people living in the diaspora and unwelcome almost everywhere. This admonition and the many other ethical precepts of Mosaic doctrine—to provide for the poor, support the weak, regulate the manumission of slaves and the distribution of property (the Jubilee Year), for example—are best understood as addressed to those no longer enslaved and already in control of their lives, those who have the authority and wherewithal to affect the lives of others. In an essay on Moses, Ahad Ha'Am indicates that Mosaic legislation was intended for an independent people within their own homeland: "But Moses made laws for the future, for a generation that did not exist."[5] In nineteenth-century Europe they may refer to a generation that no longer existed. Are these ethical ideals suited for a dispersed, homeless people which had for centuries been insulated in impoverished European ghettos, isolated from the cultural life of countries in which they resided, prohibited from participating in the world of social and historical change? Were they feasible for a people of outsiders which itself did not have the option of entertaining strangers?

Though in many instances generations of Jews had lived in a host country, restrictive conditions imposed on them all too often produced a seemingly permanent and unalterable strangeness. Even the Mosaic legacy seemed imprisoned and impotent in ghettoized, disenfranchised communities, which were sorely in need of another Moses to liberate them and their ethical tradition. This Moses did not materialize, but the Enlightenment and the French Revolution did. And within the ensuing century the Jews of Europe were politically emancipated and therewith confronted with the extraordinary tasks not only of adjusting to a society that for so long had been regarded as superior and inaccessible, but of maintaining their own Jewish identity and, as it were, emancipating a Mosaic legacy without violating or losing it.

In the introduction to a book of his essays, *Emancipation and Assimilation*, Jacob Katz notes that although forms of assimilation took place in all countries in which Jews achieved civil rights, "in no other country did it assume the character of a social program, hailed by the supporters of emancipation, Gentiles and Jews alike, as in Germany. The emancipation of the Jews was conceived there as constituting the beginning of a process of social adaptation which would ultimately lead to full social integration."[6] Here Katz refers to Germany, but the movement toward integrating Jews into Austrian society was similarly intense, though acculturated Jews in Austria retained connections with the Jewish community more readily than in Germany.[7] While emancipation was in fact but a small accompaniment to the extensive modernization of European society that included the development of secular nation-states as well as profound political and economic transformations,[8] Jews who had gained or anticipated emancipation were faced with a myriad of problems: considerable resistance and opposition in the larger population; ongoing legislation which attempted to limit recently acquired civil rights and to qualify "equality"; and a struggle with a Jewish tradition which, especially for those who sought greater political and social freedom, was seen as outmoded and superfluous.

Legal emancipation did not solve or dissolve the problems of the diaspora; it merely transferred them from the political to the social arena.[9] No longer did restrictive legislation disable the Jewish population; instead, external and internal pressures interfered with the realization of equality. Externally, many non-Jews, even those who advocated a truly emancipated society, wanted Jews to alter their lives radically so as to conform with the conventions of the larger society.[10] Assimilation was expected to result in a Jewish population indistinguishable from that of the dominant society, which in Germany and Austria was regarded as Christian. "In the mental map of the future drawn up by the emancipators," Reinhard Rürup observes, "the emancipation of the Jews was tantamount to the liquidation of Jewry, the process by which Jewry was to be absorbed as it were, into the great melting pot of the civic society, leaving no residue."[11] Internally, those Jews who wanted to or did assimilate were not always willing to fulfill the emancipators' expectations, namely, to change occupations, move to rural areas, and relinquish Jewish communal or religious allegiances.[12] Moreover, in the majority society persistent dissatisfaction with the results of modernization, with the "inadequate assimilation" of the Jews, and even with their accomplishments fueled, especially in the latter decades of the nineteenth century, the onset of intense antisemitism and Jewish nationalism.[13] Both activities serve as clear signs of the pragmatic failure of emancipation.

Emancipation may have provided legal entry into the dominant society, but the terms of admission were determined by the majority, whose persistent and increasing demands made it very difficult for Jews to enjoy the benefits of equality. Indeed, the perception of the Jew as a worthy equal was slow in coming. Since ultimately emancipation was controlled by those in power, its realization made it a gift of the dominant society to a minority in their midst, a gift which spoke, on the one hand, to the largesse and the power of the grantor and, on the other, to the inferiority and impotence of the grantee. In fact, the entire process of emancipation, even when pursued with the best of intentions, reinforced perceptions of the Christian population as powerful and virtuous and of the Jews as an alien, deficient, and generally undesirable people, who could be tolerated only when sufficiently improved or completely assimilated. These perceptions with which Jews had to contend made emancipation and integration desirable and necessary, but also demeaning; in addition, they called into question the values of the dominant society as well as the value or efficacy of the minority community. Such difficulties notwithstanding, Jews now had the possibility of choice: they could, as German or Austrian nationals, adhere to Judaism and the Jewish community; assimilate into the dominant culture; or participate in the national and European culture while maintaining their allegiance to Jewish tradition. This opportunity became, for many, the occasion of a profoundly disturbing identity struggle, which is reflected in many writings of even the most assimilated Jews who used German, their native language, to communicate their insights.[14] It is with reflections of this struggle with identity that this study is largely concerned.

INVESTIGATIONS into the experiences of Jews in Germany and Austria can hardly illuminate all the particular ways in which so varied a population understood and contended with their lives during this time of social and political transformation. And while there does exist an abundance of material that focuses on the struggle with their identity as Jews and as Germans or Austrians— memoirs, autobiographies, interviews, essays, fictional accounts, to mention some of the more obvious sources—no one avenue provides an accurate account, nor can all avenues be expected to yield an adequate picture of the multifarious experiences of the diverse groups. The problem which confronted me was how best to commence an inquiry into the significant characteristics of diaspora life in the age of emancipation; or, more precisely, how most effectively to approach the issues of Jewish-German identity when, in addition to the social and mental life of Jews in the German-speaking world, one is concerned with specific cultural representations and the distinctive texture of literary texts and artistic forms.

Heine, Kafka, Freud, and Schoenberg were all marginal Jews in that they regarded themselves as not primarily Jewish and considered their work to be essentially part of the dominant European culture; nevertheless, all turned to biblical history and interpreted significant aspects of the Mosaic tradition in works which explored their own world and lives. Wittingly or not, they thereby affirmed a dual conception of history, for within the context of modern social history and cultural expression, they helped revive the biblical story and preserve that tradition.

All were born and educated in German-speaking countries; all lived in a period of emancipation when equality for Jews was not a social reality;[15] all considered themselves Germans or Austrians and wrote their major works in German; all were Jews who, to varying degrees and at different times in their lives, considered their Jewishness to be of lesser importance than their participation in the European cultural milieu. The earliest of these, Heine, was born in 1797 after the French Revolution, but before any proclamations of emancipation in Germany; the final figure, Schoenberg, lived in the period of full emancipation and died six years after the end of World War II, during which the Germans decimated the European Jewish community. Coincidentally, both converted to Protestantism and both regretted their conversions, though only Schoenberg returned to Judaism. Although all four had written about Moses more than once, it was mainly in their later years that they created their most probing interpretations: Heine in his 1854 *Confessions (Geständnisse)*, written two years before his death; Kafka after 1920 in conversations with the young poet Gustav Janouch and two years before his death in his 1922 diary; Freud in *The Man Moses and Monotheistic Religion (Der Mann Moses und die monotheistische Religion)*,[16] completed in 1938, a year before he died; and Schoenberg in his opera *Moses and Aaron (Moses und Aron)*, still unfinished at the time of his death in 1951.

One intriguing aspect of these works is the resemblance between the depictions of Moses and salient aspects of the writers themselves, who seem, in part, to have created Moses in their own image. In doing so, they carved into the bedrock of Judaism their own painful portrait as artist or thinker living in an age of assimilation even as they inscribed the founder of the nation Israel into the documents of their German culture. Thus, in the waning years of his life, Heine described Moses as a nascent socialist and a great artist who had forged out of an inchoate mass a monumental nation, thereby gracing the prophet with the two characteristics Heine most valued in himself. In a bleak vision Kafka characterized himself as having wandered, like Moses, in the desert for forty years, but still struggling for liberation; and in a more confident moment, he saw a resemblance between Moses and a writer who, like the prophet, had the task of leading people toward a higher and purer existence. Freud's perception of his own mission in life resembles that of the last Moses he constructs, the Moses of *Moses and Monotheism*. With a "revolutionary" theory as the foundation for liberation, he, like Moses, will lead people out of bondage; he too will leave behind his prophets, the psychoanalysts, to keep his great message alive; and he hopes that his impending death—like the murder of Moses that he invents—will help to disseminate more widely his monumental idea, psychoanalysis, and grant it permanent, if not eternal, life. Schoenberg shares with his Moses an overwhelming concern about the inadequacy of available expressive means to deliver a message, especially if that message is spiritual and, like the biblical God himself, defies limitation. While it is difficult to know why these writers focused so intently on Moses and why they did so at the close of their lives, it is clear that whatever cultural reward and social accomplishment they had attained did not eliminate the importance of Jewish tradition. Their works about Moses reveal powerful efforts to come to terms with their origins and the origins of Jews as a people—origins that assimilation and even acceptance did not erase.

The discourses about Moses that these writers create are so different in subject, content, and idea, and in genre, form, and discipline, that one may forget that these various Moseses derive from a single figure. Heine was actively involved in politics and social criticism, but his interests, like Kafka's, were essentially literary; however, though Heine wrote much poetry and fictional prose and Kafka stories, parables, and aphorisms, their writings about Moses are largely discursive and, at times, clearly autobiographical. Freud's major work on Moses is a psychoanalytic interpretation of aspects of the Moses story and of the legacy that lives on in the Jewish people, though he insists on its historical factuality; he titled the earliest (1934) draft of this work *The Man Moses, an Historical Novel (Der Mann Moses, ein historischer Roman).* And Schoenberg was essentially a composer who, in addition to writing the texts to his songs and opera, wrote an unpublished drama, "The Biblical Way" ("Der Biblische Weg"),[17] in which aspects of the Moses story inform the contemporary subject matter.

Particular concerns with the biblical Moses may differ widely among the four, but their works disclose a special attraction to the contrasts and tensions in the Moses figure and legacy. Although a conflict between the ineffability of the divine message and the limitations of human communication forms the overt primary issue of Schoenberg's *Moses and Aaron*, other tensions inform works of the other writers in more subtle ways, namely, as implicit yet presumably self-evident aspects of the Moses story. Three general tensions or contrapuntal aspects strike me as having central significance, though not all of them are present in each work, nor is their presence always of equal intensity or importance. While a more detailed exploration of the separate texts has been reserved for later chapters, it is perhaps useful to introduce here the salient aspects of these tensions and to suggest their larger significance for European Jews who were struggling with the cultural and social contradictions of their time. The three tensions are: (1) Moses as quintessential diaspora Jew/human being and Moses as creator of the nation Israel; (2) Moses as liberator and universal lawgiver and Moses as unassimilable Jew; (3) Moses as a remarkable coalescence of individual fulfillment and social accomplishment and Moses as solitary and isolated figure.

(1) *Moses as quintessential diaspora Jew/human being and Moses as creator of the nation Israel.* Moses, liberator and leader of the Jewish people, is not permitted to enter the promised homeland. He lives in the diaspora throughout his life and may indeed have acknowledged the significance of this position in naming his eldest son Gershom. He did in fact name the child for himself, specifically for his status as resident alien in Midian: "And he called his name Gershom for he said, I have been an alien in a foreign land."[18] Traditional rabbinical commentary indicates that *ger* means 'alien resident' and *sham* means 'there'. Since, in addition, the proper name *Gershom* contains within it the letters of the verb root, *g.r.s.*, which means 'to drive out' or 'to banish', there is also the possibility that this status may refer as well to Moses' earlier sojourn in Egypt, suggesting an ongoing diaspora existence. That the next generation will bear the mark of the alien points to the great significance of that status.

Yet it was, of course, the sojourn in the desert that provided Moses and the Jewish people with a unique and common national history, a history which documents the genesis of the Jews as a people and records the conditions necessary for the preservation of the nation. While the people are educated and prepared for nationhood in the desert, they are promised a permanent home in which Israel will thrive. Moses, however, who liberated his people and led them to the promised homeland, dies where he had always lived—in the diaspora. But because Moses was a truly exceptional person and led a thoroughly productive and fulfilled life without setting foot in the new national home, his life in the diaspora may be perceived as a model of what every human life could and should be, namely, a continuous readying of oneself and others for the task of leading an ethical and productive life.

(2) *Moses as liberator and universal lawgiver and Moses as unassimilable Jew.* Moses is traditionally regarded as the one who liberated the Jews from Egyptian slavery and led them toward a promised homeland, though the Bible again and again credits God with those deeds and the Passover Haggadah, the text for the ritual commemoration of that event, makes no mention of his name. Indeed, Moses has become a heroic emancipator for people other than Jews, as his role, for example, in the spirituals and literature of African Americans attests.[19] However, he is regarded as a liberator not solely because he freed his people from Egyptian slavery, but because through legislation—ethical and ritual, civil and criminal—he created the foundation for permanent liberation, for a future just society. One may question the universality of the legislation, but it is clear that the laws, especially the ethical tenets, were meant to apply alike to everyone, Jew and alien, citizen and stranger, master and servant.[20]

While Moses as liberator and lawgiver is generally regarded as a universal figure, he is also perceived as an exemplary unassimilable Jew. Moses had since infancy led a privileged life in Pharaoh's palace, but when as a young man he witnessed an Egyptian beating a Jew, he slew the slavemaster. As a result of this act, he had to flee the country, returning only to lead the enslaved Jews out of that alien land. Basing Moses' unassimilability on this episode is problematic, for it assumes he acted as he did primarily because the victim was a Jew, whereas a strong sense of justice may have evoked a similar reaction to any maltreated person, Jew or not. Of course, acting out of a sense of justice and acting on behalf of a Jew who is being brutalized are not mutually exclusive, but in neither instance can it be assumed that Moses' behavior is explained by his unassimilability. Nevertheless, the view that he is the "prototype of the unassimilable Jew" persists.[21]

(3) *Moses as a remarkable coalescence of individual fulfillment and social accomplishment and Moses as solitary and isolated figure.* Moses is an active and constructive leader; in fact, the more Moses fulfills himself as leader, lawgiver, and teacher, the more he accomplishes his goal of creating out of a group of former slaves a just nation capable of self-governance. Ultimately, he forms himself as he forms his people, that is, he transforms himself into a leader in the process of transforming his people into the nation Israel. Individual fulfillment and social mission are thus intimately and inextricably intertwined.

Yet despite his intense social involvement, Moses is a solitary figure whose solitude is, in large part, connected with his relationship to God. Alone, he encounters God, whether at the burning bush, for forty days on the mountain when he receives the Decalogue, or in the tent outside the people's encampment. However, he also keeps his distance from the people, and this separation is intensified when, on returning with the Decalogue a second time, he veils his face to conceal his shining skin. Although he mediates between God and the people, he remains separate from them even as he labors to transform these recalcitrant multitudes into a coherent and ethically committed nation. Quite apart from Moses' special relationship with God, there seem to be two deep-seated struggles that account for his solitude: one is internal and involves his own sense of inadequacy in the face of divine expectations; the other is an external struggle with a people who, unlike himself, neither understands nor can keep faith with an uncompromising monotheism and its rigorous demands.

What seems to be common to all three tensions is the contrast between a larger condition which is of social or universal import and one which is essentially limited to the particulars of an individual. The Moses who struggled with these tensions was, however, also able to fulfill antagonistic conditions: he completed his great social mission, namely, creating a nation of which he was part, and yet retained a unique individual identity. German and Austrian Jews living in the period of legal emancipation and social inequality could, it seems to me, recognize in Moses' experiences their own difficult struggles to succeed as individuals and socially committed citizens. After all, they knew what it was to be offered opportunities to integrate into European society and participate in its highly valued culture and, nevertheless, to be frustrated continually in that effort; and they knew too how difficult it was to express their individuality in a society in which prejudice and intimidation persisted. Jews who wanted to assimilate were suspended between a Jewish world in which they were no longer at home and the dominant society in which they were not welcome. Just when they thought they might be able to settle comfortably into a European homeland, they found themselves inhabiting a lonely, unstable space with no firm ground on which to build their lives or secure their identities.[22]

Like the Moses who struggled with conflicting tendencies, German and Austrian Jews were confronted with seemingly insurmountable obstacles to individual and social fulfillment. However, unlike Moses, who realized that no liberation was possible for a powerless minority within an alien nation, most European Jews persistently sought equality and justice in the countries in which they lived. Whereas the tensions Moses experienced came to pass largely after the exodus and during the forty years spent in the wilderness, modern, acculturated Jews were still wrestling in and with their own Egypt. Heine, Kafka, Freud, and Schoenberg spent a lifetime absorbing the culture and values of the dominant population, but they also struggled for opportunities to fulfill themselves as unique individuals and social beings. How interesting, then, that at the end of their lives they should turn to a Moses who had left Egypt and, isolated with his people in the diaspora of a desert, had finally learned the lessons of true liberation. And how enviable must this Moses have appeared, a person whose struggle with great tensions and hardships resulted in national solidarity as well as a strong personal identity.

LET ME CONCLUDE this introduction by reflecting on some of the methodological difficulties. Not only does this study explore the texts about Moses of four Jewish writers who, for the most part and for most of their lives, strove for acceptance as part of the European intelligentsia; it also examines the political and cultural significance of these works in nineteenth- and twentieth-century Germany and Austria. I focus largely on close readings of the texts and probe their relationship to the historical and political interactions which concerned the Jewish population in those countries. Making the connections between these texts and contexts, however, was not easily accomplished. In my view, it is not the primary function of texts to document historical and social processes, although they may indeed do that; nor should historical information be expected to explain the cultural content of texts. Texts perceived simply as either embedded in a social order or having absorbed social ideas and values tend to be regarded as coterminous, if not identified, with the context. But how then does one understand a text which adopts a critical or oppositional stance to the context? Or a text which is significantly related to more than one context—here, for example, the dominant Western European tradition as well as the minority Jewish one—if these contexts have conflicting values and expectations?

I found that if I wanted to understand the interrelated literary, cultural, and social dimensions of these writings about Moses, the most compelling and productive cross-disciplinary approach would be to maintain, where possible, separate yet interrelated spheres of inquiry and discourse. And, hoping to illuminate not only each text as a complex of individual creativity and social and political factors, but some aspects of the cultural and historical contexts as well, I have opted to move back and forth between texts and contexts. Such a procedure, of course, presupposes the separability of text and social context, that is, a rejection of both extreme positions: that everything is textual; that everything is "reality-based." The conceptual discreteness of text and contexts creates a basis for a dialectical and critical relationship between them that is especially important when considering such issues as inequality and the interplay of dominant and subordinate traditions. A major problem that occurs in societies of social and political inequality is the valorization of the ideas and values of the dominant sector at the expense of those of a minority population, particularly if the minority is regarded as inferior or inconsequential. Within the social and cultural agenda of mainstream societies in which heterogeneity, inequality, and the importance of power have interlocking roles, oppositional ideas and values are often resisted, deemed unimportant, or even subjected to erasure. Under such conditions, texts perceived as either having absorbed social values or being embedded in the social context tend to be identified with the dominant social values. It is precisely this coalescence that needs to be scrutinized if the oppositional stance of the text as a challenge to the social context is to be recognized. Indeed, the distinctness of text and context allows for the intersection of a text with more than one context and with contexts other than that of the majority society.

Heine, Kafka, Freud, and Schoenberg—who were eager to assimilate into the mainstream and for whom Jewishness and Judaism were, for a large part of their lives, of negligible importance—provide an opportunity to probe significant connections between the attachment of these Jewish German and Austrian writers to the dominant culture and social order and their engagement with Jewish tradition. A vital element that plays a role here is the function of particular cultural contexts in which the writings on Moses are understood. Considered within the European tradition of letters, a tradition to which they had long declared allegiance, their writings about Moses and their interest in Judaism occupy a place close to the margins, but they are absolutely central within Jewish cultural tradition. Thus, within the discourse of the dominant culture, these works may be viewed as reflecting the writers' despair with the unfulfilled promises of emancipation, assimilation, and equal social opportunity; while within that of Jewish tradition, these texts about Moses may, through this seminal figure instrumental in the liberation of an entire people, articulate an alternative positive paradigm of freedom and national Jewish identity. Best regarded as complex responses to hostile political conditions, the works reflect, depending on the perspective assumed, either a continuing, albeit disillusioned, commitment to the dominant culture or a return to the Judaism of forebears—more likely both. Since these writers, who for most of their lives regarded themselves as European intellectuals, were moved primarily by adverse social and political conditions to come to terms with their Jewishness, their texts about Moses must be understood in their complex relationship to both social contexts, the German or Austrian and the Jewish.

While the great variation among these writings about Moses may be attributed to the predilections or particular interests of the individual writers, it seems to me that the role of the Moses figures as differing interpretations of social and political factors should not be underestimated. There has been a general tendency to regard these works as primarily reflecting Jewish interests, but they were written by Jews who in fact saw themselves as participating in the dominant cultural traditions and published in mainstream presses. To consign these texts solely to a minority cultural context is also to remove them from the complex cultural contexts within which they were conceived, and ultimately to divest them of much of their political significance. If many of these texts explore and interpret the very painful historical experiences of Jews in a hostile world, should they not be understood within the contexts of that world? It is, after all, in the dominant society where legal and social antisemitism threatens the Jewish population and its traditions; and it is within that context that these works attain their full meaning and their value as social and cultural critiques. These texts may also be interpreted as central to Jewish tradition; but that context must be understood in its uneasy and subordinate relationship to the dominant society. Of course, the political significance of these works may also be repressed if, conversely, within the context of the dominant culture the texts are "de-Judaized"—that is, if the social conditions of the Jews are ignored and the Moses figures are perceived, for example, merely as general metaphors for freedom. For their political and social critiques to be available, these texts must not be ghettoized, but must be read in relation to their multiple contexts. Indeed, reinscribing these writings about Moses, which are rooted in the Jewish tradition, into the dominant culture within which they arose may prevent their erasure as cultural and political critiques of consequence.

The very diverse experiences among the four writers considered here account for both the considerable differences and the cohesiveness in this study. These writers lived in different environments—Heine in Germany and Paris, Kafka in Prague, Freud in Vienna and finally in England, and Schoenberg in Vienna, Berlin, and the United States—and their lives span a century and a half, from Heine's birth in 1797 to Schoenberg's death in 1951. Their differences extend to their interests, politics, values, and even the media in which they worked—literature, psychology, and music. Yet, as Jews in an age of flawed emancipation and troubled assimilation, they shared a common experience of prejudice and persecution. At one point or another in their lives, each of them articulated views about the dominant political and social conditions in writings about Moses. And Moses was, for them, less a figure of religious history than a cultural metaphor that varied widely with the individual writer's particular interests. Heine and Freud even had substantially different conceptions of Moses at different times in their lives, but in each instance they were clearly concerned with the tensions experienced by Jews disadvantaged in antagonistic societies.

The differences extend not only to the particular interpretations of Moses, but to the magnitude of the texts as well. Heine's writings about Moses appear in 1840 and after 1848, Kafka's in the early 1920s; and although these texts are brief—perhaps a handful of pages—they are significant and powerful. Both writers were, after all, superlative crafters of aphoristic statement; complex and profound experiences were often articulated in a single phrase or simple sentence. Neither the brevity of their texts nor that of the chapters devoted to them in this study should imply a diminished significance. By far the longest chapter is the discussion of Freud's writings; and it is also true that his most complex work on Moses, *Moses and Monotheism,* is the most extensive and comprehensive of any of the texts considered. The length of the chapters varies with the differences between the texts under discussion; and a good argument could be mounted that the attention to Moses in these works reflects significant changes in political, social, and cultural conditions. If these writings about Moses are regarded, in part at least, as responses to hostile activities directed toward Jews, then it is probably not fortuitous that the most comprehensive works, namely, the Freud and Schoenberg texts, were written during a period in which virulent antisemitism proved cataclysmic for the Jewish people: from the time the National Socialists were coming to power through World War II into the postwar period. Both Freud and Schoenberg were to experience in the dislocations of their own lives the force of Nazi brutality; only Schoenberg lived to learn about the decimation of European Jewry during those years. Schoenberg's experience as a Jew may explain, at least in part, not only an ongoing preoccupation with the opera *Moses and Aaron* for almost a quarter of a century until his death, but also his inability to complete it.

The most prominent of the disciplinary contexts relevant to the subject of this study are social and political history, the dominant and minority cultural traditions, and the social context of family history, which often corresponds to the social history of an epoch. By following a trajectory between these contexts and the individual texts, by calling attention to the boundaries and the evidence of interaction, I try to allow for the recognition, on the one hand, of idiosyncratic characteristics in individual experience and particular texts and, on the other, of a commonality of experience that haunted many Jews in nineteenth- and twentieth-century Germany and Austria. The result is not a completed tapestry, but rather sets of warp and woof and intimations of a design so infinitely varied and changing that even an endless number of weavers will not make it appear in its entirety. The validity of such a project, however, lies not in completion, but in the quality of the materials and a design that is continually generated and reshaped by the complex assemblage of experiences.

2

Heinrich Heine: Hellenism, Christianity, and the Triumph of Moses

In 1797, the year of Harry Heine's birth—Heinrich was the baptismal name he acquired almost three decades later—Europe was on the threshold of the modern era. Enormous advances in technology, industry, and commerce were transforming England, France, and Germany; feudal institutions and absolutist governments which did not facilitate progress were dissolving or being dismantled; and new capitalist bourgeois systems, founded on the primacy of individual rights and private property, were being constructed. The idea was also beginning to emerge that unequal and humiliating treatment of the Jewish population was an archaic medieval vestige. Emancipation had already been a concern in Germany during the second half of the eighteenth century, when Enlightenment thinkers such as Gotthold Ephraim Lessing, Moses Mendelssohn, and Christian Wilhelm Dohm argued that equality was the only solution demanded by reason.[1] It was not, however, until the French Revolution, with its Declaration of the Rights of Man (which did not originally apply to Jews), and the introduction of the Napoleonic Code into French-occupied Germany that the status of Jews became a significant political issue and one also not limited to them.[2]

Because the political changes and social dislocations during Heine's lifetime are generally representative of an ongoing situation that fomented turmoil and uncertainty among Jews in European countries for almost a century of struggle for emancipation, a summary of significant moments in his early life may illuminate the overall situation of German Jews in that period. Heine was born in the Rhineland in Düsseldorf, a city with three hundred Jews in a total population of 15,000, largely Catholic. Because no ghetto existed, there were relatively free personal and professional relations between Jews and Gentiles. In 1809 the Napoleonic Code was introduced into the French-occupied Rhineland, and Jews enjoyed legal equality, with the limitations, however, imposed by Napoleon's 1808 "Décret infâme," which restricted certain economic practices by Jews for a ten-year period.[3] Although after the fall of Napoleon this decree was not renewed in France, it remained in force until 1847 in regions of the Rhineland which in 1815 became part of Prussia. Actually one of the most critical events for Prussian Jews was the 1812 "Judenedikt" which, under certain conditions, granted residency and Prussian citizenship to Jews living in Prussian lands. Jews could now hold academic posts and serve in the military, though not as military officers or administrators. In 1815, however, progress suffered a major blow at the special international Congress convened in Vienna to attempt the reconstruction of Europe after Napoleon's defeat. Because a number of delegates, including those from Prussia, were seeking a uniform European formula for improving the political lot of the Jews, the assembly took up the "Jewish question." Article XVI, which was to have assured Jews the same equal rights in every state, had been adopted, but was surreptitiously altered so that in the final version these rights were allotted *by* individual states. Now particular states retained the option of enacting whatever discriminatory legislation they desired, and many did.[4]

In the ensuing years the situation of Jews in Germany became even more insecure and volatile. Fomented by Napoleonic policies, severe economic crises and food shortages fueled reactionary nationalism and encouraged anti-Jewish activity, the most notable of which were the Hep-Hep riots of 1819.[5] Liberties were retracted and restrictions reinstituted. In Prussia, for example, there were eighteen new restrictive laws, one of which—an 1822 ordinance prohibiting Jews from holding academic positions—was the primary impetus for the conversions of Heine and Eduard Gans, Heine's colleague in the university and the Society for Culture and Science of the Jews (Verein für Cultur und Wissenschaft der Juden). Shortly after converting, Gans was appointed to a university post he had sought.[6] In 1848, a time of revolutionary fervor in Europe, an upsurge of liberalism brought significant progress in the movement toward emancipation. This was, however, short-lived; for soon thereafter reaction set in, gains were annulled, and conditions in some instances became worse than before. In Prussia, for example, constitutional changes of 1848 that eliminated exceptions which applied to Jews were annulled in 1851, and not until almost two decades later was full emancipation instituted. For those who wanted emancipation the paths were hazardous and unpredictable, the solutions illusory or inadequate, and their ambitions and accomplishments again and again undermined or endangered. Remaining a Jew was problematic and being accepted as a German—that is, a Christian—virtually impossible, as the course of Heine's life attests.

Heine and Judaism

Although Heine was not shy about revealing either the details of his life or his opinions and observations, assessing the extent of his involvement with Judaism and Jewish affairs is no simple task.[7] He left no systematic account of his views on these subjects; and scholars differ widely about his knowledge of things Jewish (be they Hebrew and Yiddish, customs and rituals, literature and culture), the depth of that knowledge, and when it was acquired. Readers concerned with factual information about Heine's origins and ideas may have to live with the discomfort and skepticism that at times the writer himself seemed to harbor about the details of his own life and interests. Yet entering the debate about whether Heine's family was orthodox or even observant, how long he attended Hebrew school as a child, and whether or not he was a *bar mitzvah* would, it seems to me, only impede the way to the homespun Moses that Heine discarded in his youth or to the monumental one he created at the end of his days for his own final exodus. Actually, for the purposes of this study the barest outline of his involvement should suffice.

The Jewish commitments of Heine's family show the effects of the process of secularization, modernization, and nascent emancipation that had begun in the eighteenth century. He was born into a Jewish family which was probably not orthodox. Although his father was a member of a Jewish community burial society and an orthodox benevolent society (Society for Humanitarian Donations and the Recitation of the Psalms [Gesellschaft zur Ausübung menschenfreundlicher Handlungen und zum Rezitieren der Psalmen]), he also belonged to the Freemasons.[8] According to Heine, whose recollections may not always be accurate, his mother was an ardent deist, but apparently also an observant Jew,[9] who nevertheless did not permit a commitment to Judaism to interfere with her exalted ambitions for her son's future: at different times she is said to have urged him to become a high military officer, an influential banker, and, in her old age, regretted that she had not directed him into the priesthood.[10] As a young child Heine did attend a communal Hebrew school for a period of between two and five years.[11] Beginning in 1804 he was educated in Catholic schools, which were the common schools of Düsseldorf, and finally at a business school.

After some months of working without success in the commercial sector, his wealthy uncle Salomon Heine sent him to the university to study law, but Heine spent his best moments there reading literature and history. In 1822, while at the University in Berlin, he joined the Society for the Culture and Science of the Jews (Verein für Cultur und Wissenschaft der Juden), a group of Jewish intellectuals—philosophers, philologists, historians, among others—who had a serious interest in Jewish culture.[12] The various aims of the Society were all directed at integrating the Jewish people, their culture, and their religion into general European society and culture; by applying scientific methods of research to

Jewish history and culture, it endeavored to make especially Jews, but non-Jews as well, conscious of a minority heritage which had great intrinsic value and was also an integral part of the dominant culture. Even though the Society had a short life (a mere five years from 1819 through 1824), and Heine's tenure there lasted only until he departed Berlin in 1823, the Society, its members, and its work seem to have impressed him significantly and left a notable mark on his development.[13] It brought him into contact not only with a variety of Jewish cultural, historical, and social materials, but also with contemporary thinkers who regarded these materials with scholarly seriousness. Jewish culture was not just a record of archaic traditions, a history of suffering, and an uncomfortable existence, but a reality which should be studied, one which could contribute much to the understanding of European and world culture. It is probably not incidental that soon after he departed Berlin, he was reading a history of Jews and their religion in the Christian era and had begun work on an epic about Jewish life in the Middle Ages, *The Rabbi of Bacherach: A Fragment (Der Rabbi von Bacherach: Ein Fragment).*[14] The novel treats the persisting conjunction of liberation and persecution in the attempt made by strangers to fabricate a case of ritual murder against the Jews during the Passover Seder meal, the event that celebrates the liberation of the Jews from Egyptian oppression. Heine did not complete the work; but significantly, sixteen years later, in 1840, reviled at the blood libel charges against Jews in Damascus,[15] he returned to this work of medieval persecution. Once again, however, it was left unfinished.

In June 1825, just a year after he had undertaken *The Rabbi of Bacherach* and a month before he received a doctorate in jurisprudence, Heine was baptized in the Lutheran church. Although the motivation for his conversion seems to have been largely opportunistic, the circumstances surrounding his decision bespeak a complexity which helps to explain the dynamics that moved others to baptism. Without financial means and having to rely on income solicited from a wealthy uncle, he hoped that his law degree would lead to a lucrative career, but letters to his good friend and Society colleague Moses Moser express fears that it would not.[16] The 1822 Prussian prohibition of academic positions for Jews and general prejudice against appointing Jews to administrative posts made it highly unlikely that he could attain a position he wanted. Baptism was, then, an avenue to which many were turning. "The baptismal certificate," he remarked in one of his aphoristic statements, "is the entry ticket to European culture."[17] Religion does not seem to have been a motivating factor. Heine may have harbored religious sentiments, but he certainly expressed throughout his life a deep antagonism to organized religion, to what he referred as "positive religions"; less than two years before his conversion, he wrote Moser that he was "the born enemy of all positive religions," but that he would nevertheless remain an outspoken advocate for "the rights of the Jews and their civil equality."[18] Yet I think it fair to conclude that while Heine's conversion from Judaism was opportunistic, opting for Protestantism and not Catholicism was more principled than not. Protestantism was of course the state religion of Prussia, but Heine also held the Reformation in high esteem for its progressive stance. It had, after all, championed freedom of thought and laid the foundation for a philosophical revolution of which Kant and Hegel were heirs and with which Heine was in sympathy.[19]

Regret about having converted was not long in coming. Six months afterward he wrote to Moser: "I would be very sorry if my own baptism could appear to you in a favorable light. I assure you if the laws had permitted stealing silver spoons, I would not have had myself baptised."[20] Baptism did not bring the work he needed for self-sufficiency, nor did his new legal status protect him from antisemitism. And in January 1826, once again to Moser: "I am now hated by Christian and Jew. I very much regret that I had myself baptized. I do not see that since that time anything has improved for me. On the contrary, since that time I have had nothing but misfortune."[21] After five years of traveling widely at home and abroad, searching unsuccessfully for a suitable position, and being hounded by the censor and the authorities because of his political writings, Heine—hoping to find a freer and more rewarding existence elsewhere—emigrated to France in 1831 and remained in Paris until his death in 1856.

Heine's Moses Figures

It is curious and perhaps not merely coincidental that Heine, already a convert to Christianity, should have turned his attention to the figure of Moses in writings composed during two significant periods of his life, both associated with revolutions. The first of these works, *Ludwig Börne: A Memorial (Ludwig Börne. Eine Denkschrift)* was written in 1839 and 1840; the discussion of Moses appears in Book 2, which consists of fictional letters or diary entries written while vacationing in Helgoland in 1830 before and after the July Revolution. There Heine contends with the Moses usually regarded as universal lawgiver, unassimilable Jew, and the creator of the nation of Israel. The second appearance of Moses is in the *Confessions (Geständnisse)*, published in 1854 and written after 1848, when he was confined permanently to bed with a debilitating ailment. In this work a reinterpreted Moses arises; the concern with universal emancipation, the remarkable coalescence of individual and social fulfillment, and the quintessential diaspora Jew were apparently now more appealing to Heine. This Moses was, for him, a revolutionary figure, a nascent socialist and a great artist who forged out of an inchoate mass a monumental nation, a hero with traits which Heine most valued in himself. In an age of increasing assimilation it is curious that a baptized Jew would have carved into the bedrock of Judaism his own painful image as artist and political thinker.

Before 1848 the Moses that Heine presented was an opponent of art and image, a proponent of strict regulation, and an antagonist of revolution, a critique generally associated with a New Testament perception of the Old. But in 1854 Moses reappeared in Heine's writing as the creator of a people and protagonist of revolution fighting for a new social order. In Heine's utopian expectations, revolution should promote not only a system of equality for all, but an environment in which the individ-

ual—not the masses or the "Volk"—would reign free and powerful. "We are fighting not for the human rights of the people,"
Heine notes in *Towards a History of Religion and Philosophy in
Germany (Zur Geschichte der Religion und Philosophie in Deutsch-
land)*, "but for the divine rights of the person . . . we are founding
a democracy of equally magnificent, equally holy, equally blissful
gods."[22] Thus, at its best a revolution would fulfill two of the
biblical Moses' ideal accomplishments: creation of a just society
and the simultaneous realization of individual fulfillment and
sociopolitical goals. From this perspective the revolutionary
Moses of the *Confessions* returns to the tradition of the Old
Testament.

1848 seems to have been the critical year in Heine's life,
when a significant shift in perspective and values mediated two
very different interpretations of Moses. In 1851, three years after
his debilitating illness confined him to bed, Heine articulated in
the afterword to *Romanzero* a conception of God that persists in
his writings until his death in 1856; and it is this conception
which, in the *Confessions* of 1854, underlies his reconsideration
of not only Moses and the Bible, but also his earlier perceptions
of art and politics.

In the Afterword to *Romanzero* (1851) Heine recalls a day
in May 1848, the last before his confinement, he says, when he
dragged himself with great difficulty to the Louvre in order to
bid farewell to the goddess of beauty. He claims that he collapsed
before the statue of the Venus de Milo and sobbed so violently
that stone would have been aroused to pity. "The goddess even
looked down upon me with compassion, yet at this same time so
hopelessly as if to say, 'Don't you see that I have no arms and
therefore cannot help?'"[23] Since in 1848 it was assistance in daily
life that the sick man needed as well as help for Europe in the
throes of revolutionary struggle that the political poet wanted, it
is noteworthy that Heine turned to a representation of the Hellenic culture he had so long championed, to an artifact now on
display in a museum.[24] For Heine, who had once regarded himself
a Hellene, Hellenism had promised an almost unbelievable unity

of the sensual and the spiritual, of a fulfilled individuality and utopian society. "Hellenic cheerfulness, love of beauty, and blossoming vivacity"[25] proffered sensuous gratification and laid the foundation for a society in which "the divinity of man reveals itself also in his physical appearance," for "a democracy of equally magnificent, equally holy, equally blissful gods" with "nectar and ambrosia, purple robes, precious fragrances, voluptuousness, and splendor, the dance, music, and comedies of laughing nymphs."[26] But now in the Louvre Heine confronted this glorious spirit of ancient Greece in a fragmented statue of a goddess and recognized its lifelessness and inefficacy, its impotence in the face of a person being consumed by a mortal ailment and a society struggling for transformation.

Now Heine also rejected the god of pantheism, whose promise of wholeness had once absorbed him: "This poor dreamy being is interwoven and grown together with the world . . . will-less and powerless."[27] He turns instead to a God with a will, to "an old superstition, to a personal God," who, unlike the Venus, had its limbs intact and could lend a helping hand: "In order to have a will," he observed, "one must be a person, and in order to manifest it, one must have one's elbows free."[28] Although terminally ill, Heine was not seeking a transcendent god to save his soul or guarantee immortality, which he assumed would be given "like the fine marrow bone, which the butcher, if he is satisfied with his customers, places free of charge in their basket."[29] Quite the contrary: the smarting jest and bitter irony in the Afterword suggest that Heine wanted an active deity able to attend to worldly needs and endeavors. He expected no more and no less tangible help from the Bible and its God.

Just as he had reevaluated and revised his conception of God, a few years later in the *Confessions* Heine re-formed the figure of Moses and admitted: "I had never particularly loved Moses before, probably because the Hellenic spirit predominated in me."[30] He was clearly referring to views articulated a decade and a half earlier in Book 2 of *Ludwig Börne: A Memorial*. There Heine noted that despair had driven him to the Bible: "And I confess to you," he wrote in one of the 1830 fictional epistles from Helgoland, "that in spite of the fact that I am a secret Hellenist, the Bible did not merely entertain me well, but also thoroughly edified me. What a book!"[31] At that time his Hellenism informed his perception not only of the Bible, but of Moses, Börne, and the Jews as well. In his view, the Jews, whom he regarded as both "the people of the book" (as Mohammed referred to them) and "the people of the spirit" (as Hegel did),[32] had a strong predilection for the abstract which was evident not only in the sharp distinction they drew between spirit and matter, but also in their insistence that the absolute existed only as spirit. Their strict and austere religious life contrasted markedly to the lives of their neighbors in the ancient world, to "the brightly colored Egypt, teeming with hieroglyphs," to the "gracious, sweet-scented Babylon," and to "Greece, the blossoming homeland of art."[33]

It was because of the threat to spiritual Mosaic religion by the sensuality of their neighbors that the Moses of the *Memorial* instituted stringent ritual laws and fostered a strong self-conscious national identity. By doing so Moses also secured the spiritual foundations of Christianity. Indeed, the further radicalization of the separation of matter and spirit in Christianity—readily apparent in Christ's crucifixion—was, in Heine's view, responsible for the lingering malaise of Western civilization. Referring to the primacy of the spirit and the evil of matter, Heine noted in 1834 in *Toward a History of Religion and Philosophy in Germany:* "This world view, the actual idea of Christianity, had disseminated with unbelievable speed throughout the entire Roman Empire like a contagious disease; the sufferings, sometimes raging fever, sometimes exhaustion, lasted throughout the entire Middle Ages, and we moderns still feel cramps and weakness in our limbs."[34] The harsh assessment of Christianity articulated in the *Memorial* is ameliorated, as we shall shortly see, by significant alterations in Mosaic religion which Heine attributed to Christ.

Actually the Moses of the *Memorial* is viewed largely from the perspective of the New Testament, that is, in relation to Jesus who continues and surpasses Mosaic tradition. Jesus, as emancipator who succeeded Moses, liberated people from the outdated rigid Mosaic codes, transcended national identity, and extended the spiritual religion to all humankind.[35] In an argument rife with contradiction, Heine, no friend of the austere spirituality associated with Judaism, showers praise on Jesus—"What a sweet figure, this god-man!"[36]—whose activity and martyrdom resulted in the glorification and hegemony of pure spirit everywhere. And while Jesus flourished, Moses declined, recalling the New Testament assessment of Moses as a servant in God's house and Christ "a son over his own house."[37] Paradoxically, this Moses, hero of abstract spirituality, dwindles to a small quotidian significance, while Jesus soars to magnificent proportions: "Moses loved his people with a touching intimacy; like a mother he cares for the future of his people. Christ loves mankind, that sun blazed around the entire earth with the warming rays of his love. What a soothing balm for all the wounds of this world are his words! What a healing spring for all sufferers was the blood that flowed at Golgatha."[38]

Contradiction, however, is not limited to Heine's admiration for a highly abstract and spiritual conception of love that he finds in Jesus; Christ's spirituality is also called into question because of its destructive powers. Speaking of the crucifixion, Heine realizes that the "white marble Greek gods were splashed with this blood and fell ill from inner horror, and could never again recover!"[39] It is not clear whether this history of the abstract spirit, in which Christianity not only supercedes the Mosaic tradition but decimates the representatives and relics of Hellenism, should be regarded as a "great drama"[40]—Heine's view of Christ's Passion—or whether the evolution which started with his homey and motherly, almost materialistic, Moses warrants hosannas or mourning.

Fourteen years later in the *Confessions* the domesticated Moses is nowhere to be found, nor for that matter does Jesus appear. In fact, the New Testament seems alien, even repellent, to Heine, while the Old Testament is credited with having reawakened his religious feelings and replaced Christ as "a fountain of salvation."[41] Now too Heine notes that "the character of Moses in the first section of the Holy Scripture has become more intelligible to me." Indeed Moses has undergone a spectacular transformation from domestic nurturer into veritable god: "This great figure," "What a giant form!," "How small Sinai appears when Moses stands upon it!" And finally Heine's most heretical observation for which he asks God's forgiveness: "Sometimes it would seem to me as if this Mosaic God were only the reflected brightness of Moses himself to whom he appears so similar, similar in anger and in love."[42] In this text Moses is understood only in terms of the Old Testament, and the New Testament ceases to be regarded as a text which continues, completes, or surpasses the Old. Any reference to Christianity here is limited to Protestants disseminating the Old Testament and Luther instituting freedom of thought.[43]

In the *Confessions* the principal interest in Moses is neither to glorify nor to demonize him, but rather to reevaluate his cultural and social accomplishments. Whereas earlier Heine had concentrated on the inhibitory function of spirituality, regulation, and nationality, he now focused on the substance of Mosaic ethical tradition. Reassessing his views of Moses and art, Heine attributes his former aversion to Moses to the prophet's disdain of "figurative representation" *(Bildlichkeit)* and art. But he has come to understand his "true artistic spirit,"[44] that is, the formative power that created a monumental nation out of a poor shepherd tribe. National identity, previously viewed as a parochialism to be overcome, is now considered a colossal achievement; the recurrence of the term "a people" *(Volk)* in the following passage testifies to that: "He [Moses] built human pyramids [*Menschenpyramiden*], he chiseled human-obelisks [*Menschen-Obelisken*], he took a poor shepherd tribe and created out of it a people that should also defy the centuries, a great, eternal, holy people, a people of God that could serve as a model, indeed as a prototype for all other peoples: he created Israel!"[45] The asceticism of the Jews, their legal codes, and their ardent nationality, once interpreted as measures for the protection of spirituality, are now deemed necessary for creating and preserving an ethical and just society, especially if it borders on temples of the neighboring countries—Babel, Nineveh, Sidon, and Tyrus—where "bloody and obscene orgies were cele-brated."[46]

Thus, Heine's late Moses is celebrated not only for his cre-ativity, but also because as lawgiver he constructed a society that guaranteed freedom, equality, and a life free of material want. Only realism and practicality prevented this revolutionary Moses from eradicating such long-established institutions as private property and slavery. He opted instead for progressive reforms which controlled the ownership and distribution of property (the Jubilee year) and the manumission of slaves. For this Moses freedom was less an abstract principle than a concrete social reality; he sought practical solutions. "Moses did not want to eliminate property," writes Heine, "he wanted everyone to pos-sess it so that no one, on account of poverty, would be a slave with a slavish disposition. Freedom was always the great emanci-pator's ultimate idea, and this idea breathes and blazes in all the laws concerning poverty."[47] Whether or not emancipation here also refers to liberation from Egypt, it certainly applies primarily to a society free of economic want and social bondage.

In the *Confessions* Heine ventures a bold insight that God may be created in Moses' image. But it also seems plausible that the Moses in that work may have been created in the best image Heine had of himself, that is, a socially committed artist who is, as he once characterized himself, also "a good soldier in the war for the liberation of humankind."[48] Heine once suggested that the remedy for a world suffering from "one-sided striving for spiritualization" could be found in "politics and art,"[49] two pri-mary concerns of both Heine and his late Moses. But there is more than self-glorification in his conception of a Moses that mirrors Heine's own best attributes. After all, Heine is addressing the larger issue of the relationship of art and politics, creativity and culture. The achievements of his late Moses suggest, for instance, that artistic activity can, together with reason and rationality, create a society in which every individual can realize freedom and justice as well as participate in a cultural environment. The discussion of Moses in the *Confessions* follows Heine's rejection of German philosophy, especially Hegel's, because of the impotence of its idealism and egotism,[50] and this distinction between Hegel and Moses seems not to be mere coincidence. In an 1850 letter Heine first assures his friend Heinrich Laube that he has not, as rumor has it, undergone any great change in his religious sentiments ("in meiner religösen Gefühlsweise"), but admits that his ideas about religion have been through a "February Revolution": "I have, namely, to elucidate the matter in a word, given up the Hegelian god or rather godlessness and in its stead have again placed a real, personal god, which is outside of nature and the human mind . . . For me Hegel has very much declined, and old Moses is flourishing [*steht in floribus*]."[51] It may seem that Heine has replaced his commitment to human autonomy and to European culture and politics with devotion to Judaism and religiosity, but this is not borne out by his writings. His new conception of Moses and Mosaic tradition may best be understood as testifying not only to an ongoing comprehensive involvement with European culture. Indeed it may be understood as an attempt to situate Germans and German culture within a broader historical context and to bring Jews and Judaism into the realm of modern social thought.

It is, therefore, worth pausing briefly to reflect on Heine's views about the connection between Jews and Germans before continuing the pursuit of Moses and the origins of the Jews as a nation. Curiously, although in his last years Heine reevaluated and significantly altered his conception of Moses and Mosaic law, his ideas and even the vocabulary of his discourse about the relationship between Jews and Germans remained relatively unchanged for almost two decades.[52] Heine detected an elective affinity (*Wahlverwandschaft*) between these two ethical peoples (*Völker der Sittlichkeit*) who shared "the most courageous hatred of Rome, a personal sense of freedom, ethics."[53] Their filiation is also evidenced in the spiritual identity Jew and German found in the Bible, which as "the great family chronicle of the Jews . . . has served as an educational text for the entire Germanic world."[54] Indeed, the Bible was perceived as having determined the character and life of Germanic peoples in many areas of the world: "The historical record of the Jews, the Bible, became the national book in the Germanic North, overflowed into flesh and blood, left its characteristic stamp on internal and external life—and those who speak about the traces of the Orient in Jews do not notice the Old Testament, genuinely Jewish physiognomy of the Germanic North in Europe and America."[55] To Heine these peoples were so similar that ancient Palestine might be taken for an oriental Germany, or "contemporary Germany for the home of the Holy Word, for the mother soil of prophesy, for the stronghold of pure spirituality."[56] However, the most significant contribution of the Jews to contemporary Europe, according to Heine, was what he referred to as "the modern principle" which informed the "most recent cosmopolitan republicans," that is, the devotion in Judaism to the primacy of the law and therewith to a religion of "freedom and equality."[57]

It is surprising that nowhere before the *Confessions* does Heine connect Moses with the religion founded on law that had such a profound influence on the Western world. In fact, in the *Memorial* Moses instituted only *ceremonial* law, whose function in protecting abstract spirituality could only rob people of genuine freedom. When in the *Confessions,* however, Heine focused on the affinity between Jews and Germans, the occidental character of Judea, and the Jewish people's "spiritualistic belief, its strict, chaste, even ascetic ethics, . . . its abstract inwardness" that distinguished it from its ancient neighbors, he had only praise for the practice of "virtue and justice" among Jews.[58] And it was this newly evaluated spirituality that Heine's late Moses combined with "Israel's love of freedom" and the demands of ethical behavior, namely, the "true law of reason."[59] This Moses, a practical man and also a socialist, was responsible for initiating moral and equitable legislation regulating property, be it real estate or slaves.

Just as the Bible was, for Heine, an index to moral behavior and an ethical society rather than a religious text, so too is his late Moses not distinguished by an intimate relationship with God, but instead by his rational and moral creative capacity to construct the social foundations of a nation.

A great artist, a socialist, a lawgiver, a leader, someone who could lead the way to the emancipation of all people—that is the Moses of the *Confessions*. Heine looks to the day when in Western nations "what is genuine, imperishable, and true, namely the ethics [*Sittlichkeit*] of ancient Judaism, will flourish just as pleasing to God in those lands as once on the Jordan and on the heights of Lebanon"; and possibly referring to his past sensualism and Hellenism, he adds, "One does not need palm trees and camels to be good, and being good is better than beauty."[60] Clearly the principles and values of this late Moses, who is both ethical colossus and artistic genius, are projected as universal and paradigmatic for all times, for all peoples. The same year the *Confessions* was published Heine wrote a short addendum to "Ludwig Marcus: Recollections" in which remarks about universal emancipation resembled Karl Marx's central argument in his 1843 "Zur Judenfrage" ("On the Jewish Question"). Heine seemed to be imploring Jews to remember their affinity with Christians and Germans and thereby to affirm the universal significance of Moses' emancipatory activity: "The Jews should finally arrive at the insight that they could only then truly be emancipated when also the emancipation of Christians is completely won and assured, and they should not as Jews desire what was for a long time due them as Germans."[61]

Final reflections about Moses in the *Confessions* concern slavery. The discussion begins with German peasants' objections to unethical property practices and concludes with a Mosaic regulation, the interpretation of which is significant, whether or not it is an accurate reading of the biblical text. The passage in question refers to Exodus 21:4–6, in which a slave, after the expiration of his servitude, might decide to remain with his former master so that he would not have to leave the master, wife, and children he loved. As a sign of his intention to remain with the master forever, the slave's earlobe is pierced. Not tolerating bondage of any kind, Heine saw the pierced earlobe not only as a marker, but also as punishment for accepting servitude. Using the Hebrew designation ("Moshe Rabenu") Heine appeals to Moses as a teacher of both Jew and German to supply what is necessary to eradicate the servility that still survives in Germany: "Oh Moses our teacher, Moshe Rabenu, noble opponent of servitude, hand me a hammer and nails to nail fast by their long ears our genial slaves in black-red-gold livery to the Brandenburg gate."[62] Moses, the activist teacher of universal emancipation, is being asked to assist in the liberation not of Jews, but of Germans, since Jews in Germany would be truly free only when Germans were. It seems then that Heine may not only have inscribed into the foundations of Judaism his own painful image as artist and political thinker, but also, in the age of emancipation, engraved in the landscape of German culture and politics the ineradicable features of the Old Testament emancipator.

A HAUNTING IMAGE clings to Heine's preoccupation with the Bible and Moses in the *Confessions*. A terribly ill German writer living as an alien in Paris, a Jew by birth, converted to Protestantism and married to a Catholic, Heine lies imprisoned in a mattress-grave; his body is wracked with pain, limbs paralyzed, muscles convulsing, eyelids unable to open of their own accord—"a poor mortally ill Jew, an emaciated picture of misery, an unfortunate human being," he called himself.[63] In these waning years of his life, the Bible, which had long been very important to him, seems even more prepossessing, perhaps because he hoped it might reconcile seemingly irreconcilable aspects of his life as Jew and Christian, German and alien. The Bible had become for him not only the record of his Jewish origins, but also the document progressive Protestants translated and disseminated along with their revolutionary idea of freedom of thought;[64] he saw it as a basic educational text for Jew and German. Now, unable to participate actively in the larger world outside, Heine lay with his

Bible as confined to his bed as the Jew had been in his ghetto. This confluence of Jew, Bible, and ghetto appears in both the *Memorial* and the *Confessions*, but in the latter with a small but significant alteration.

In the former work, the Bible is understood as the misfortune of the Jews who, bound by their singular religious devotion, remained isolated from the world:

A book is their [the Jews'] fatherland, their possession, their ruler, their fortune, and their misfortune. They live in the enclosed boundaries of this book, here they practice their inalienable civil rights, they cannot be expelled, cannot be despised, here they are strong and worthy of admiration. Immersed in the readings of this book, they noticed little of the changes that took place around them. Nations arose and disappeared, states blossomed and expired, revolutions stormed across the earth . . . but they, the Jews, lay bent over their book and noticed nothing of the wild hunt of the times which passed over their heads![65]

For these Jews the Bible was their ghetto, and the freedom within its confines was gained by excluding the world and accepting a nationhood of words. Even the Moses in this text exists in the ghetto, one which he constructed of ceremonial laws and national adherence and which Jews for almost two thousand years in exile inherited and maintained. The ghetto insulated the Jewish people, time stopped, and their Bible sealed their fate; there was no tangible freedom, no perceptible movement here.

In the *Confessions* the same configuration of Jew, Bible, and ghetto appears, but with a difference: no longer are the Jews presented as culturally moribund, shards from the past that can be overlooked, an idea that must be overcome. They are alive and vital in their ghettos, they have preserved their Bible and therewith the ethics of justice and liberation, and hidden behind the walls their biblical scholars tutor Europe's most progressive thinkers, the Protestant reformers. Here Heine acknowledges the change in his sensibility that may account for his altered views:

> Now in my later and more mature days, when religious feeling again has stirred in me overwhelmingly, and the shattered metaphysician clings firmly to the Bible: now I value Protestantism quite remarkably because of the merit it has earned by its discovery and dissemination of the Holy Book. I say discovery because the Jews, who rescued it from the great conflagration of the second temple, and in exile dragged it around with them like a portable fatherland, throughout the entire Middle Ages, they kept this treasure carefully hidden in their ghetto, to which German scholars, predecessors and instigators of the Reformation, sneaked in order to learn Hebrew, to gain the key to the chest which contained the treasure . . . Indeed to the Jews, to whom the world owes its God, it also owes His word, the Bible.[66]

Here the salutary aspect of the ghetto is noted, for it is the place where the great treasure and its vitality were preserved; and along with the Bible the Jewish people—"people of the book," "people of the spirit"—were preserved as a nation by keeping alive and active "the great realm of the spirit, the realm of religious feeling, of love of neighbor, of purity and of true ethics [*Sittlichkeit*], which cannot be taught by dogmatic conceptual formulations, but by image and example, as they are contained in the beautiful holy educational book for small and large children, in the Bible."[67]

Thus, while Heine has maintained his former views of the primacy of spirit and ethics in the Bible, in the *Confessions* he writes more about biblical values of loving one's neighbor, justice, freedom of thought, and liberation. It is as though Heine had penetrated the walls, moved into the ghetto so that he could perceive the concrete, material aspects of Moses and Mosaic Judaism he had formerly overlooked. From his earlier sublime position of sensualism and Hellenism, he had seen from afar the walls of the ghetto covered only with ceremonial laws, endless restrictions, and prohibitions.

What motivated Heine's reevaluations is difficult to ascertain—it may have been aging or his illness and confinement—but the change in perspective is significant. His approach to the Bible and Moses is largely secular; thus, nowhere does he regard the role of a transcendent God with any seriousness. But he does take the Bible and Moses very seriously; for Heine, they seem necessary for the cultural, social, and political foundations of modern life. They are also vital to the understanding of his own value. Faced with his own physical impotence, he seemed especially attracted to the practicality of ability and strength. He sees, for example, the inadequacy of Hegelian philosophy in the face of active deism: "The cobweb-like Berlin dialectics can not lure a dog out of a hole in the oven, it can kill no cat, much less a god."[68] And of the Jews, he writes: "I now see that the Greeks were merely beautiful youths; the Jews, however, were always men, powerful, unyielding men, not only then, but until the present day, despite eighteen hundred years of persecution and misery." Then he adds, "The writer of these pages could be proud of the fact that his forefathers belonged to the noble house of Israel, that he was a descendent of those martyrs who gave the world a god and morality, and had fought and suffered on all the battlefields of the idea."[69]

In the *Confessions*, the Bible, the lawgiver and "overseer" (*Werkmeister*) Moses, and his "work," the Jews, have all been resuscitated and invested with ancient power—and the writer Heine with them. So powerful have they become that cultured and revolutionary Western Europeans, representatives of the outside world, are seen coming into the ghetto to unearth texts that may contribute to the re-formation of Western society. Heine has returned to one of the most challenging ideas of the Society for the Culture and Science of the Jews, namely, to the contributions Jews made and continue to make to the contemporary Western world. In his waning years, Heine seems to be extending an invitation to enter the ghetto, be it segregated territory, Bible, or sickroom, where suffering may still fuel the struggle for justice, freedom of thought, and a liberated life.

3

Between Bondage and Liberation:
Kafka and Moses in the Wilderness

Franz Kafka's father, Hermann, owes his very existence to emancipation legislation, and some of the major decisions of Hermann's life may be attributed to the tensions between the resulting new freedoms and aggravated antisemitism.[1] In 1848 the new Emperor Franz Josef realized that an economically progressive Austria needed Jews to be fully mobile in order to advance industrial production and distribution. To this end he instituted a constitution which, while not granting Jews full civic rights, lifted the existing prohibitions on marriage, residence, and occupation.[2] It was the revocation of marriage restrictions to control the Jewish population, which had heretofore permitted only the oldest son to marry, that allowed the thirty-five-year-old Jakob Kafka to marry and raise a family.[3] Hermann, the second of six children, was born in 1852 (the year ghettos throughout the Austrian Empire were legally abolished) into impoverished circumstances in the village of Wossek in Czech Bohemia. Although he was but four years older than Sigmund Freud, he was more closely related, sociologically and economically, to the generation of Freud's father, Jakob, who—owing to the confluence of a declining economy, growing nationalism, and anti-Jewish activity—migrated from his parental village to larger urban areas, finally settling in Vienna. The fathers of Freud and Kafka were representative of a transitional generation in the process of assimilation and acculturation: they were born into relatively traditional Jewish communities in small towns of the Austrian crown lands and moved into the secular life of the metropolis in search of social and economic security.[4] They and their children had to contend with the legacy of modernization and secularization in European society as well as with the erosion of Jewish traditions and community. "Restless wandering," Christoph Stölzl notes in an informative social history of Bohemian Jews in the nineteenth and early twentieth centuries, "is the leitmotif of Hermann Kafka's generation, from the one home village, which had been a compulsory residence, into the next (even Wossek was a 'new' Jewish settlement founded only after 1848), into the town, into the German-Bohemian industrial settlements on the outskirts of Bohemia, to Prague, to Vienna."[5]

Kafka's father had to work from the age of ten, but at fourteen poverty forced him out of his village to seek a livelihood elsewhere. He became a peddler, a trade common among Jews; worked in shops; and finally, in 1882, after fulfilling his military obligation, settled in Prague. In September of that year he married Julie Löwy, the daughter of a well-to-do brewer who had earlier moved from Podiebrad to Prague. The migrations of this generation to the cities were not just fortuitous adventures, but part of a persistent search for protection and better work opportunities at a time when antisemitic activity and the erosion of the emancipatory guarantees threatened the Jewish population, especially the poor and vulnerable. Difficult social and financial circumstances in the mid-nineteenth century endangered the lives of Czech Christians and Jews, though not in the same ways. A look at changes in production suggests the scope of the problem. Before 1848 Jews had long been barred from crafts and agricultural work and were, therefore, for centuries largely involved in merchandising and money-lending; and in more recent times they were also engaged in industry and finance. Increasing industrialization after 1848, however, slowly but surely made the work of the small craftsperson and peasant obsolete, thereby impoverishing many Czech communities. Thus, Jews were finally offered new and broader economic opportunities at a time when modernization and expanding capitalism had already begun to disrupt the lives of Czech workers. In addition, with growing animosity toward the politically powerful German-speaking minority, Czech nationalism grew even more intense than it was before 1848; and the lower classes, including the petite bourgeoisie, workers, and peasants, now felt that, in the wake of the new emancipation, Jews as well as German-Bohemians threatened their lives economically and politically. As a result of these developments, Jewish and German Bohemians became the target of Czech nationalists' attacks, and antisemitic activity as well as new restrictive legislation made the recently instituted freedoms very difficult to realize.[6] Indeed, the severity of antisemitic attacks in spring 1848 motivated Jews to welcome suppression of the revolution by the Austrian military, something not easily forgotten by the frustrated and defeated Czechs.

Throughout the ensuing two decades, which encompassed Hermann Kafka's youth, antisemitic activities—violent demonstrations and hostile literature attacking Jews—occurred almost everywhere in Bohemia.[7] In 1861 anti-Jewish riots broke out in Bohemian cities, such as Straknowitz, which was but a few miles from Wossek where the Kafkas lived, and in Prague; and as a result of the severe economic crisis in 1865–66, the Young Czechs, a radical nationalist group of largely workers and petit bourgeois, published newspaper attacks on Germans and Jews, both of whom were viewed as aliens deliberately destroying a wholesome native society. Not surprisingly, the most impoverished workers carried out the anti-Jewish riots and conflagrations, which only the Austrian-Prussian war in 1866 would temporarily quell.

During the second half of the century the opportunity for assimilation on the one hand and the extreme insecurity and peril experienced by the Jewish population on the other created conditions unfavorable for stability and a settled life. Nevertheless the 1867 political victory of liberalism in Austria brought a new constitution, which this time granted Jews full civic equality; but fierce antisemitic literature continued to circulate, exacerbated no doubt by the stock market crash of 1873 and the ensuing depression, which lasted two decades.[8] Thus, even in the era of emancipation and assimilation, an impoverished young Hermann Kafka —like many others of his generation trying to eke out a living— was made to repeat again and again the wanderings associated with a precarious life in the diaspora.

The children of transitional figures who had lived through the vicissitudes of two cultures did not easily evade the strife their parents had known. Social conditions and family ties again and again reminded apparently assimilated children of a heritage and tradition which, though distant and still fading, persistently intruded into their lives.

Kafka and Assimilation

Born in Prague in 1883, Franz Kafka was among the first generations of Jews who could assimilate easily because of their clear legal access, from birth, to political and professional opportunities not available to their parents. Given these advantages and their almost negligible bonds with religion or religious observance, the members of his generation might have been expected to regard themselves not as Jews, but as Czech or German Bohemians. This, however, was not the case. Most often Jews of that generation continued to live among Jews and, in Bohemia, were far less assimilated than in Germany, Austria, or Hungary. During the last decades of the century the numbers of conversions in Vienna, for example, were considerable, but there were virtually no instances of baptism in Prague.[9] While it is difficult to document why the situation in Bohemia was so different, Ezra Mendelsohn suggests that, instead of giving Jews real options, the binational-bilingual groups (Czech and German) with outspoken nationalist and antisemitic attitudes rejected possibilities for Jewish integration;[10] and although many Jews had supported liberal politics, the liberal tradition of Prague Germans, waning after the crash of 1873 and defunct in the Bohemian parliament in 1883, was not particularly receptive to Jews.[11] In this era of intensifying nationalism, Jewish nationalism developed as an active alternative to that of the Germans and Czechs. Kafka became especially interested in Zionism toward the end of World War I. He subscribed to the Zionist weekly *Selbstwehr* and in 1916 and 1917 published several stories in *Der Jude,* a Zionist journal edited by Martin Buber; but unlike Max Brod, Hugo Bergmann, and other friends, he did not join the movement.[12] In 1917 he began to study Hebrew and became so proficient that in the last years of his life he could not only read the Bible with Rashi's commentary and difficult modern Hebrew literature as well, but also write and converse in the language. In the waning years of his life, he considered the prospect of emigrating to Palestine, but his writings suggest that, because of a deteriorating tubercular condition and wavering commitment, he was essentially flirting with unrealizable possibilities. In July 1923, for example, he wrote Else Bergmann, wife of his friend Hugo, that he could not join her on the trip to Palestine; "it would be no voyage to Palestine, but in a spiritual sense something like the voyage to America of a cashier who has embezzled a lot of money; and the voyage that would have been made with you would have very much increased the spiritual criminality of the case."[13] Later that same year, in a letter to his friend and Czech translator Milena Jesenská, he admitted that a trip to Palestine planned for October "would never of course have come about, it was a phantasy, the kind someone has who is convinced he will never leave his bed. If I never leave my bed, why should I not travel at least as far as Palestine?"[14]

Kafka was neither a religious nor a practicing Jew, but throughout his life, as his diaries, notebooks, and letters attest, he was preoccupied with Jews, their social significance, and their profound importance for his own life and writing. Speaking about the "frightful inner predicament of these generations" of young Jews drawn to the German language, Kafka notes in a 1921 letter to Max Brod that their problems arose from their relationship with "the *Jewishness* of the fathers" (emphasis mine): "Most of those who began to write German wanted to leave Judaism, mostly with the unclear approval of the fathers (this unclarity was

what was so shocking), they wanted to, but with their little hind
legs they were still glued to the Jewishness [*Judentum* generally
means 'Judaism' or 'Jewry'] of their fathers and with their little
front legs they found no new ground. The despair about that was
their inspiration."[15] The irony and anxiety, as Jew and writer, of
being fixed and immobilized in a transitional situation are painfully dramatized here; and many of Kafka's writings indicate just
how powerfully his understanding of himself as a Jew was affected
by historical and social conditions which informed his and his
family's life, just how burdened he was by the legacy of transition
from traditional Jewish society to Western European culture in an
ambivalent era of emancipation and virulent antisemitism. The
experience of this very difficult, often destructive transition and
unresolved assimilation is poignantly reflected in so many of
Kafka's works, from *America (Amerika)* and "A Report to an
Academy" ("Ein Bericht für eine Akademie") to *The Castle (Das
Schloss)* and his reflections on such biblical figures as Abraham and
Moses. Before turning to his wandering Moses, I would like to
explore—in several texts from the letters and diaries—Kafka's
relationship with Jewish life and Judaism, so intimately intertwined with this burden of change.

Kafka's brief description in his October 1, 1911, diary entry
of the *Kol Nidre*[16] service he had attended the previous day in the
Old-New Synagogue communicates not merely an antipathy to
the people assembled and to their religiosity, the evidence of
which he not always finds convincing, but also a sense of his
position as indifferent and perhaps lonely outsider. Surveying the
scene as though it were a busy Brueghel setting, he notes the
muted murmuring about the stock market; the collection box in
the foyer; three pious, seemingly Eastern Jews praying, the gen-
uineness of whose tears he questions; the disoriented small boy
who moves about, shoving and being shoved; the clerk whose
large emphatic gestures at prayer seem designed to compensate
for a quiet voice; and the family of a bordello owner. His conclusion seems perfunctory and aloof, the response to an event staged
for a visitor's benefit: "In the Pinkas synagogue I was incompa-

rably more strongly moved by Judaism."[17] Four years later, however, again on the eve of the Day of Atonement, his attitude is remarkably altered: "Sight of the Polish Jews, who are going to Kol Nidre. The small boy, who, with prayer shawls under both arms, runs alongside his father. Suicidal, not to go to the temple."[18] At this time Kafka could witness the life and practices of a rather large community of Eastern European Jews who had, in the early months of 1915, sought refuge in Prague from the Russian army advances through Galicia. His cryptic diary entry reveals a profound awareness of the power of Jewish religion or, at the least, tradition to maintain the cohesion of generations and to sustain life itself. Here the longing of an assimilated outsider to become an insider seems especially intense. And this was apparently not a fleeting experience. Five years later, when he wrote his friend, Milena Jesenská, about Russian emigrés cramped into a room of the Jewish town hall, his longing had not abated: "If I had been given the choice of being what I wanted, then I would have wanted to be a small Eastern Jewish boy in the corner of the room, without a trace of worry, the father in the center discusses with the men, the mother, heavily wrapped, rummages in the traveling rags, the sister chats with the girls and scratches in her beautiful hair—and in a few weeks one will be in America." Even after detailing their horrible and dangerous conditions, Kafka concluded that they were, after all, a community, "*one* people."[19]

Although it is difficult to account for Kafka's changed attitude to Eastern European Jews, there can be no question of the importance of his encounters with a Polish Yiddish theater troupe that performed in Prague from the fall of 1911 to the following spring. In fact, it was just four days after Kafka's visit to the Old-New Synagogue that he saw his first performance of the Yiddish theater at the Savoy Cafe. From that time until its departure from Prague, he was absorbed in their work and drawn to several performers, especially Jizchak Löwy, with whom he established a close and long friendship, and Mania Tschissik, a woman he adored. His copious commentary on the troupe in his diary indicates just how involved and excited he was. From January 1911 to October 5 of that year, when he comments on the first performance, the diary consists of 43 printed pages; from October 5 to the end of the year there are 144 pages, many of them lengthy discussions of the plays, performances, and people connected with the theater. What the Yiddish theater represented, at least in part, was the reality of a Jewish people who, in their language and art, addressed their own people and measured themselves only by the standards of their own community.[20] His commentary on his first visit indicates the overwhelming effect that Yiddish culture and the autonomy of its community had on him: "Some songs, the expression 'jüdische Kinderlach' [from the Yiddish for 'little Jewish childen'], many a glance of this woman—who on the podium, because she is a Jewess, draws us to her because we are Jews, without longing for or curiosity about Christians—caused my cheeks to tremble."[21] Indeed it was during this period that Kafka made note of the difference between Eastern and Western European Jews, a distinction he maintained, judging by his letters and diaries, throughout his life.

These two groups of Jews constitute, for Kafka, the extremities of the transition which Western Jews underwent in the process of assimilation in the nineteenth and early twentieth centuries. At one extreme was Eastern Jewry, a Jewish community in the diaspora with its own culture and values intact; they measured their worth by the standards of the group and remained indifferent to the judgments and expectations of the dominant society. In part Kafka accepted the myth that there was a kind of primeval originality about this group, an independence and wholeness untouched by Western history and intellectual currents, by secularization and industrialization. "[T]hey are *one* people," he wrote Milena.[22] On the other hand, he does not idealize them, but sees their crudeness as well as their piety, their destructive behavior as well as their warmth and closeness. Kafka seems so attracted to them, however, because their closed community is able to uphold its own deeper values even when their behavior, judged by the standards of "polite" Western society, seems to belie them. In the diary entry of November 24, 1914, Kafka poignantly captures these qualities of Eastern Jewry. Speaking about the wonderful demeanor of a Mr. Chaim Nagel—his Jewish given name suggests that he has not been thoroughly Westernized—who was involved in the distribution of used clothing to Galician refugees, Kafka generalizes about the insularity of people in a way that may also refer to the Jewish refugees: "People, who fill up their sphere so completely that one thinks they succeed with everything within the entire sphere of the world, but what also pertains to their perfection is that they do not reach out beyond their sphere."[23] He concludes the entry with the description of an episode that characterizes the value of such a closed context: after rummaging for a long time through children's clothing and being loudly rebuked for it by Mrs. Brod (the mother of writer Max Brod),[24] one Mrs. Lustig, a refugee, replies "even more loudly and with a large wild movement of her hand: 'The *Mitsve* [good deed] is worth more than all these *shmattes* (rags).'"[25] The Galician woman's response calls into question Mrs. Brod's values about both the value of clothing and the grateful behavior apparently expected from the recipient. By quoting her retort enclosed within Yiddish words which together comprise two significant aspects of that culture—*Mitsve* from the Hebrew *Mitzvah* and the religious tradition and *shmattes* (in parenthesis Kafka adds *Hadern*, a slang word for *rags*), which derives from the Polish *szmata*—Kafka records the more bounteous, even humane moral perspective of Eastern Jewry while recognizing its penurious situation.

The comparison of his own lot with the communal cohesiveness and shared traditions of Eastern European Jews more sharply demarcates the outsider status of emancipated Western Jewry and Kafka's own complex anxiety. For the dozen or so years from his first encounter with the Yiddish theater troupe until his death, Kafka's attention to Eastern Jewry and Jewish tradition most often elicited reflections on the predicament of Western Jews of his generation, that is, those who had little experience of Judaism, but in whose lives it nonetheless survived, however minimally. In almost all of his reflections on Jewish life, any participation on his part is almost always mediated by his role as distant observer. As observer, he can hover without commitment between involvement and detachment, between the community and isolation. At the ritual circumcision of his nephew in December 1911, for example, Kafka, as distant from the traditional ceremony as any of those present, focused on the remoteness of all the others, who—apart from the grandfathers (namely, those of his father's generation)—could experience the tradition and ritual as something only historical. "I saw before me," Kafka noted in his diary, "Western European Jewry caught in a distinct immeasurable transition, about which those most closely affected don't worry, but, as genuine people in transition, bear what is imposed upon them."[26] Caught in a transitional process that had no adequate resolution—the hind legs adhering to a fading parental Jewishness, the front ones dangling in midair—Kafka's anxiety seemed later in his life to become even more oppressive for him, if his letters and diaries afford an accurate index. Again and again he articulates the despair of being suspended between a fast disappearing origin or point of departure (a meaningful tradition and community) and a terminus which either could not be attained or, if reached, would at best be unfulfilling.

Although, on some level, Kafka understands the human condition as one in which socialized individuals have to create their present and future lives, he finds that he alone, so bereft of any meaningful traditions, has perhaps the "most original task" of all, namely, to create the very "ground, air, commandment" of life.[27] In 1920 he wrote to Milena:

We both know abundantly characteristic examples of Western Jews; I am as far as I know the most Western Jew among them, that means, expressed with exaggeration, that not one calm second is granted me, nothing is granted me, everything must be earned, not only the present and future, but also the past, something which perhaps every person has brought with them, even that must be earned, that is perhaps the most difficult work, if the earth turns right—I don't know whether it does—I would have to turn left in order to recover [*nachholen,* which may also mean 'to make up for'] the past.[28]

Kafka may be glued to his father's Jewishness, but he can no longer retrieve the traditions his father had already left behind, those not bequeathed to him. These would have to be created anew, though Kafka is not optimistic about the likelihood. Indeed, his works, so many of them fragmentary, may be viewed as attempts to articulate this dilemma. Kafka perceived his father as one of the "transitional generation of Jews that emigrated from the comparatively still pious countryside into the cities."[29] And although he realized that his father's life was to a great extent determined by objective social conditions, Kafka nevertheless felt cheated out of a "past," of a meaningful cultural heritage, which might have supplied him with the "ground, air, commandment" he so desperately needed. Kafka seems not fully to understand that his father too had not inherited the cultural traditions for which the son longed. "You really had brought from your small ghetto-like village community something of Judaism, it wasn't much and a little more of it disappeared in the city and during military service, but still the impressions and memories of your youth just about sufficed for some kind of Jewish life . . . but for a child it was too little to be passed on, it trickled away entirely while you were passing it on."[30] Even at this stage of his life—at thirty-six years of age and conscious of the massive social and political renovation of his society—Kafka believed that Judaism itself could have supplied the communality he had felt among Eastern European Jews, the closeness of the young boy and father going together to the synagogue or, as he wrote his father, the "possibility of establishing new connections between us."[31]

Kafka understood that the pain he experienced was not his personal misfortune, but the lot of his generation which, having virtually no contact with a communal past (or present, for that matter), must forge a present and future out of thin air, as it were. But, for him, hope or despair about such estrangement was perhaps breeding ground for "inspiration," as he wrote in the 1921 letter to Brod noted above, for a new beginning rather than an end. In his fourth octavo notebook, Kafka articulates this possibility in a passage in which his own plight is intertwined with that of his age; indeed, he conceives of himself as its representative:

> I have brought with me nothing at all of the demands of life, as far as I know, but only general human weakness. With this—in this regard it is a gigantic strength [*Kraft*]—I have powerfully received [*kräftig aufgenommen*] the Negative of my time, which is indeed very close to me, which I have the right never to oppose, but to some extent to represent. I had no inherited share in the easy Positive nor in the extreme Negative tilting toward the Positive. I have not, like Kierkegaard, been led into life by the already heavily sinking hand of Christianity and have not, like the Zionists, grasped the last tip of the Jewish prayer shawl fluttering away. I am end or beginning.[32]

Once again Kafka positions himself *between* alternatives, not opting for elusive positive solutions, whether Christianity or Zionism, but remaining instead with the negative stance. With "the lack of ground, air, commandment," it was his task to create them; with no past, present, or future granted him, "everything must be earned."[33] Suspended between "end or beginning"—there may be more optimism here, "beginning" being the last word—he once again occupies the space between two possibilities and, as such, remains the most Westernized of Jews. This Jew, in the course of modernization and secularization, has been divested of a communal past, yet holds fast to some vestige of it and, rejecting an alternative Christian or Zionist community, may be prepared to become a beginning, to begin to create anew the absent "ground, air, commandment."

The tension between a seemingly comforting traditional communal life and a lonely, estranged existence within atomized Western society appears in a variety of forms in Kafka's writings during the last years of his life. This tension informs powerful experiences that are both intimately personal and socially mediated; and awareness of it allows insight into the nexus of Kafka's personal pain and the plight of an acculturated Jew under conditions of problematic emancipation. A few examples may illuminate the complexity of this intersection of experiences. In October 1921, a few days after he had refused to join his parents in a card game, Kafka agreed to keep score for his mother, but had to admit that no intimacy resulted; "and even if there were a trace of it, it would be overwhelmed by weariness, boredom, sadness about time lost. That's the way it would always have been," he writes in his diary, then generalizes about the condition of his life: "This borderland between loneliness and communality I have only extremely seldom crossed, I have settled therein even more than in loneliness itself." And Kafka adds, almost as an aside, "What a lively beautiful land was Robinson's island in comparison to this,"[34] implying that happiness and beauty may be realized where isolation and fellowship coexist. Given the reality of his generation, however—unable to release itself from the father's Jewishness and the demands of family and tradition, to divest itself of Western culture and the appurtenances of massive industrial and commercial developments, to live simply as an Eastern European Jew—the borderland with all of its conflicts and contradictions may be the best, if not the only, option.

In the paralipomena to a series of aphoristic formulations entitled "He" ("Er"),[35] one segment specifically focuses on a person in the diaspora who lives isolated not from a traditional community, but from the general population. In very few sentences the narrator compresses both the experience of life in the diaspora and the moral dilemma such a life raises: "He lives in the diaspora. His elements, a horde living freely, roam the world. And only because even his room belongs to the world does he sometimes see them [in German, this *sie* is ambiguous, referring either to 'elements' or to 'the world'] in the distance. How shall he bear responsibility for them? Can that still be called responsibility?"[36] Here the tension between involvement and detachment is communicated not merely in the subject matter, but in the expressive means. The speaker simultaneously communicates an experience of the life of the character "he" and his own observations in such a way that it remains unclear whether the final two sentences reflect the thinking of the character "he" or the narrator. The relationship of character and world in the passage reinforces the stylistic tension, for though "his" living arrangement is part of the world, he lives apart and can observe his "elements," the populace, and also the world, from afar. Here the opposition between the character who, on the one hand, lives in the world as the object of an observer and who, on the other, observes those living anarchically and ruminates about responsibility seems to account for the confining quality of life in the diaspora. What is, of course, crucial in this paradigm is the attention accorded to the outside world by the room-dweller who, despite his insularity, is nonetheless concerned about moral obligation. Though this passage presents an abstract reflection, in that same year, 1920, Kafka's response to an antisemitic riot functions as a concrete analogue to that abstraction. Kafka writes Milena that he had been in the streets and "bathed in Jew-hatred," that not emigrating is a sign only of the heroism of cockroaches which cannot be exterminated; he then adds: "Just now I looked out of the window: mounted police, gendarmerie prepared for bayonet attack, screaming crowd running asunder, and up here in the window the repulsive shame, always living under protection."[37]

Clearly, the hostility of the majority society to the Jewish population ruled out any rapprochement or alliance and may have made it well nigh impossible for this Westernized Jew to extricate himself from his father's Jewishness or to relinquish a vanished ideal. Kafka suggests in another of the "He" segments that yearning for an unrealizable, disappearing world may be useful, for it can make living and creating feasible. The passage begins: "He was once part of a monumental group," which had a rational and meaningful social structure. However, "the group has dissolved a long time ago or at least he has left it and makes his way alone through life." The fact that he has forgotten the past and can't even remember his former profession causes him "a certain sadness, insecurity, uneasiness, a certain longing for times past that has spoiled the present. And yet this longing is an important element of vitality and perhaps vitality itself."[38] The insights expressed here—the past lost to experience, irretrievable memories, discomfort, and longing because of the loss of memory—account, at least in part, for Kafka's persistent attraction to Eastern European Jewish culture (and his father's Jewishness) long after it was clear that there was no way of incorporating it into his life. The impossibility of adopting that culture resulted in the "negativity" that allowed Kafka—neither mired in the reckless life of the horde nor completely cut off from a receding past—to live with possibilities.

The 1921 letter to Max Brod cited earlier indicates that Kafka's relation to Jewishness is neither merely academic nor idiosyncratic, but encompasses larger social and cultural dimensions. He writes to Brod in June 1921 that he is principally interested in understanding the attraction of young Jewish writers to the German language which, in his view, is for them an "alien possession, not earned, but stolen in a (relatively) hasty snatch, and which remains an alien possession even if not even a single grammatical error could be shown."[39] He concludes that the roots of this attraction are to be found within the society, in the relationship of young Jews to their Jewishness, to "the horrible inner condition of *this* generation" (emphasis added).[40] Kafka consciously shifts the locus of the issue from the emotional-psychological arena to the sociological, clearly favoring the latter when he significantly changes Freud's Oedipal model: "Better than psychoanalysis I prefer in this case the understanding that this father-complex, from which many have been intellectually [*geistig* may also mean 'spiritually'] nourished, does not concern the innocent father, but the Jewishness of the father."[41] Kafka interprets the generational problem, in which Freud perceived innate Oedipal competition for authority and power, as a struggle socially and historically conditioned by the experience of emancipation and assimilation.

The dilemma for these young Jewish writers is serious and unrelenting. They may, on the one hand, concede—"in this small world of German-Jewish literature"[42]—to participate in "Mauscheln," which derives from the name Moishe (Yiddish for Moses) and, in the past, referred either to the way Yiddish-speaking Jews spoke German or to the coarse and embarrassing discourse associated with "uneducated" Eastern Jews; but according to Kafka, who like other Westernized Jews of Kafka's generation had begun to lionize Eastern Jewry,[43] "Mauscheln" was one way to vitalize a linguistic middle ground that "was nothing but ashes, which could be brought to apparent life only when exceptionally lively Jewish hands stirred it up."[44] For Kafka, "Mauscheln" was "the organic connection between bookish German and the language of gesture,"[45] between the intellectual language of the educated Western Jew and the nonverbal discourse of the gesturing Eastern Jew. On the other hand, the young Jewish writers might try to write German literature, but since their hind legs still adhered to their father's Jewishness, the literary works in which they "discharged their despair could not be German literature, which it appeared externally to be."[46] It seems that they, like Kafka, could hardly be expected to succeed in adopting, stealing, or producing what was "positive" in their world. They could thus live and write honestly only by realizing the necessity of negation or, as he put it in this letter, of impossibility: "the impossibility of not writing, the impossibility of writing German, the impossibility of writing differently, one could almost add a fourth impossibility, the impossibility of writing."[47] Depending on their expectations these Jewish writers were either condemned to live with the negative or free to do so: condemned to a fate of incomplete assimilation or free of the need to adapt and conform. Thus, like Moses in his desert wanderings or the most Westernized of Jews in the diaspora, they faced the possibility of being an end or a beginning; the choice was their struggle.

Kafka and Moses

Apart from a short piece about Sinai that appears among the "Fragmente" and whose date of composition is unknown,[48] references to Moses in Kafka's writings occur after the spring of 1920 in the diaries and in his conversations with Gustav Janouch.[49] Unlike Kafka's interest during the last four years of his life in the patriarch Abraham, which was limited largely to the personal dilemma of child sacrifice rather than to religious or social concerns,[50] his writing on Moses is focused less on the person or figure than on the cultural and social ramifications of the lawgiver's activity and life. His Moses is responsible for constructing not only the foundation for a just and productive nation, but those norms and principles that make out of a Jewish life a quintessentially human one. Kafka's reflections on Moses may best be understood as encompassing four major concerns: the character of existence in a diaspora; the nature of the human condition; the value of creative activity; and Jewish identity in his contemporary Europe.

Kafka explores the significance of Moses as a leader of his people and the quality of his wilderness life in an October 1921 diary ·entry:

> The essence of wandering in the wilderness. A person, who as leader of his people [*Volksführer seines Organismus*] goes this way, with a remnant (more is unthinkable) of consciousness about what is happening. He is on the trail of Canaan for his entire life; that he should see the land only just before his death is incredible. This last prospect could only have the purpose of demonstrating how incomplete a moment human life is, incomplete because this kind of life could go on endlessly and yet would result in nothing other than a moment. Not because his life was too short does Moses not reach Canaan, but because it was a human life.[51]

In this passage the first two segments (they are not sentences) articulate two integrally connected ideas which together establish its subject: namely, the essence of life in the wilderness, and the person who with some semblance of consciousness leads a people whom he forms into a nation. The unusual locution "Volksführer seines Organismus" articulates not only Moses' leadership, but emphasizes his inseparable alliance with his people: both the term "Volksführer" and the phrase "seines Organismus" suggest a people, a "living whole," which is both his and of which he is a part.

The life presented here is that of a people moving through a desert toward Canaan, a goal which when attained will conclude the struggle for liberation. Although this Moses has been on the trail of Canaan his entire life, his own destiny is merely to see, but not to enter, that land. According to this text, his lot is not a personal or particular one, but rather one shared by all human beings. Human life is, thus, understood as an unceasing struggle toward liberation and a homeland; death, as a conclusion to that struggle. Those who live consciously will pursue these goals even knowing that they cannot be achieved in any one person's lifetime. It is not clear from this text why Moses continues his struggle, whether he is motivated by the value of the goal or by the importance of living with such goals. Yet even the unending struggle, the brevity of life, and its inevitable fragmentariness do not seem to obliterate the value of striving for a place, a home that promises freedom and fulfillment. This representation of a Mosaic life and a human one is also that of a homeless existence in which people constantly contend with a wilderness and make conscious efforts to achieve what Canaan promises. Thus, a life in the diaspora is itself analogous to a human life: "Not because his life was too short does Moses not reach Canaan, but because it was a human life."

The depiction of Moses and his people in this passage refers to an existential condition of Mosaic and human life; although political implications are suggested, they are not explicit. In conversations with Janouch, however, the political and social character of the Moses story is emphasized. In one instance, in the course of explaining to Janouch that the increasing interest in Zionism among Jews was largely a defensive measure, Kafka accounted for this intensified nationalism by alluding to the social significance of Moses' endeavors to create a nation: "Jewish nationalism is the strict, externally imposed maintenance of a caravan which moves through the frost of a night in the wilderness. The caravan does not want to conquer anything. It only wants to reach a securely enclosed home [*Daheim*) which would give the caravan's men and women the possibility of a freely developed human existence."[52] Here the struggle and the goal are valuable only because of their political significance, of the possibility of creating an enduring, productive community for a people, whether that people is wandering through Sinai or settled in Western Europe.

The centrality of Moses for Jewry in the diaspora, only hinted at in the previous passage, is elaborated in another exchange with Janouch shortly thereafter. In response to his question about the meaning of the word *diaspora,* Janouch reports that Kafka replied: "This is the Greek designation for the dispersion of the Jewish people. In Hebrew it is called 'Galut'," and then added:

> The Jewish people is scattered, as a seed is scattered. As a single seed absorbs matter from the environment, stores that within itself and enhances its own growth [*das eigene Wachstum höher führt*], so is it the fated task of Jewry to absorb the strengths of humankind, to purify them, and thus to enhance them [*so höher zu führen*]. Moses is still a current reality. As Abiram and Datan opposed Moses with the words "Lo naale! We shall not go up!" so the world acts in opposition with the cry of antisemitism. In order not to ascend to the human level, people throw themselves into the dark depths of the zoological doctrine of race. They strike the Jew and murder the human being.[53]

Several separate, yet interrelated, issues are striking in this passage: the understanding of the Jews as a people even though they are dispersed; the idea that creative integration rather than adaptation or assimilation is vital for a productive relationship of Jews to their environment; the conception of Moses as a current reality suggests that Jewish life in the diaspora need be neither fantasy nor fossil, but a vital actuality; and finally, the identity of Jew and human being (not merely zoological entity) is related to the reality of Moses. This passage addresses the general relationship between people and their environment, and the particular instance of the Jewish people, who live in hostile surroundings. The hostility aimed specifically at the Jews does not, in Kafka's view, strike only its target, for antisemitism dehumanizes the antisemite and the very society in which it arises.

Antisemitism notwithstanding, nowhere in the passage is the value of life in the diaspora called into question. Indeed, within the text, the sentence "Moses is still a current reality" mediates between the creative human potential of life in the diaspora and an antisemitism that threatens the foundation of human society. This confluence of a positive diaspora experience and antisemitism seems to reflect the tension in Kafka's environment between legal emancipation and continuing hostility to Jews. In this text, however, the reality of Moses establishes a profound, concrete connection between past and present, not only for Jews, but for all people. The fate of the Jews as pariahs in a hostile environment and their determination to live a free and meaningful life are characteristics not peculiar to them alone, just as Moses' sojourn through the wilderness—though one of the seminal events of Jewish national history—may also represent a universal struggle of all human beings for a just and liberated community. For Kafka, the destinies of Jew and human being seem to converge around the figure of Moses; and because of the identification of Jew and human being, those who smite the Jew destroy not only that person, but also what is human in themselves and their world: "They strike the Jew and murder the human being."

It is not the fact of diaspora existence that Kafka finds destructive, but rather that antisocial behavior that threatens creativity, morality, and community. When, speaking about antisemitism, Kafka noted, "In order not to ascend to the human level, people throw themselves into the dark depths of the zoological doctrine of race," he distinguished between moral activity on the one hand and determined instinctual behavior on the other. The comments of Samuel Hugo Bergmann, coincidentally a close friend of Kafka, in a relatively recent essay on Judaism and morality read like a gloss of Kafka's remark. "The philosophy that paved the way to Nazism," Bergmann writes, "belonged to the 19th century. It was that outlook, which—under the continuously mistaken influence of the methods of natural science, which were correct in their place—taught men to see humanity as a zoological species and sought to eliminate the abyss between man and beast. This philosophy attempted to forget the truth that man had made himself by his moral freedom, that thereby he had cut himself off from the laws of biological nature."[54] Thus, people are considered human when they behave consciously and ethically, animal when their behavior is merely biologically determined. And it is precisely the ethical position that Kafka believes is undermined in his own time by hostility to Jews.

Janouch notes that in conversation with him, Kafka indicated that what, for him, distinguished the Jewish people and "the world of the Bible and Judaism" from the formless, anonymous masses was the commitment to law and the fulfillment of moral duty. Kafka added:

> The human race becomes a grey, formless, and therefore nameless mass only by falling away from form-giving law. Then, however, there is no longer any above and below; life is flattened out to mere existence; there is no drama, no struggle, but merely the deterioration of matter, decay. That is not, however, the world of the Bible and of Judaism . . . The people of the Bible is the union of individuals through a law. The masses today, however, resist every union. They struggle away from one another because of their inner lawlessness . . . The human being has lost its home here.[55]

Estranged from history, tradition, and community, the nameless, formless masses are the antithesis not only of Moses, the resolute, conscious leader, but also of his people, for whom freedom consists in the binding commitment to law. The alliance of freedom, commitment, and conscious activity, which Kafka in a conversation about Zionism associates with Moses' wilderness existence, has contemporary relevance, for it indicates a significant way in which a people may overcome their alienation and always be at home: "The old home [*Heimat*]," he notes, "is again and again new if one lives consciously; with the alert consciousness of one's ties and obligations to others. Only in this way, through one's ties, will the human being really be free. And that is of the utmost importance in life."[56]

In Kafka's understanding of Moses, Jewish life, and Judaism, the concept of leading is of unmistakable significance. In the diary entry of 1921, it is clearly Moses who is a "leader of his people" *(Volksführer seines Organismus)*. And in the conversations with Janouch, leading does, in fact, provide a nexus for Kafka's ideas about the diaspora, his personal experience as European and Jew, and his understanding of art, particularly literature. In the course of the conversation concerning the "people of the Bible" and the anonymous masses, Janouch reports the following interchange. Kafka remarks:

> "Sin is retreat in the face of one's own mission. Misunderstanding, impatience, and indolence—that is sin. The writer has the task of leading over what is isolatedly mortal [*das isolierte Sterbliche*] into infinite life, the accidental into the lawful. He has a prophetic task."
>
> "Then to write means to lead," I observed.
>
> "The correct word leads, the incorrect leads astray," said Kafka. "It is not an accident that the Bible is called Scripture. It is the voice of the Jewish people which is not something historically belonging to yesterday, but is thoroughly present."[57]

Clearly this kind of leading is not that of a heroic figure who guides others and stands apart from those who follow; he is surely not the "great man" protagonist of Freud's *Moses and Monotheism*. Here the person who leads and undertakes the prophetic task is, like the biblical Moses, a part of the people he directs—truly a *Volksführer seines Organismus*—and does for others what he does for himself. But it is also the task of the writer to lead, to transcend his mortal experience and lead "what is isolatedly mortal over into the infinite life." In the same way that, in Kafka's formulation, Moses exists only in relationship to his people and community and a people as such exists because of a Scripture that binds them, the writer through his work is bound to the community of readers. Kafka actually enunciated this idea almost a decade earlier when, in a diary entry of December 1911, he referred to minority literatures as a "keeping of a diary of a nation," which, among other things, could unify national consciousness in the face of a hostile environment.[58] The writer, then, has a mission and obligation to lead (not to lead astray) and himself be led toward that which is infinite, lawful, and meaningful. This poet does not sing privately of personal experience alone, but must, if he is to fulfill a prophetic mission, become the voice of the people, for his role at its most profound level is that of maintaining the community.

Of the allusions to Moses in Kafka's writings there are two in which he seems to view himself as a Moses figure and to experience his own life as a wilderness existence: in the first, which is reported by Janouch, Kafka characterizes his own artistic creativity, in the second, a diary entry in January 1922, he reflects on his problematic personal life. In the former, Kafka spoke about his drawings, in which he recognized "traces of an old, deeply anchored suffering." "Of course," he continued, referring to the suffering, "it is not on the paper. Here there are only the traces. The suffering is in me. I always wanted to be able to draw. I wanted to see and hold fast what is seen. That is my suffering" (*Leidenschaft*, which may also be translated as 'passion'). In response to Janouch's question about whether he had studied drawing, Kafka answers, "No. I tried to circumscribe what is seen in a completely unique way. My drawings are not pictures [*Bilder*, also 'images'], but a private figurative script [*eine private Zeichenschrift*] . . . I am still in Egyptian captivity. I have not yet crossed the Red Sea."[59] Quite apart from the effort to circumscribe what is seen, Kafka emphasizes the private character of his art ("in a completely unique way," "private figurative script"), and it is apparently this characteristic that either keeps him imprisoned in Egypt or is a sign of his presence there. Thus, this condition of enslavement in hostile territory bars him from entering the wilderness, that is, the place where the law was given, the nation formed, and "the voice of the Jewish people" created. If it is incumbent on the artist, whose graphic language is after all also a script, as it is on the writer to lead over "what is isolatedly mortal into infinite life, the accidental into the lawful," then Kafka would have to transcend his "private figurative script" and cross over into that arena where binding law and commitment to a people can liberate. When Janouch reminds him that beyond the Red Sea looms the wilderness, Kafka replies: "Yes, that's the way it is in the Bible and in general,"[60] thereby suggesting that the way out of captivity, the way of genuine liberation and of a committed life and art, is the way through the wilderness, the way that Moses walked with his people.

In the diary entry of January 28, 1922, Kafka presents a contemporary landscape that is likened to the one Moses knew. Canaan is the established quotidian world of Kafka's father, of family and personal relationships, and the wilderness a desolate place where only the isolated and solitary wander. Although only thirty-eight at the time of this entry, Kafka indicates that it has been forty years—the number of years Moses spent in the wilderness moving toward Canaan—since he had wandered out of Canaan; and his life has seemed like a "reversed wandering in the wilderness with continuous approaches to the wilderness and with childish hopes: (especially with regard to women)."[61] Being in the wilderness was apparently preferable to inhabiting his father's world, for which Kafka felt himself to be unprepared and ill suited. But he asks himself "why he wanted to leave the world," and his answer brings him face to face with the wilderness:

> Because "he" [the father] did not let me live in the world, in his world. Of course now I don't have to judge it so clearly, for now I am already a citizen in this other world, which is related to the ordinary world as the wilderness is to cultivated land (I have been forty years wandering from Canaan), look back as a foreigner, am of course also in that other world—that I have brought along as paternal inheritance—the smallest and the most anxious one and am only capable of living there because of the special organization there, according to which even for the lowliest ones there are

exaltations that come like lightning, of course also millenial shat-
terings that crush like the weight of the sea. Should I not be
thankful in spite of everything? Would I have had to find my way
here? Could I have not been crushed at the border through "ban-
ishment" there, combined with refusal here? Was not because of
my father's power the expulsion so strong that nothing could
withstand it (not me)? Of course, it is like a reversed wandering in
the wilderness with continuous approaches to the wilderness and
with childish hopes (especially with regard to women): "I shall
nevertheless perhaps remain in Canaan" and meanwhile I have been
in the wilderness for a long time, and there are only visions of
despair, especially in those times when even there I am the most
miserable one of all, and Canaan must represent itself as the only
land of hope, for there is no third land for human beings.[62]

The landscape in this passage suggests that the goal and meaning
of the biblical Moses' life have been realized and surpassed—Canaan has been settled and the struggle for liberation and community has ceased. Nor is the wilderness any longer the arena for the
preparation of a people for nationhood, but rather barren territory which provides sanctuary from the constrictions and expectations of the settled world. While this desert refuge may allow
for exaltation, it offers no guarantee of protection from misery
and despair. Unlike Kafka's earlier perception of the continuing
creative reality of Moses, the view here of a quotidian Canaan and
a wilderness populated by solitary escapees from the promised
land presents a world emptied of tradition, continuity, and pro-
ductivity. Indeed, the wanderer in this wilderness seems trapped
between two forms of imprisonment: Canaan requires confor-
mity, and the desert, which may provide refuge from the misery
of Canaan, cannot protect against despair and illusory hopes.
Given a choice only between these two possibilities ("there is no
third land for human beings"), Kafka surmises that Canaan—
where family, relationships, and community, however inadequate
or destructive, are at least possible—"must represent itself as the
only land of hope" *(Hoffnungsland)*,[63] a comment which seems
like a hope beyond all hope rather than a realistic possibility. The

prospects might be brighter had Canaan remained what it was for the biblical Moses, namely, the promised land *(das Gelobte Land)*, a land promised to a committed and just nation; and had Kafka, seeking emancipation in a hostile world, not had to give up the metaphorical desert of his father's world in order to return alone to a desolate contemporary "reality" of Moses' wilderness.

4

From Rome to Egypt:
Freud's Mosaic Transformations

Sigmund Freud was born less than three months after Heine's death;[1] he was the eldest child of the third marriage of Jakob,[2] a textile merchant, to Amalie Nathansohn, a woman twenty years his junior. The opening sentences of Freud's autobiographical portrait ("Selbstdarstellung"), written in 1925, offer pertinent information about his birth, but reveal as well that in his older years Freud perceived in his origins a familiar saga of Jewish life in exile: "I was born on May 6, 1856 in Freiberg in Moravia, a small town in what today is Czechoslovakia. My parents were Jews; I too have remained a Jew. I have reason to believe that my paternal family had lived for a long time on the Rhine (in Cologne), that because of the persecution of Jews in the fourteenth or fifteenth century they fled to the east and in the course of the nineteenth century undertook the journey back from Latvia through Galicia to German Austria."[3] The significance of his Jewish heritage is underscored by the outright assertion of his parents' and his own Jewishness, which is here connected not with religious or cultural affiliation—although these are certainly not denied—but with the enforced wandering of diaspora Jewry. Members of the Freud family would continue this heritage of wandering soon after Sigmund's birth in 1859 and 1860 because of economic distress and again in 1938 in the wake of Nazi persecution. In May 1938, just months before he fled to England,

Freud recognized in himself what many Jews perceived as the prototypical diaspora Jew—the wandering Jew, eternally abused, eternally pursued: "I compare myself sometimes to the old Jacob whom in his very old age his children took with them to Egypt . . . I hope that there won't follow, as it did then, an exodus from Egypt. It is time that Ahasuerus comes to rest somewhere."[4]

The threat posed to the Jewish population by the confluence of historical, political, and economic conditions in the years following 1848 was probably responsible for the exodus of the Freud family in 1859 from Freiberg to Leipzig and in 1860 to Vienna. It was not long after the reforms instituted in the 1848 revolutionary period that the promise of equality for Jews was abrogated and many Jewish disabilities were reinstituted.[5] Equally important in the many territories of the Hapsburg empire was nationalistic fervor, which revolution moved to the foreground. These struggles for independent nationhood were especially perilous for Jews in Moravia and Bohemia who, because of their identification with the German-Austrian ruling class and with German language and culture, were viewed as an enemy by the Czech populace.[6] Competition with a growing Czech middle class as well as inflation, unemployment, and a decline in business threatened the livelihood of both the local, largely merchant, Jewish population and new Czech business entrepreneurs. The deteriorating relationship between Jewish and Christian Czechs in the 1850s could only have added to Jakob Freud's concern about his declining business; and when Freud was three years old the family moved first to Leipzig and a year later finally settled in Vienna.

The general political and economic turmoil in the Hapsburg Empire, including the loss of Italian territories in 1859, provided the impetus for political reforms designed to rescue a disintegrating empire; but any implementation of reforms by Emperor Franz Josef, an obstinate conservative, were slow in coming. Only when the Prussian defeat of the Austrian army in 1866 ended the Hapsburg influence in Germany and exposed the enormous instability and fragility of the Empire did Franz Josef approve a constitution which offered full political and civil rights to all national and religious groups. Complete emancipation was instituted unexpectedly in 1867, and Jews were suddenly free to reside where they would, enter any profession or occupation, and seek any office, with the exception of civil service positions, which remained outside the purview of the emancipation legislation. This sole prohibition actually affected only a few, though it was probably responsible for the conversion in 1897 of Gustav Mahler, who sought the directorship of the Vienna State Opera, a civil service post. After 1867 many Jews participated so energetically in the cultural and social life of Vienna that in the last decades of the nineteenth century, when intellectual and artistic innovation were at their zenith, Jews were prominent in virtually every scholarly discipline—be it physics, medicine, linguistics, or psychology—and every branch of the arts, including architecture, painting, literature, theater, music, and journalism.[7] During these years and within that environment, Freud completed his academic studies, lectured at the university, and wrote his pioneering work on psychoanalysis, *The Interpretation of Dreams* (*Die Traumdeutung*, 1900).[8]

The last quarter of the century generated not only new possibilities for Jews, but increasing antisemitism as well.[9] The vitality of liberalism and its program of middle class access to constitutional power, resuscitated after the 1859 military defeat by France and Piedmont, were brought to a halt by the stock market crash of 1873 and a depression that endured until the waning years of the century. The burden of the disastrous economic and social conditions was suffered overwhelmingly by the poorer segments of the masses and precipitated enormous hostility against those deemed responsible, namely, liberals, who were largely German Austrians, and Jews. Carl E. Schorske has captured the complex political reactions in that period:

> During the last quarter of the nineteenth century, the program which the liberals had devised against the upper classes occasioned the explosion from the lower. The liberals succeeded in releasing the political energies of the masses, but against themselves rather

than against their ancient foes. Every shot aimed at the enemy above produced a salvo from below. A German nationalism articulated against aristocratic cosmopolitans was answered by Slavic patriots clamoring for autonomy. When the liberals soft-pedaled their Germanism in the interest of the multi-national state, they were branded as traitors to nationalism by an anti-liberal *petite bourgeoisie*. Laissez faire, devised to free the economy from the fetters of the past, called forth the Marxist revolutionaries of the future. Catholicism, routed from the school and the courthouse as the handmaiden of aristocratic oppression, returned as the ideology of peasant and artisan for whom liberalism meant capitalism and capitalism meant Jew.[10]

Indeed, antisemitism in this period informed three very different major political movements founded by former liberals who had repudiated the values and practices of liberalism: Georg Ritter von Schönerer, fanatic both in his pan-Germanism and antisemitism, introduced the politics of violence; Karl Lueger, who was elected Mayor of Vienna in 1895 but received Imperial approval only two years later, made political use of antisemitism in his attacks on capitalism and liberal values; and Theodor Herzl, as a result of reporting on the Dreyfus trial, became convinced that antisemitism would continue to pursue even the most assimilated Europeanized Jews and concluded that the only solution was flight to a Jewish homeland.

Freud and Antisemitism

Although most Viennese Jews, including Freud, did not support Herzl's Zionism, they remained profoundly troubled by the effects of antisemitism on their lives. Freud's attitudes toward Judaism and the Jewish people were also influenced by antisemitism, and they shaped his two confrontations with the figure of Moses.[11] In order to explore these attitudes I will concentrate on one specific instance, Freud's "Rome-phobia," which affords both historical and psychological perspectives on Freud's choices and positions. This episode in Freud's life is especially relevant to his first Moses, "The Moses of Michelangelo" ("Der Moses des Michelangelo"); it also sheds light on the Moses of *Moses and Monotheism,* which he began to construct in 1934, a year after Hitler had come to power in Germany, and completed after the annexation of Austria by the Nazis.

In *The Interpretation of Dreams* Freud treats the dynamics of what is commonly referred to as Freud's "Rome-neurosis" or "Rome-phobia," that is, his yearning to visit Rome and his inability to do so until years later. That segment, "The Infantile as Dream Source" ("Das Infantile als Traumquelle"), investigates how childhood experiences may reinforce current wishes that excite dreams; and one example on which Freud draws is the experiential complex concerning his longing for Rome and his failure to fulfill that longing. This complex is presented in three parts: the first, a series of four dreams which, Freud suggests, will have to satisfy, at least for the time being, his wish to go to Rome; then, a memory from his youth that he recalled during his most recent visit to Italy when, not fifty miles from Rome, he turned homeward; and, finally, the recollection of his powerful response to a story his father had told him three decades earlier. Although experiences of Jews are mentioned in all three sections, only the final two are concerned with the reaction of a Jew to experiences directly involving Jews.[12] The focus here will thus be on these latter sections which are, in fact, essentially concerned with the ways in which antisemitism may motivate behavior, desires, and the choice or construction of ideals.

There is, however, in the first section, a dream which is especially important for this inquiry because of the dreamer's identification with Moses; but this identification is problematic because in choosing Rome over Jerusalem, Freud carves out a history for himself in Rome amidst classical culture and Christianity, not in Canaan among the Jews. In this dream someone takes the dreamer to the top of a hill from which he views in the far distance Rome shrouded in mist, yet incredibly distinct. "The motif," Freud explains, "'to see the promised land from afar,' is easy to recognize therein. The city which I had first seen in the mist is—Lübeck; the hill has its model in—Gleichenberg."[13] Here Freud-Moses sees Rome-Canaan, which is, if the biblical parallel proves correct, enemy territory that must be conquered, but also a place the viewer is destined never to reach. While, in the Bible, Canaan is an old homeland which must be regained, the promised land for Freud is alien territory, the home of Catholicism. Despite this difference, if Freud the dreamer is nevertheless like Moses, then failing to reach the promised land will affect neither Freud's future influence nor fame: the significance of Moses has, after all, survived for millennia. And if the wish fulfilled by this dream is to be like Moses, then the dream may be less about entering Rome than about being assured of one's heroic status if one does not.

What is unexplained in this dream, even by those who focus closely on the Rome-phobia,[14] is the identification of Rome-Canaan with Gleichenberg and Lübeck. Gleichenberg was a health spa in Austria where in 1883 Freud visited his sister-in-law's fiancé, Ignaz Schönberg, who was ill with tuberculosis. Several years later Schönberg died of his illness. By analogy with Gleichenberg, Rome would seem to be a place where one could not expect recuperation or resurrection.[15] The reference to Lübeck, however, at that time one of the free Hanseatic cities, is more difficult to understand. Not alluding to this particular passage, Ernest Jones notes that Freud associated Lübeck with his wife Martha: she had vacationed there before their marriage, and that is where the Freuds spent the first days after their wedding. From that city the newlyweds wrote Martha's mother a joint letter, which Freud concluded with a remark that identified marriage and perhaps Lübeck as hostile arenas: "Given at our present residence in Lübeck on the first day of what we hope will prove a Thirty Years' War between Sigmund and Martha."[16] Lübeck does, in addition, play a role in recent Jewish history, but there is no evidence that Freud knew this. It was one of the places which, after the defeat of Napoleon, cancelled emancipation legislation and gained attention at the Congress of Vienna (1814–15) for openly opposing the enfranchisement of the Jews in

Germany.[17] Indeed, in 1824 all Jews were expelled from that city. The differences between Rome, Canaan, and Lübeck are suppressed in the dream. Inscribed in the dream, however, is territory hostile to the Jew that needs to be conquered—be it Christian Rome, Canaan, or the Lübeck of the battle of the sexes or antisemitism; all are apparently elements which Freud deemed necessary for the construction of the monumental conquering figure that informs the subsequent sections.

In the second section Freud discusses the importance of youthful impressions for his intense yearning for Rome, and he searches his past for the origin of his ideal. He notes that new insights into his behavior and motives became evident to him when, on his previous Italian trip, he turned back a mere fifty miles from Rome. He began the journey to the roots of his attraction by recognizing his identification with the military commander Hannibal and not with the scholar Winckelmann, both of whom were preoccupied with reaching Rome. Hannibal had indeed been one of his boyhood heroes, and even now as an adult Freud conceives of himself as following in his footsteps—like the Carthaginian, he too had gone to the Campania and had failed to reach Rome. Freud recalls that he, like many of his fellow Gymnasium students, favored the Carthaginians and not the Romans in the Punic wars. But the figure of Hannibal loomed especially large for him at that time: "The initial understanding about the consequences of being descended from a race alien to the nation arose, and the antisemitic reminders among my classmates exhorted me to take a stand . . . Hannibal and Rome symbolized to the youth the opposition between the tenacity of Jewry or Judaism [*Judentum* may signify either] and the organization of the Catholic Church."[18] Freud adds that current antisemitism has helped him retrieve these youthful experiences.[19] Thus, antisemitism seems to be responsible for both his early interest in the alien conquering hero and the recollection of that youthful experience. Clearly Freud's strong early identification with Hannibal had thirty years later activated—perhaps because of the prominence of antisemitism in the last decades of the century[20]—his desire to enter Rome as an antagonist who possessed the tenacity and persistence of the Semitic general.

Freud's response to antisemitism is indeed central not only to his youthful choice of and identification with a warrior, but to the significance of this hero for his adult life as well. Since for Freud the antagonism seems to be between the *organization* of the Church and the *tenacity* of Jewry or Judaism, not conflicting theologies, what concerns him here seems to be the resistance of the Jews to pressures by the Church. And with what better model to wage battle against such antagonism and antisemitism than with a Semitic warrior! But with a Semitic warrior who is not a Jew? Can it be that Freud expects through his association with Hannibal to shed his identity as Jew, which had recently interfered with his professional advancement (he had been hoping for a professorship), and nevertheless to remain a Semite who will heroically destroy the Church organization that had such an uncompromisingly powerful presence in Hapsburg Vienna? That may be. After all, forty years later Freud would transform Moses, with whom he identifies here at the turn of the century, into an Egyptian who is the founder of Jewish monotheism. But why then choose a hero who, defeated in the Campania, had never reached Rome? Perhaps because a defeat of the hero that does not destroy the hero's reputation—Hannibal's greatness did indeed survive his defeat—may in fact safeguard the dreamer, the constructor of monuments and ideals, and ensure his preeminence. And Hannibal shares with the dreamer's Freud-Moses not only the failure to reach a fateful destination, but also lasting renown despite that frustration.

In the third and final section, while apparently still trying to understand his preoccupation with Hannibal, Freud just "happens upon" an experience from his past, an event once again concerned with antisemitism. This time he recalls an incident his father related to him when he was ten or twelve years old. To illustrate that times had indeed changed for the better his father told a story about himself as a young man in Freiberg. One Saturday he had gone out for a stroll wearing a new fur hat, which was knocked from his head into the mud by a Christian shouting, "Jew, get off the sidewalk." To his son's query about how he had responded, the father replied that he had gone into the gutter and picked up his hat. Freud's reaction is not sympathetic, and his observation seems more appropriate for a child half the age of a ten- or twelve-year-old:

> That did not seem to me heroic of the big strong man, who led me, the small one, by the hand. I juxtaposed this situation, which did not please me, with another, which conformed better to my sentiments, the scene in which Hannibal's father, Hamilcar Barcas, had his son swear on the household altar that he would take vengeance on the Romans. Since that time Hannibal has a place in my fantasies.[21]

Once again antisemitism and the response to it are motivating forces behind the necessity for a hero, this time for one who himself wants or needs an authoritative father. In this instance, Freud's father is rejected because of his weakness and would be replaced by a powerful patriarch. But it may be that the father is rejected also because he is a Jew—after all, as Freud tells the story, his father is readily identified as a Jew by a passing pedestrian[22]— and replaced by a Semite who is not a Jew, but might nonetheless fight antisemitism. Freud could then be a warrior who has not abandoned the Jews.

In a kind of coda to the attempt to discover the roots of his preoccupation with Rome and Hannibal, Freud mentions other heroes, two military men, with whom he was concerned as a child: Marshal Masséna, whom he thought to be of Jewish descent; and Napoleon, who, like Hannibal, crossed the Alps. Although Freud notes that Masséna may be a Jew, he does not consider the importance of Napoleon for the emancipation of Jews, something of which many nineteenth-century European Jews, including, of course, Heine, were all too aware. Freud concludes that weakness and vulnerability may indeed be significant determining factors for the adoption or creation of a person's martial heroes: "And perhaps the development of this warrior ideal can be traced even further back into childhood to wishes which the alternately friendly and warlike interchange during the first three years with a boy a year older must call forth in the weaker of the two playmates."[23] Freud is here speaking about his childhood relationship with his half-brother's son, John, who was older than he. The antisemitism, however, which was so prominent in Freud's discussion of his prepossessing interest in Hannibal and Rome, is absent from this interpretation. It seems almost miraculously to have either disappeared as Freud moved more deeply into his past or been vanquished by the rather speculative explanation for his interest in heroic warriors. The possibility then lingers that by going down deep enough and back far enough in time, psychoanalysis, like the warrior-psychoanalyst, may merely by interpretation conquer even the most destructive social ills.[24] Of course, like Hannibal, it might also not be successful.

Freud's interpretive journey into how desire and ideals are produced—specifically his Rome-phobia and the relationship of this phobia to antisemitism—reveals something more and other than how psychoanalytic procedure can unearth the origins of behavior in childhood experience. It also discloses that the value Freud attributes to social and historical reality diminishes as one moves, in the process of psychoanalysis, further back into a past increasingly inaccessible to memory. Freud's ultimate evidence for his Rome-phobia is, after all, not recollected data, but *probable* childhood experience in a situation of the unequal age/power distribution among toddlers. In her work on Freud's Jewish identity, Marthe Robert notes that *The Interpretation of Dreams* and *Moses and Monotheism* together comprise Freud's "family novel" (a kind of autobiography of his struggle with Jewish culture and a Jewish father), but that the works differ significantly in the ways in which reality and history are comprehended and retained. In the former, Robert concludes, "the fantasies of Freud's nights are presented in their constant relation to the realities of his days and then subjected to an analysis which . . . is carried on with perfect impartiality," while in the latter, "the novel takes its leave of history and the real world of necessity and pursues its own aims."[25] Freud's presentation of Rome-phobia, on which, incidentally, Robert dwells at length,[26] does not entirely support her claim about the significance of "realities of the day." Those realities, especially antisemitism, are not explored in their social or psychological context, but provide the impetus for investigating the general emotional life of the adult and child. I would, therefore, suggest that there is in fact less substantive change than Robert supposes in the "autobiography," which extends from *The Interpretation of Dreams* to *Moses and Monotheism*. An exploration of Freud's concern with Moses will, I hope, disclose that realities, be they social or textual, when not simply absent, are persistently transfigured and even selectively eliminated in the course of the interpretive process. A cautious and critical journey through the Moses texts may help to bring us closer to an understanding of Freud's complex and changing responses to Jews and Judaism at different times in his life.

IN 1900 FREUD characterized his own adventurous nature in terms of conquest: "I am actually not at all a man of science, not an observer, not an experimenter, not a thinker. I am by temperament nothing but a *conquistador*, an adventurer, if you wish to translate this term—with all the inquisitiveness, daring, and tenacity characteristic of such a man."[27] Whether in the guise of *conquistador* or Semitic warrior, Freud apparently conceived of himself at that time as conquering Rome in the name of Jewry, which the Roman Church, in his view, had persecuted and continued to threaten. But what did happen when he finally reached Rome? Freud indicates that on his return from Rome his "zest for life and work" had grown sufficiently that he could actively lobby for the professorship he had quietly awaited for several years. Since it is commonly accepted that he was denied the position largely because of Education Minister Wilhelm von Härtel's antisemitism, being promoted to *Professor Extraordinarius* in 1902 was indeed a victory connected with Rome.[28]

There is, however, evidence—and his Moses (of Michelangelo) may be a prime witness at a later date—that Freud did not enjoy a significant conquest, but that Christian Rome may have altered the Jew in Freud. Freud finally reached Rome in the summer of 1901 and admitted to his friend Wilhelm Fliess that although it was "an overwhelming experience," it was also "slightly disappointing." The presence of ancient Rome and the modern metropolis posed no problems for him, but that was not true of medieval Rome: "But while I was completely undisturbed by ancient Rome . . . I could not freely enjoy the second [medieval] Rome, the meaning disturbed me; being incapable of putting out of my mind all my misery and everything else I knew, I could not readily tolerate the lie of mankind's salvation, which reared its head to heaven."[29]

It was apparently the Christian Rome of Michelangelo and Pope Julius II with which Freud was preoccupied every day of a three-week visit in 1913. He contemplated Michelangelo's statue of Moses and created of that figure a Moses "superior to the historical or traditional" one, a new rational and controlled Moses who surpassed the Old Testament hero—a new Christian Moses who would not rise from his place atop the eternal resting place of a pope. If Freud was a *conquistador,* one wonders whether it was Rome he had conquered or the biblical Moses.

"The Moses of Michelangelo"

Like Heinrich Heine, who in Paris stood before a representation of Hellenic culture, a statue of a pagan goddess, and pondered the importance of that culture for his life,[30] Sigmund Freud spent hours, so he tells us, each day of a three-week visit to Rome, looking at a representation of the most significant biblical figure of Jewish history, a statue of Moses, and sought an explanation for its powerful and intimidating effect on him. Their accounts of the encounters with these artworks indicate that both Heine and Freud were wrestling with ideas and values which were of great significance to them and which were reflected not only in the subject of their works, but in the discrepancy between those sculptures and the places in which they were housed.

Heine saw the Venus de Milo prominently exhibited in the

Louvre, one of the most renowned museums of western Europe, and ruefully acknowledged at that time in 1848—a year in which he saw all hope dashed for the recuperation of his own health and of that of France and Europe—that this Venus, whose limbs had not weathered the centuries, could hardly be expected to rescue an ailing poet or nation. Recognizing the futility of trying to reawaken the living reality of a fragmented ancient relic which, along with the culture it represented, was preserved for the aesthetic pleasure of museum visitors, Heine had come to the Louvre to take final leave of the Hellenic ideals which had for so long informed his poetic muse and political ideals. A few years later he noted that his previous preoccupation with the "Hellenic spirit" had interfered with a judicious assessment of Moses.

Michelangelo's statue of Moses is a prominent part of the tomb of Pope Julius II located in the Church of Saint Peter in Chains. It is clear from his essay "The Moses of Michelangelo" that for Freud the church functioned as a museum where during his visits to Rome he could study the statue of Moses, although the fact that the church was still used for religious practice could not have eluded him. The essay reveals an awareness of not only the incompatibility between the "Lawgiver of the Jews"[31] and this sanctuary of Western Christendom, but also the dilemma of the European Jew confronted with the attractions of the dominant culture, be it Christian or classical. Indeed, a statue of Moses by a great Christian artist ensconced in an edifice dedicated to the glorification of Christianity reflects the fundamental disparity between Christianity and Judaism, between a European universe and the Jewish place within it. And in Freud's dream it is difficult to overlook the irony of Moses and Freud in the promised land, in Rome, home of Catholicism. Freud's preoccupation with the art and ethos of the dominant European and Christian culture may not be obvious in this essay because of the Old Testament subject matter, but it becomes apparent when, in the course of his interpretation, he relinquishes the traditional understanding of the biblical hero for a "new and different" Moses.

In 1901 Freud finally reached Rome and saw the Michelangelo Moses, the first of many viewings during repeated visits to Rome. But it was only during the summer of 1912, Ernest Jones reports, that Freud indicated his interest "in the meaning of the statue";[32] and later that year, he wrote his wife, Martha, from Rome that he had seen the statue every day and was thinking of writing about it. In a concluding paragraph of that letter he writes: "Daily I wear a gardenia and play the rich man who lives out his passions,"[33] a remark which echoes the opposition between exterior pose and concealed emotion he perceived in Michelangelo's statue. It was not, however, until December 1913, a few months after he returned from yet another trip to Rome, that he began to write "The Moses of Michelangelo," which he completed on New Year's Day 1914. Jones attributes Freud's hesitation about writing to insecurity about his interpretation; it is certainly true that Freud was doing extensive research on this statue and had expressed misgivings about his views.[34] But other, more problematic, motives may have also played a part.

The years just preceding this undertaking had been very difficult for Freud. Two founding members of the Vienna Psychoanalytic Group left Freud and the group: Alfred Adler in 1911 and Wilhelm Stekel the following year. The year 1913 brought the most devastating defection of all, the break with Carl Jung. Freud had looked to an alliance with Jung to extend the boundaries of psychoanalysis beyond his circle of generally Jewish adherents and disciples. His correspondence with Karl Abraham indicates that Freud had expected that the inclusion of Jung in their group would secure the psychoanalytic project from criticism of being parochial and from antisemitic attacks; in May 1908, he wrote Abraham: "You are closer to my intellectual constitution because of racial kinship, while he [Jung] as a Christian and a pastor's son finds his way to me only against great inner resistances. His association with us is then all the more valuable. I would almost have said that only his appearance has removed psychoanalysis from the danger of becoming a Jewish national affair."[35] And in December of that year, in reference to an article he had written which he thought would elicit strong negative reactions, Freud wrote: "Some German ideals again in danger! Our Aryan comrades are nevertheless indispensible to us, otherwise psychoanalysis would succumb to antisemitism."[36] Hoping to groom Jung, who was nineteen years younger, for leadership, Freud wrote Jung in 1909 that "you will as Joshua, if I am Moses, take possession of the promised land of psychiatry, which I am only permitted to glimpse from afar."[37] But almost as though to immunize his movement against usurpation by the prevailing culture, Freud converts Jung—the pastor's son who was to universalize psychoanalysis—into a Jew, and a warrior Jew at that, thereby assuring the dominance of Jewish authority. In 1915, after the break with Jung, Freud wrote to James Putnam, an American follower, that he did not find religious-ethical conversion inviting. "Jung, for example, I found sympathetic as long as he lived blindly, as I did. Then came his religious-ethical crisis with higher morality, 'rebirth,' Bergson, and at the very same time, lies, brutality and anti-Semitic condescension towards me."[38] Following the Nazi reorganization of the German Society for Psychotherapy as the International General Medical Society for Psychotherapy, Jung did become its president, retaining this post although publicly denounced by his Swiss colleagues. He also edited the Society's journal and was responsible for investigating the differences between Aryan and Jewish psychology.[39] Whether or not Jung harbored antisemitic sentiments in the early decades of the century during the period of his association with Freud is open to question; but Freud clearly thought so. Yet, until the final break with Jung, Freud was willing to compromise greatly in order to maintain good relations with Jung. He wrote to Abraham in 1908: "I harbor the suspicion that the suppressed antisemitism of the Swiss that wants to spare me is deflected in reinforced form upon you. I only think that as Jews we must, if we want to participate anywhere, develop a bit of masochism, be ready to permit some injustice done to us. Otherwise there is no getting it together."[40] That he tolerated antisemitism in the case of Jung—a position he found unacceptable in his father's behavior—and nevertheless had finally to sever connections with him affected Freud's emotional life and professional plans. In October 1912 Freud wrote to Sandor Ferenczi: "At the moment the situation in Vienna makes me feel more like the historical Moses than the Michelangelo one."[41] It was with the volatile emotional residue of defections, antisemitism, condescension, and failure that in 1913 Freud once again traveled to Rome and stood before Michelangelo's Moses, this time trying to articulate its meaning.

Freud's first response to the statue indicates that this Moses had a very powerful and intimidating presence, displaying such a "powerful bodily mass and forcefully vigorous musculature" (*gewaltige Körpermasse und kraftstrotzende Muskulatur*)[42] that it left him "overcome and as it were paralyzed by the general effect [of the statue]."[43] By essay's end, however, Freud discovers that Michelangelo had actually created a "different" Moses, one stoic and controlled, whose enormous physical power "becomes only a corporeal means of expression for the highest mental achievement possible in a human being."[44] It is this transformation in the interpretation of the Moses statue from Freud's idea of the traditional biblical Moses into a civilized and controlled hero, from the overwhelming threat of a figure of commanding, even physical, power into one of constrained quiescence—a transformation that is the result of Moses' mental decision—with which the essay is largely concerned and which needs to be explored.

FREUD'S INITIAL REMARKS in "The Moses of Michelangelo" address those aspects of aesthetics which will inform his discussion of the Moses statue and, out of concern for the nature and intensity of the spectator's response, focus on the artist's intention as expressed in the work of art. Since Freud expects to discover this intention primarily in the "meaning and content" of the work,[45] he proceeds with an analysis of it. His methodological procedures, while not systematically articulated, become apparent as he develops an understanding of the statue, an understanding which, he hopes, will disclose Michelangelo's intention and therewith explain his own overwhelming reaction. It is not entirely clear whether Freud believed that the artist's intention was completely available in the artwork or that the artwork provided an external index to Michelangelo's concealed or unarticulated experience; while a large part of the discussion in the essay leads to the former conclusion, there is evidence, especially in the concluding insights, that he was especially interested in the sculptor's hidden agenda. The assumption that Michelangelo's unexpressed emotional life and intentions will be conveyed by the artist's work suggests Freud's critical naiveté and perhaps also a hidden agenda of his own.

Freud begins the discussion of the statue with a brief review of a number of texts about the work and notes not only the considerable diversity of interpretation, but also the ample disagreement about the figure's specific physical features and gestures, its demeanor, and the intention of the artist. His analysis of detail convinces him that this work does not represent "a timeless image of character and mood,"[46] as some have maintained, but rather a "particular, but then most significant moment of his [Moses'] life,"[47] which can only be precisely ascertained if the movements of the figure that preceded the instant fixed in stone could be reconstructed. Thus, the exploration of the manifest data urges a consideration of the figure's past and latent life whose discovery, Freud expects, will explain his own bewildering and inscrutable response to the statue.

Freud indicates that in this instance his method of interpreting cultural texts is basically no different from the psychoanalytic exploration of behavior and dreams. Yet perhaps because he sees himself as "merely a layman" in the area of art interpretation,[48] he seems especially anxious to defend his approach as one that in the past—even before the advent of psychoanalysis—had been used for artistic investigation. Referring to the art connoisseur Ivan Lermolieff, whose emphasis on "the characteristic significance of minor detail" assisted him in distinguishing original works of art from copies, Freud notes that psychoanalysis, like Lermolieff's method of inquiry, "is accustomed to detecting what is secret and concealed in lightly valued and unnoticed features, in the rubbish heap—the *'refuse'*—of observation."[49]

An important question that arises is, however, less concerned with the validity of Freud's methodology than with how to evaluate his understanding of Michelangelo's statue, a product of his hermeneutic strategy. Does Freud present an accurate account of the artist's intentions, or is his reading an unacknowledged creation of his own Moses in a performance so stunning that he himself does not recognize his own underlying impulses and maneuvers? It is difficult to know whether his insights have actually fathomed Michelangelo's intentions, but if that is the case, Freud must have arrived at his conclusions by means other than the analytic process, for, as I hope to demonstrate, his assertions and conclusions are too often not sustained by the evidence and arguments he offers. These difficulties notwithstanding, the Moses Freud constructs in the process of interpretation is important because it illuminates his own interests and intentions, which may best be understood by clarifying his interpretive procedure.

Freud's first reference to the Moses statue suggests that the tomb of Pope Julius II and its statuary represent the kind of power and violence, albeit repressed and potential, which arouses enormous dread; at their mere sight, an eminent professional man in his fifties feels anxious, intimidated, and impotent:

> [Michelangelo's Moses], as is known, is only a portion of that monumental tomb which the artist was to have erected for the mighty *(gewaltigen)* Pope Julius II . . . For from no other sculpture have I had a stronger impression. How often have I climbed the steep steps of the unattractive Corso Cavour to the lonely square where the deserted church stands, have always tried to withstand the disdainful angry glance of the hero, and sometimes I have cautiously sneaked out of the semi-darkness of the interior as though I myself belonged to the rabble toward whom his eye is directed, who can hold on to no conviction, who don't want to wait and trust, and who rejoice when they have regained the illusion of their idols.[50]

It is not merely to the power and anger of the hero that Freud as spectator reacts but, as we learn two lines later, to Moses as "Lawgiver of the Jews, holding the tables of the Ten Commandments," in whose presence he feels himself to be part of a rabble that possesses neither the tenacity nor the resolve to maintain its convictions. Confronted with what he considers an inscrutable statue to which he has a debilitating response, Freud undertakes an interpretive adventure, as it were, during which he gains control of his sense of overwhelming inadequacy. At the conclusion of this venture, Michelangelo's Moses has mastered his enormous rage at the disobedient idolatrous Jews, and Freud seems to have shed his anxiety, parted company with the rabble, and virtually identified with Michelangelo's "different Moses" who has now attained "the highest mental achievement possible in a human being."[51]

Curious difficulties arise when one tries to explain the transformations of Michelangelo's Moses from enraged to restrained hero and of Freud's response from cringing fear to tranquil admiration. On the one hand, the changes are presented as results of analysis and products of interpretation; through scrupulous attention to detail, Freud arrives at what he considers an accurate description of the statue and assessment of its posture. On the other hand, however, the recognition of a restrained "different Moses" and the experience of Freud's new salubrious response to it seem also to affect hermeneutic procedures; thus, for example, there are significant instances in Freud's essay when his perception of a transformed Moses in Michelangelo's work seems to determine the ways in which the biblical narrative is read and misread. What need to be clarified, therefore, are the nature of the evidence and the use to which Freud puts it.

FREUD AGREES WITH a number of nineteenth-century critics that Michelangelo's Moses is looking at worshippers of the Golden Calf; but he does not concur that Moses is about to rise up in rage against them or let loose the tables of the law. A close study of hand, head, and leg positions and of the general pose of the body led Freud to believe that this figure had contained its enormous wrath, leaving only traces in the gesture of the hand interacting with the beard. In Freud's assessment, this Moses has checked his fury about the idolatrous activity and decided not to act so that he might preserve the tables which would have slipped from under his arm and shattered had he yielded to his passions. Indeed, it was to save the Decalogue that "he has overcome the temptation, and he will now remain sitting in this way in restrained rage, in pain mixed with contempt. Nor will he throw away the tables so that they break on the stones, for it is on their account that he has overcome his anger, for their preservation mastered his passion."[52] Moreover, Freud interprets Moses' act of checking his anger and behavior not as spontaneous activity, but as a carefully reasoned decision: "He [Moses] remembered his mission and for its sake renounced the gratification of his passion."[53] Freud presents a vague but very interesting overview of the statue that supports the importance of mental resolve and restraint, an idea which some twenty-five years later in *Moses and Monotheism* he identified as a prominent characteristic of the Jewish people: "A threefold stratification is expressed in the figure when viewed vertically. There are reflected in the countenance of his face the passions which have become dominant, in the middle of the figure signs of repressed movement are visible, the foot still shows the position of the intended action, as though mastery had advanced downwards from above."[54] Whether Michelangelo's sculpture in fact portrays this "more than human" Moses as having mastered his "own passion on behalf of a destiny to which [he] has dedicated [him]self,"[55] is not at issue here; what is important, it seems to me, is an understanding of the connection between Freud's interpretive procedure and his conception of the Moses figure as well as of the significance of that conception.

Freud expends great effort in "The Moses of Michelangelo" to determine the function of even insignificant features and gestures of the statue; yet it is curious that once he has decided that this work is not a character study but the portrayal of a moment in Moses' life, he does not question whether this particular moment occurs when Moses catches sight of the revelry around the Golden Calf. He presents no other possibilities, though others are plausible. One interesting alternative that comes to mind is Moses' subsequent return from the mountain with two new tables, which he did not break. This possibility would account for the horns on Moses' head. The idea of Moses' horns resulted from a misunderstanding in Exodus 34:35 of the Hebrew verb *karan*, whose meaning is 'shone'. The translators of the Vulgate mistook this verb for the noun *keren*, meaning 'ray of light' or 'horn'. Instead of understanding that the skin of Moses' face shone or radiated after he returned with the new tablets, the Vulgate translation had Moses acquire horns, a characteristic that gained some prominence in the art of the Middle Ages and Renaissance.[56] I am not here defending this particular interpretation, but merely want to suggest that other possibilities deserve consideration.

The idea of Moses comfortably and easily holding the two new tables would no doubt conflict with Freud's conception of the sculpture as representing the mastery of a powerful and potentially destructive emotion. In fact, his interest in the figure's restraint of anger is apparent throughout this essay, even in the deviations from Scripture and tradition for which he holds Michelangelo responsible: the biblical Moses had a fierce temper and acted on his anger, unlike Michelangelo's Moses as interpreted by Freud; and the traditional Moses destroyed the tables, while Michelangelo's (as seen by Freud) preserved them. These deviations form the foundation for the possibility of Michelangelo's new, "civilized" Christian Moses, and it is the quality of this new Moses which draws Freud's attention: "But Michelangelo has placed on the tomb of the Pope a different Moses, who is superior to the historical or traditional Moses."[57] Indeed Freud readily discards the biblical Moses, or rather his conception of that Moses, for the new hero he has uncovered in a Renaissance work that is informed by classical models and created by a Christian artist.

Although Michelangelo's Moses is, in Freud's view, a master of restraint and preservation, it is worth noting that this new and superior hero also does not act, he remains seated and still. But the historical Moses to which Freud alludes does act, if only in fits of passion. There are, however, indications in the essay—one in a misreading, the other in selectively deleted passages—that Freud was familiar with a biblical Moses who even in his wrath was rational and restrained and took very deliberate action. In the first instance, to exemplify the consequences of Moses' fiery temper Freud refers to one of Moses' earliest aggressive acts: "In such a fit of divine wrath he slew the Egyptian who was maltreating an Israelite, and therefore had to flee out of the land into the wilderness."[58] The passage in the Bible reads somewhat differently: "And he spied an Egyptian smiting a Hebrew, one of his brethren. And he looked this way and that way, and when he saw that there was no man, he slew the Egyptian, and he hid him in the sand" (Exodus 2:11–12). A person who makes certain there are no witnesses before acting can hardly be perceived as operating "in a fit of divine wrath." Although Moses' behavior may have been unwise and was no doubt grounded in moral indignation and righteous anger, it seems at the least to have been the considered response of a rational subject.

The omissions of the scriptural texts present a more difficult problem primarily because the deleted texts are very provocative. They occur in Freud's liberal quotation from Exodus 32 when he tries to account for Michelangelo's deviation from the Bible. Noting that he will cite that portion which treats "Moses' behavior at the scene of the Golden Calf,"[59] Freud omits the first six verses, which record the making of the idol in Moses' absence, then cites the rest of the chapter, excluding verses 12–13 and 21–29. One can only speculate why these passages were suppressed from such a comprehensive quotation (there are 35 verses in this chapter), but an examination of these segments suggests plausible reasons.

Verses 12 and 13, which follow Moses' plea to God not to consume the people whom God had worked so mightily to liberate from Egypt, record the overall design of Moses' argument. He begins by suggesting that God consider how Egyptians will regard a God who delivers people from bondage only to decimate them, and concludes by asking God to remember promises made to the Patriarchs to increase the population and bestow land to be theirs forever. The argument is successful; God relents and does not consume the people. The great effort to convince God to restrain his wrath indicates that Moses, in addition to his concern for the welfare of the people, is devoted to a principle of behavior that echoes Freud's conception of Michelangelo's "different Moses" who "remembered his mission and for its sake renounced any gratification of his passion."[60] The biblical Moses is after all asking God to restrain his great and justified anger so that his plan for the salvation of Israel could be fulfilled; and his plea that a wrathful God practice rational restraint is, incidentally, not an anomaly in the Bible (see, for example, Numbers 14:11–20). The suppression of these verses suggests that the Old Testament may not have been the place where Freud hoped to find his new Moses; a pope's tomb in a Roman church was apparently more appealing.

The other passage Freud omits, verses 21–29, may be divided into two parts, one in which Moses interrogates Aaron about how the idolatry came to pass, the other in which he orders persevering idolators to be punished. When questioning Aaron, Moses' great anger is reflected in Aaron's response, "Let not the anger of my lord wax hot," and seems to be a continuation of the rage in which just previously Moses had destroyed the tables of the law (32:19). Since it is difficult to imagine how Aaron's perfunctory statements justifying the weakness of the people, which one commentator calls "threadbare excuses,"[61] could have stilled such passion, one can but assume that the sight of the continuing revelry only exacerbated Moses' fury. Nevertheless, the action he undertakes, though most cruel and vile, is rational and deliberated. After first gathering to him those "on the Lord's side," he orders them to slay their relatives, companions, and neighbors, and when they have carried out the punishment and slain some three thousand idolators, he calls them blessed because they acted in God's behalf. In this episode there is no apparent conflict or contradiction between Moses' powerful, even violent, emotion that is expressed and that restraint and reason which Freud detected only in Michelangelo's hero. Here emotion and restraint culminate in decisive action.

The omission of these texts strongly suggests that Freud was acquainted with a biblical Moses different from the one whose burning anger drove him to such irrational acts as killing the Egyptian or destroying the tables, but that he excluded this Moses from his conception of the traditional figure. The Moses Freud confronted at the beginning of the essay must have conformed to his idea of the biblical hero, the one whose "angry scorn" was menacing; otherwise why would Freud have cowered in fear before the statue? Through a process of interpretation, however, which also included the deletion of significant material and the misreading or misunderstanding of texts, Freud constructed a conception of Michelangelo's Moses who, "seated and still," was no longer a threat to the viewer and was moreover "a corporeal means of expression for the highest mental achievement possible in a human being, for the conquest of one's own passion on behalf of a destiny to which one has dedicated oneself."[62]

At first it might seem that such an achievement could apply as well to the controlled biblical Moses who must contain his passions in order to act appropriately, but there are substantial differences. For Freud, the Moses of Michelangelo is involved in a mental struggle *against* emotions in order *not* to act or destroy the documents of the law; while in Exodus 32, Moses is wrestling *with* his emotions but also—and this seems far more significant— with the moral imperative of readying a people to become an ethical and pious nation. For this latter Moses, the highest achievement is not merely psychological or mental, but social and political as well; his concern seems not to be how to restrain himself from acting out his feelings, but rather how to act passionately, yet judiciously and productively.[63]

On the heels of the statement about the "highest mental achievement" Freud announces that his interpretation of the statue is now completed, but it is not clear whether he thinks that the exposition of the artist's intention is also completed or whether that remains to be explored; for immediately thereafter Freud inquires about "what motives were active in the sculptor when he decided on Moses, and indeed such a greatly transformed Moses, for the tomb of Julius II."[64] Freud's reply is speculative and illuminating, and since he himself participated substantially in the "transformation" process, one might also expect it to reveal something about his own intentions and motivations.

Noting that many had sought to account for Michelangelo's motives by examining the character of Pope Julius II and Michelangelo's relations to him, Freud considers three areas of their relationship: first, the character of Pope Julius II, an enormously ambitious man of action who intended to carry out his goals by dint of an iron will and through violent means; then, the characteristics shared by this pope and Michelangelo, namely, "the same vehemence of aspiration" and the pursuit on a grand scale of what is great and mighty;[65] and finally, the abuse which the artist suffered at the hands of the hot-tempered and impatient pope. The personalities of these men and their relationship created the conditions under which, according to Freud, Michelangelo had to make artistic decisions. Since Michelangelo was perceived as the more introspective of the two and "may have had a presentiment of the failure to which they were both doomed,"[66] he created the kind of work through which he was able to transcend his own destructive and self-destructive impulses, or so Freud suggests. "So he put his Moses on the pope's tomb, not without a reproach against the dead man, as a warning to himself, through this criticism elevating himself above his own nature" *(sich mit dieser Kritik über die eigene Natur erhebend).*[67] Thus, in Freud's view, what Michelangelo intended in this statue of a "new and more than human" Moses was not only a critique of Julius' and his own violent, potentially dangerous passions, but also the remedy: restraint and quiescence.

It must be more than mere coincidence that Freud himself shared the desire for great and powerful achievements that he identified in this pope and in Michelangelo;[68] like Michelangelo,

Freud wanted not only to elevate himself above his own hostile impulses, but also to create a monumental work—psychoanalysis—with its origins in Judaism, refined by Christian restraint, and housed in the heart of Christendom. With the defection of Jung earlier that year, Freud's hopes for protecting his work against antisemitic attacks seemed shattered. However, faced with the figure of the stoic Jewish lawgiver in the church of St. Peter in Chains, Freud could devise a Moses-Michelangelo-Julius II text which would reflect not only his own crisis, but the remedy for transcending it as well: a solitary, stony Christianized Moses, restrained for an eternity, seated on the inert remains of an entombed warrior pope.[69]

Curiously, the concluding words of the essay indicate that Freud had serious misgivings about whether great passion was expressed in Michelangelo's statue: "Perhaps he was not completely successful in the case of Moses if it was his intention to have the storm of passionate excitation detected in the signs, which, after it [the storm] subsided, remained behind in the calm" (*wenn es seine Absicht war, den Sturm heftiger Erregung aus den Anzeichen erraten zu lassen, die nach seinem Ablauf in der Ruhe zurückblieben*).[70] This statement without qualification or discussion conceals an uncomfortable silence not only about the absence of strong emotion which may indeed have reflected the artist's intention, but also about the special significance for Freud of both powerful emotion and powerful restraint. Moreover, investing Michelangelo's statue with this "storm of passionate excitation" suggests that Freud may have actually accomplished two awe-inspiring interpretive feats: on the one hand, he embedded in Michelangelo's solemn and calm figure his own conception of a biblical Moses who was subject to fits of passion and divine wrath; on the other, he has Michelangelo's different and Christian Moses vanquish the volatile Jewish hero and condemn to silence the very passion which Freud saw as a dominant trait of the historical Lawgiver of the Jews.

But where does this leave Freud the essayist at essay's end? After an arduous interpretive journey, no longer anxious and intimidated in the face of a menacing Moses, Freud seems to have mastered his own emotions by mastering Michelangelo's Moses. Delving into this Moses' past and inner life, he discovered the suppressed anger which initially had made him feel frightened and diminished, but through the outward calm and containment of the seated figure, Freud found a way to restore his own self-mastery. As "The Moses of Michelangelo" reveals, accomplishing this task was far from simple. For Freud to achieve self-mastery required more than the creation of a new, exemplary Moses. The Moses of the Old Testament was rebuked and discounted, and one of the greatest artists of Western civilization and Christendom had to fulfill the mission of constructing a new Moses, and fulfill it in an environment not traditionally experienced as salutary by Jewish people: in Christian Rome, in a church, in the presence of a monumentalized pope. Only then, through the application of all his interpretive wit and skill, did the essayist Freud finally achieve the transformation of Moses as well as himself, thereby perhaps assuring himself that he had risen, as he said of Michelangelo, "above his own nature."[71] Michelangelo's Moses remained, interpreted and still, in the Church of Saint Peter in Chains when Freud, bearing a chastened Christian Moses within him, returned to his seat of power in Vienna and wrote his story of what had transpired in Rome. At about the same time that he wrote "The Moses of Michelangelo," he also elaborated on his differences with Jung in a long essay, "On the History of the Psychoanalytic Movement" ("Zur Geschichte der pyschoanalytischen Bewegung"), which Peter Gay notes "was Freud's declaration of war. As he wrote it furiously, he sent drafts to his intimates, and he came to call it affectionately the 'bomb'."[72] This work's epigraph, "Fluctuat nec mergitur" ("It tosses but is not sunk"),[73] suggests Freud realized that, unable to vanquish Christian Rome—however much Rome may have played havoc with the Jew in him—he nonetheless remained afloat.

FREUD FIRST PUBLISHED "The Moses of Michelangelo" in 1914; he claimed authorship in 1924 when it was included in the

Gesammelte Schriften (Collected Works). His reasons for anonymity are not clear. He wrote to Jones: "Why disgrace Moses by putting my name to it? It is a joke, but perhaps not a bad one."[74] To Karl Abraham he explained that, in addition to his thinking it a joke, he had misgivings about the essay's amateurishness and strong doubts about its conclusion.[75] Since Freud himself understood that a joke, like a dream, is one way of expressing what is repressed by outwitting the mechanisms of repression, this joke is perhaps a deadly one, what the Germans call "Galgenhumor" (humor of the gallows).[76] Freud just might be trying to get away with murder, perhaps even two: the murder of the biblical Moses, whom he buried in misreadings and omissions; and the murder of the enraged, threatening Moses whom Freud enclosed and silenced in the interior of Michelangelo's statue. One is left to wonder whether Freud thought that he had for eternity silenced the Jew or preserved the Lawgiver in Michelangelo's monument to a pope.

Moses and Monotheism

In 1934, about a decade after "The Moses of Michelangelo" appeared, Freud told Arnold Zweig about a new work he had written whose title was *The Man Moses, a Historical Novel (Der Mann Moses, ein historischer Roman).* In an introduction to this text, Freud noted the inadequacy of the material about Moses, relying as it does on one source, the Bible, "fixed in writing only in a later period, in itself contradictory, certainly revised several times and distorted under the influence of new tendencies, while closely interwoven with the religious and national myths of a people."[77] Freud undertook in this work to account for what he saw as contradictions and gaps, "to give preference to the assumption that can claim the greatest possibility. That which one can obtain by means of this technique can also be taken as a kind of historical novel, since it has no proven reality, or only an unconfirmable one, for even the greatest probability does not coincide with the truth."[78] Though Freud did not dispute that a Moses actually existed, he called into question the facts of his life: fictionality seems to cling to the biblical narrative as well as to Freud's text. But in this later work, Freud does not attribute his Moses to another person, some great artist, but acknowledges the figure as his own creation, a statue of his own making, as it were. Several times, in fact, in *Moses and Monotheism* and in letters, Freud referred to this Moses as a statue, one that rests on a shaky foundation, and he voiced misgivings about the arguments and evidence that supported his conception. Thus, in a 1934 letter to Arnold Zweig he explained that although he had no "inner difficulties" about his ideas, he was nonetheless disturbed by having been "obliged to construct a terribly grand statue upon feet of clay, so that any fool could topple it."[79] And in the second part of his work—the entire work published in 1938 as *The Man Moses and Monotheistic Religion*, a title which deletes the earlier suggestion of fictionality[80]—while referring to his hypothesis that Moses was an Egyptian, Freud once again likened his Moses to "a bronze statue upon feet of clay."[81] From yet another reference to this new work and its problematic foundation, it becomes clear that the statue with the clay feet refers not only to the Moses Freud had constructed, but also to views about the psychohistorical origins of Jewish monotheism and Mosaic teachings and their significance for the development of civilization. Writing to Zweig just a month before the letter quoted above, Freud agreed with Zweig that there would be some risk in publishing his work on Moses, and added, "What is worse is that the historical novel won't stand up to my own criticism. I require yet more certainty and would not like it if the entire project's final formula [*Schlussformel*], which I regard as valuable, were endangered by its mounting on a higher foundation."[82] One wonders why this "formula" was so necessary and valuable that he would risk creating a statue that might turn out to be his golden calf—an attempt to realize wishes and illusions that could not be concretely attained.

Moses and Monotheism is a puzzling work whose structure and rationale are not easily fathomed. The statue of Moses that Freud erects consists of two parts: the main portion—Freud's "bronze" statue—is solid, but is only tenuously supported on the rest, its "feet of clay." The bronze part seems to represent theories concerning the origin of religion which Freud first presented in *Totem and Taboo (Totem und Tabu)* and in whose complete correctness he was confident. The "feet of clay" is an allusion to the very problematic evidence he had mounted to explain the origin of Jewish monotheism. Although Freud maintained that his findings about the beginnings of the Jewish religion supported his previous interpretation of the origin of religion and were therefore part of the solid bronze body, his sense of the precariousness of his argument persisted. In March 1938, just months before publication, he continued to express his discontent in the second prefatory note to the third part of the work.[83] Here the clay-footed statue has somehow been transformed into an agile toe dancer:

> This [conviction about the correctness of my conclusions] I acquired a quarter of a century ago, when I wrote the book about *Totem and Taboo*, 1912, and it has only grown stronger since. Since that time I have never doubted that religious phenomena can be understood only according to the model of the individual's neurotic symptoms familiar to us, as the return of long forgotten, significant events in the primeval history of the human family; that they owe their compulsive character to just this origin and thus by virtue of their content of historical truth have an effect on human beings. My uncertainty only sets in if I ask myself whether I have succeeded in proving these propositions for the example of Jewish monotheism chosen here. To my critical faculties this work, which emanates from the man Moses, seems like a dancer balancing on the tip of one toe.[84]

From 1934 to shortly before his death in 1939, Freud's comments on *Moses and Monotheism* indicate that despite considerable misgivings he remained engrossed in the figure of Moses and the origin of Jewish religion. Indeed, rather than becoming discouraged by either the weaknesses he recognized in his interpretation or the negative reception he anticipated from Christians and Jews alike, he did not relinquish the most questionable of his views about Moses, even when presented with convincing scholarly rebuttal. The conclusions as well as the subject had acquired overwhelming significance for him. "Don't say any more about the Moses book," he wrote Zweig in the same letter in which he spoke of the statue. "That this effort to create something, apparently my last, has been wrecked depresses me enough. Not that I can get away from it. The man, and what I wanted to make of him, pursues me incessantly."[85] Exploring what Freud "wanted to make" of Moses and how he accomplished his end leads to the heart of this complex and perplexing work and may, in addition, disclose why he found this task so compelling.

Although *Moses and Monotheism* begins with a discussion of Moses' origin and early life and only later investigates the consequences which the man and his teachings had for the Jewish people and Western civilization, there are indications that Freud's conviction about Moses' significance for the future of that people conditioned his abiding interest in Moses.[86] In his efforts to explain the sense of the work to both Zweig and Lou Andreas-Salomé, Freud noted that the upsurge in attacks on Jews motivated his inquiry into antisemitism and the destiny of the Jews, and that, in turn, led him to the importance of Moses. To Zweig he wrote: "The starting point of my work is familiar to you . . . In the face of new persecutions one asks oneself again how the Jew had become what he is and why he has attracted this undying hatred. I had soon discovered the formula: Moses created the Jews."[87] Apparently the new and alarming hostility toward Jews motivated him to seek the origins of what he considered a social condition that had persisted for millennia; and in this instance, as in his preoccupation with Hannibal and Michelangelo's Moses, antisemitism provided the impetus for his construction of a heroic figure. He clearly assumes not only that there is something about the victims that have made them targets,[88] but that the origins of this "something" may be traced to Moses. This idea is reaffirmed in a letter to Lou Andreas-Salomé: "It started out from the question about what has really created the particular character of the Jew, and came to the conclusion that the Jew is a creation of the man Moses."[89] And in *Moses and Monotheism* we find the same connection between the character of the Jewish people; the one person, the man Moses; and antisemitism: "It was the one man Moses, who created the Jews. To him this people owe its tenacity, but also much of the hostility which it experienced and is still experiencing."[90] Thus at a time when Hitler had already secured power in Germany and before he had advanced into Austria, when Nazi antisemitic rhetoric and persecution had become state policy in Germany, Freud passionately explored why the Jewish people had become the object of so much hostility and how they had been able to resist extraordinary persecution for centuries and survive as Jews.

His "formula," namely, that the *man* Moses had created the Jew, generally neglects Moses' abundant teachings and those of other Jews throughout the centuries; nor does it acknowledge the culture and institutions Jewish people created throughout the centuries in many corners of the world in order to maintain their lives and values. Instead it focuses largely on the person of a single man as the sole creator of a people now thousands of years old. Such a conclusion suggests a conception of Moses and his influence that is indebted to Freud's particular views not only of history and cultural development, but of the dynamics of human behavior as well. In fact, in *Moses and Monotheism* Freud recapitulates many of his theories of psychology and history which do more than merely support a view of Moses; they function as an intrinsic aspect of the interpretive construct that may be called Freud's Moses. And since this construct will be the focus of attention here, Freud's approach to methodology and interpretation deserves scrutiny.

Methodology: Distortion and Its Secrets

Not unlike the methodological procedure in "The Moses of Michelangelo," the conception of Moses in *Moses and Monotheism* began, Freud says, with an analysis of the distortions and discrepancies in the biblical narrative. He further maintains that his studies of the Bible led him to conclude that the distortions were meant to conceal realities that the Jewish people felt were not in their interest. Because the record of such realities had to be altered or eliminated, Freud thought the biblical accounts were "like gravestones, under which the true information about those early things, about the nature of the Mosaic religion and the violent removal of the great man—all of which were withdrawn from the knowledge of later generations—should, as it were, find its eternal rest."[91] Freud's major concern was how to recover "truths" that had been not only long buried, but also "distorted through the influence of powerful trends and embellished by products of poetic invention"; and having already been "able to divine one of these distorting trends," he thought continued efforts would bring further positive results.[92] The difficulties for readers of his work, however, are similar to those confronting Freud, namely, to be able to recognize and interpret both the distortions and "truths" of the text. When Freud had originally called this work "A Historical Novel," he took note of its fictionality. Were it not for this subtitle, however, his interpretations would suggest nothing fictional about Moses and monotheism. *Moses and Monotheism,* therefore, purports to expose the realities which the Bible conceals; and in this effort Freud's own cogent observations about the genesis of biblical distortions and the possibility of retrieving "truths" provide valuable methodological clues to the dynamics of his own text.

For Freud, distortions in the biblical account of Moses, which signal discrepancies between historical reality and the reporting of that reality, are the result of two opposing activities: one falsifies, mutilates, and extends texts in accordance with "secret intentions"; the other wields "an indulgent piety," disregards all contradictions, and retains everything as is. "Thus, there have come about almost in all sections conspicuous gaps, disturbing repetitions, tangible contradictions, indications which betray to us things never intended to be communicated."[93] Such contradictory activities, one of which defaces and represses while the other preserves, are familiar psychic operations in Freud's perception of individual and social behavior. They participate in the dream-work through which unconscious thoughts and wishes are transformed into a dream-content whose distortions both conceal and reveal the dreamer's latent life; they are fundamental psychical activities not only of neurotics and the psychologically impaired, but of anyone who must adapt to the requirements of civilization. In understanding the biblical text, such activities constitute the dynamics of narration and interpretation, particularly when these are motivated by or subject to what Freud referred to as "secret intentions."[94]

While few interpreters of the Bible, and perhaps only the most fundamentalist religious adherents, would object to an investigation of the correspondence between historical reality and the biblical account of it, many might question the efficacy or wisdom of claiming verity for material repressed thousands of years ago and for which there are proofs no more reliable than intuition and interesting conjecture. Curiously, Freud, who generally considered himself a committed rationalist and scientist, did not hesitate to follow a tenuous course of speculation; and the construction of his Moses, so fraught with difficulties, often seems informed by his own "secret intentions," the illumination of which will, I hope, shed light on his bold interpretive venture.

The distortion of a text is, according to Freud, criminal transgression twice over: "The distortion of a text is similar to a murder. The difficulty lies not in the execution of the deed, but in removing its traces."[95] However, the improbability of eliminating all signs of the deed makes it possible for the crime to be unearthed. An understanding of distortion *(Entstellung)* should include, according to Freud, the term's literal meaning, which is not in current usage. "It should mean not only: 'to change in its appearance,' but also: 'to bring to another place,' 'to shunt elsewhere.'"[96] Thus the interpreter of a distorted text becomes a kind of criminal investigator or detective whose goal is the discovery of evidence that a crime had been perpetrated or, better yet, of the victim's remains. Since it is unlikely that a centuries-old victim could be found, the textual investigator is left to search for the evidence necessary to reconstruct the circumstances of the crime and its victim. This is precisely what Freud attempts to do in *Moses and Monotheism:* in the process of tracking down the distortions in the biblical text, he finds indications that, on the one hand, the origins of Moses have been effaced and replaced—the Egyptian nobleman has been transformed into a Jewish commoner—and, on the other, that Moses never set foot on Mount Sinai, but had earlier been murdered by those liberated from Egyptian bondage. By odd coincidence, this investigator of a "murdered" text uncovers a murder, the murderers, and the victim. From Freud's perspective, the murder of Moses stands at the beginning of the history of the Jews as a nation and was necessary for their subsequent development. But since it repeats a much older crime that, according to Freud, had initiated the first society, namely, the murder of the father of the primal horde by his sons,[97] one might say that murder—and not just metaphorical murder[98]—was on Freud's mind when he was constructing or reconstructing this Jewish hero. But more of that later.

When in *Moses and Monotheism* Freud discussed the "truth" of Moses and the Jewish multitude, he was referring to their historical existence and social function. His recognition of their truth did not, however, extend to their deity, whose physical existence was unverifiable. In a 1935 letter to Lou Andreas-Salomé, in which he acquaints her with the subject of this work, Freud identifies the problem of "truth" and the "formula which has so totally fascinated me." Religions, he wrote, "are reawakened memories of very ancient, forgotten, highly emotional events of human history. I have said this already in *Totem and Taboo,* express it now in the formula: what makes religion strong is not in its *material,* but in its *historical* truth."[99] That same year, in a "Postscript" to his *Autobiographical Study,* Freud suggested that this new "formula" corrects an earlier view of religion he held: "In *The Future of an Illusion* [*Die Zukunft einer Illusion*] I expressed an essentially negative valuation of religion; later I found a formula which does better justice to it: its power is to be sure based on its truth content, but this truth is not a material but a historical one."[100] Freud is here alluding to *Moses and Monotheism,* specifically to the segment in Part Three entitled "The Historical Truth." There the formulation that religion contains only historical truth becomes the basis for understanding all religions, including monotheism, as having no divine origin, but deriving from specific events and behavior which took place at some time in the very distant past. Thus, he notes:

> we do not believe that one great god exists today, but that in primeval times there was one single person who at that time had to appear gigantic and who, raised to the status of a deity, returned in the memory of the people . . . When Moses brought to his people the conception of a single god, it was nothing new, but it signified the resuscitation of an experience out of the primeval times of the human family that had long ago disappeared from the conscious memory of the people.[101]

While the origin and development of Moses and monotheism cannot be verified, a historical interpretation of the evidence is possible and would result, according to Freud, in truths which are not material, but historical. These truths, he believes, will save him from being "classed with the scholastics and Talmudists who are content to show off their ingenuity, unconcerned about how distant from reality their assertion may be."[102] However, his insistence on the factuality of the unverifiable events that gave rise to civilization and religion, including Jewish monotheism, may not save him from being classed with the dogmatists.

Since it is impossible here to cover all the various and important aspects of *Moses and Monotheism,* it is perhaps best to chart a course of discussion that includes the significant elements of Freud's Moses, the Mosaic teachings, and monotheism, as well as some of the more general theoretical considerations concerning the origins, development, and psychology of religion and civilization. An approach that seems prudent to me would focus on the character of both the "great man" and his followers, the "masses," which for Freud encompass the Jewish people not only in Moses' time, but also in the ensuing five millennia. Freud's interest in both the past and present manifestations of Moses' influence was already apparent in "The Moses of Michelangelo." There he discussed not only the two Moses figures as he conceived them— the biblical one and Michelangelo's—and their relationship with the disobedient revelers around the golden calf, but also his own confrontation with the Moses of the statue, in whose presence he felt himself to be part of the contumacious, faithless rabble. The overall importance of Moses is reflected in Freud's numerous assertions that the character of the Jewish people was the creation of this single individual. Moreover, *Moses and Monotheism* also reflects Freud's more general concern for the dynamics of leader and mass which he discussed in a number of important works, among them *Totem and Taboo* (1912), *Mass Psychology and the Analysis of the Ego* (*Massenpsychologie und Ich-Analyse*, 1921),[103] *The Future of an Illusion* (1927), and *Civilization and Its Discontents* (*Das Unbehagen in der Kultur*, 1930).

The Birth of the "Great Man": Nationality and Status

The title *The Man Moses and Monotheistic Religion*, the former title *The Man Moses, a Historical Novel*, as well as Freud's many comments on this work emphasize that the Moses in question is a man—a male being ("der Mann Moses"). Although Freud does not indicate precisely why he refers so often to the biblical hero as the "man Moses," his usage suggests several possibilities: he may want to distinguish the human from the divine, the individual from the mass, man from woman; or he may very well want to retain all of these possibilities. In juxtaposition to "monotheistic religion," the idea of "the man Moses" seems to declare a relationship between the human and the divine which encompasses both separation and intersection. Of course, to establish the relationship between the human and divine, the term *Mensch*, meaning 'human being', would be more appropriate than *Mann*, meaning 'male person'.[104] One encounters the same difficulty if one perceives in the title an implied contrast between the individual and the mass; the term *individual* or *person* would be more appropriate than one marking gender. The term *man* does distinguish Moses from women, but one wonders why this is important, since there is no likelihood of confusing him with a "woman Moses" or with a woman who created monotheism and the Jewish character. But for Freud, maleness in gender and in behavior is a requirement for the hero: "A hero [the masculine *Held*] is one who courageously rises up against his father and in the end has victoriously overcome him."[105] Had Freud wanted to distinguish Moses from God and from the masses and in addition call attention to masculinity, he accomplished that masterfully and simply with the phrase "the man Moses." And it is precisely the alliance of male, individual, and mortal—rather than, let us say, social human being—that constitutes the configuration of the protagonist of this work.

Freud locates the first indication that the Bible presents a revisionist history of the hero's life in Moses' beginning, his infancy. Of the three essays that comprise *Moses and Monotheism,* the first treats Moses' nationality almost exclusively. Freud contends that Moses was an Egyptian by birth and most likely a nobleman, basing his conclusions on two principal arguments: Moses has an Egyptian name; and because his birth and very early life conform to the myths about heroes, he must surely be of noble blood. Freud admits that his arguments are indecisive and his conclusions problematic, but he is nonetheless convinced that if "one tries to take seriously the assumption that Moses was a distinguished Egyptian, then very interesting and far-reaching perspectives result."[106] While it is true that Freud was primarily interested in the consequences which an Egyptian Moses as liberator and lawgiver had for the development of the Jewish people, he furnishes evidence and arguments—often grounded in an unarticulated value system that is nonetheless accessible in the text— which have an important role in the formulation of his views of heroes and society and deserve cautious scrutiny.

The first of the arguments Freud presents to establish nationality is that Moses' name is Egyptian. This may very well be accurate, but nowhere in the text does he entertain the possibility that a person with an Egyptian name may also be a Jew, just as, for example, a Sigmund, Heinrich, or Franz living in Germany or Austria may be Jewish. Because he assumes that a person with an Egyptian name cannot be a Jew, Moses' name has great importance for him. "Mose" (the final *s* was an addition in the Greek translation of the Bible) is, he notes, the Egyptian word for *child* and often appeared in proper names appended to the name of a god or king, thus Ptah-mose and Thut-mose (Thotmes). He quotes J. H. Breasted's *The Dawn of Conscience* as an example of what other scholars have claimed, namely that the name is of Egyptian origin and that "the divine name was gradually lost in current usage, till the boy was simply called '*Mose.*'"[107] Freud dismisses the accuracy of the biblical naming event ("and he became her son. And she called his name Moses: and she said, Because I drew him out of the water," Exodus 2:10), indicating first that it is ridiculous to believe an Egyptian princess would know Hebrew and then that her etymological explanation of the name is inaccurate. Even if he were correct and the name is inaccurate, there remains the possibility that an Egyptian princess might have known, but not been fluent in, Hebrew, something Freud does not even consider.

When Freud says that "it is nonsensical to attribute to an Egyptian princess the derivation of the name from the Hebrew,"[108] it is difficult to know whether he is calling into question her ability as an Egyptian or as a woman, or both. However, if we look at the biblical account to which Freud alludes (Exodus 2:10), there is reason to believe that he is more likely referring to gender than to nationality. If, as the biblical narrative has it, the princess did name the child "Moshe," which in Hebrew means "the one who draws out," because, as she says, "I drew him out of the water," she named him for herself, for she was the one who drew the infant from the river. Since, as Freud notes when discussing birth myths, the act of drawing from the water a basket housing a baby is "an unmistakable symbolic representation of birth,"[109] her naming of the child acknowledges her parenthood. And when later in life Moses draws out of bondage an oppressed people through the Red Sea, he may be acknowledging that he is indeed his mother's son by proving true to his name, "the one who draws out." However, Freud, usually so attuned to etymological nuances and their implications, seems to have turned a deaf ear to similar possibilities in the biblical text.

It is to names which establish paternal heritage that Freud turns when he seeks support for his contention that 'Moses' is an abbreviated Egyptian name. Referring to Breasted's idea that a name like Ptah-mose meaning 'Ptah-child' was actually an abridged form of 'Ptah-(has given)-a-child', Freud questions only why Breasted had omitted "analogous theophanous names that are found in the list of Egyptian kings, such as Ah-mose, Thut-mose (Thotmes) and Ra-mose (Ramses)."[110] In an illuminating, as yet unpublished, manuscript on the naming of Moses in *Moses and Monotheism,* Ilana Pardes has suggested that by following Freud's own advice, textual distortions may be clarified by seeking the displaced material elsewhere in the text.[111] Thus one ought to be able to find in *Moses and Monotheism* evidence that would jusify a naming process that affirms the paternal prerogative. In the final essay of this work, Freud discusses the superiority of intellectual processes to sense perception and concludes that because maternity is proved by the senses and is therefore inferior to paternity which can be proved only through deduction, "the child should bear the father's name and be his heir."[112] Thus, giving a child the father's name is not compensation for uncertainty about parentage, but rather a sign of the "progress in spirituality [intellectuality]" (*Geistigkeit* may refer to either), a "triumph of spirituality [intellectuality] over the sensuality."[113] From this perspective, the princess who names the child and furthermore names him for herself contradicts Freud's theory and values, which require the boy to be named by and for the father, thereby assuring continuation of male dominance. If Freud had his way, Moses would then be the father's son, the text notwithstanding.

Examining the implications of Freud's interpretation of the naming of Moses, Pardes notes that in fact "naming speeches are primarily a feminine discourse in biblical narrative," and that in this instance the princess may be undermining her father's authority not only by rescuing the child, but by giving it a name that may be Egyptian or Hebrew, or both.[114] "Yet while feigning to use the dominant discourse," Pardes concludes, "she undermines the name of the father by assigning a Hebrew etymology to the name of her son, an etymology which commemorates her as the procreator of Moses and the one who violated her father's law."[115] While I find Pardes' insight into a dual function of languages interesting, I am not convinced that the naming process is best understood as a subversive act against the father, and I hesitate to discard the literal reading of Moses' rescue and proclaim the princess the procreator of Moses. In my reading, the princess is the adoptive mother who chooses her maternal role and, through the process of naming, establishes her parenthood.

Freud's second argument in support of Moses' Egyptian nationality is grounded in an understanding of myths associated with the origins of heroes. Essentially following Otto Rank's treatise, *Der Mythus von der Geburt des Helden (The Myth of the Birth of the Hero),*[116] Freud makes several salient points. First, within the tradition of the exposure myth, birth parents are usually nobility, the family which raises the child is "humble or degraded,"[117] and the child becomes a hero by overcoming his humble situation and rising to his noble origin or even transcending it. Because in the biblical narrative Moses is born into a humble Jewish family and reared in a royal Egyptian one only to return to the people of his humble origin, Freud and Rank agree that the Jews adapted the story to their own national interest, in this instance to make a native son of the Egyptian who was their liberator and lawgiver. Second, although in the myth the hero has two families, psychoanalytic interpretation concludes that there is in fact only one, but that the hero as a child overestimates parents and experiences them as exceptional and noble, while as an adult he makes a more accurate assessment and perceives them as the ordinary folk they are. Since this conception surely contradicts the circumstances of the biblical Moses, who was born to humble parents, Freud assumes that the biblical account was altered. Third, if there is actually only one family, then, Freud maintains, the first family is fictitious, the result of the child's naive assessment, and the second one, the humble one, is the real family: "If we have the courage," Freud asserts, "to accept this thesis as a generality to which the Moses legend is also subject, then all at once we see clearly: Moses is an—apparently noble—Egyptian whom the myth was meant to transform into a Jew."[118]

Freud's specific arguments about Moses' nationality show signs of speciousness even apart from the serious difficulties that arise when trying to reconstruct historical data from the study of myths and from biblical materials for which there are few corroborating sources. But contradictions may not necessarily be an obstacle to reaching conclusions.[119] If, as Freud indicates, the biblical story has been altered to accommodate Jewish national interests and the original story conforms to hero myths such as that of Oedipus, Moses would have been born to Egyptian nobility; but if the biblical account is accurate and if also the real family is the second one, as Freud suggests, here too Moses is an Egyptian nobleman. Moses is an Egyptian nobleman whether the biblical version is accurate or altered. In other words, if Freud wants Moses to be an Egyptian, that is easily accomplished any which way, a sorry commentary on Freud's historical methodology. Content with his conclusions, though decidedly uncomfortable about his proofs, Freud entitled the second part of *Moses and Monotheism* "If Moses was an Egyptian. . ." ("Wenn Moses ein Ägypter war . . .").

Freud loses some of his credibility as biblical interpreter because of the ways in which he establishes the status of Moses' birth and nationality, although that birthright is, as critics have noted and as he himself recognized,[120] not vital to his conceptions of Moses or the development of the Jewish people. The issues that are actually of primary importance for him are two "truths" which lie buried beneath the distortions of the biblical narrative about Moses: the murder of Moses and the nature of the Mosaic religion. Mosaic religion, as Freud understands it, and its powerful impact may exist independent of whether Moses was an Egyptian nobleman or a Jewish commoner or whether the origin of monotheism was Egyptian or Jewish. The values, however, that inform Freud's contentions about nationality and status, including those of power and authority associated with masculinity, are significant and will be considered here in due course.

Moses the Father: Superiority and Power

Since Freud's conceptions of Moses and his importance for the destiny of the Jewish people are grounded in an unconventional biography of the biblical hero, the following brief summary of Freud's revision of Moses' adult life and of the beginnings of Jewish monotheism will perhaps facilitate the continued discussion of *Moses and Monotheism:*

MOSES WAS AN Egyptian nobleman during the reign of the pharoah Ikhnaton, who had renounced the prevailing polytheistic religion and pursued a new one, a strict monotheism. This was the earliest incidence of monotheism in world history, and its universality was well suited to Egypt's expanding imperialism.[121] However, when the pharoah died after a short reign, his people eagerly abandoned the austere and demanding monotheism and returned to the sensuality and comfort of polytheism. Moses, probably a provincial governor, was an adherent of Ikhnaton's monotheism and after the ruler's death adopted a plan "of establishing a new empire, of finding a new people, to whom he wanted to give for veneration the religion that Egypt disdained."[122] In order to accomplish this he chose a new people, a Semitic tribe that had probably settled in a border province, placed himself at their head, and "carried out the Exodus 'with a strong hand'."[123] Moses apparently accepted the full burden of transforming this tribe into a people of his own liking: "We must not forget that Moses was not only the political leader of the Jews settled in

Egypt, he was also their lawgiver, educator, and forced them into the service of a new religion, which is still today called the Mosaic religion after him."[124] He instituted a number of restrictive and repressive practices—among the most important, the Egyptian practice of circumcision—which functioned to separate this group from others encountered on their journey and, more significantly, to give those who adopted these measures a sense of pride and superiority to others. Recalcitrant followers, however, who wanted to be free of the restrictions and renunciations Moses and his religion demanded, murdered their leader and abandoned his religion. The religion was eventually revived, and the way this came about had a profound effect on the power of Mosaic teachings to shape for millennia to come the character of those who zealously adhered to them.

THE DIFFERENCE in status between the leader Moses and his followers in *Moses and Monotheism* is marked and reveals inequalities which actually resemble the distribution of power in Egyptian society. As a member of the privileged Egyptian nobility, Moses had been superior to Egyptian commoners and to Jews, who were an oppressed alien minority; and later as tribal leader he maintained superiority to his subservient Semitic followers. Thus, the inequality within the tribal group merely reproduced Moses' situation as a nobleman in that society. Indeed, Freud affirms the values of the ruling society when he unquestioningly accepts the superiority of nobility to commoners and of Egyptians to Jews.[125] And nowhere in *Moses and Monotheism* does he entertain the possibility of different group dynamics which, for example, would attribute lesser worth to oppressors or greater worth to a humble group without a power elite; nor does he judge superiority by standards other than the prevailing views of status. Thus, in the first part of this work Freud notes that "the heroic life of the man Moses began by descending from his exalted position [*von seiner Höhe*], lowering himself to the children of Israel";[126] and in the final part of the work, in a segment entitled "The Great Man," the inequality has increased in intensity and scope: "Without doubt it was a powerful father prototype [*gewaltiges Vatervorbild*] which in the person of Moses stooped to the poor Jewish compulsory laborers [*Fronarbeitern*] in order to assure them that they were his dear children."[127] In this latter passage, Moses is not just another nobleman with a paternalistic attitude to his followers, but the powerful abstract figure of a great father, the quintessential authoritative father of all fathers, while his "children" are presented in greater concreteness, perhaps to compensate for a loss in status. No longer are they "children of Israel," but compulsory laborers whose activity seems only to emphasize their debasement; and Moses, their possessor, condescendingly assures them that they are *his* dear children.

For Freud, the relationship with the chosen people is a sign of Moses' greatness, his heroic nature. While he accepts Rank's view of the hero as someone who stands up to his father and overcomes him, his Moses may not conform to that pattern. Although he may have defied the will of the Pharaoh, a father figure, Moses' heroic activity is essentially directed toward the conquest of the people he adopted as his children, for it is through them that his ideas can be realized. Moses' only other connection with a father figure in *Moses and Monotheism* is a salutary relationship with Ikhnaton, whose ideas, according to Freud, Moses actually brought to fulfillment. If indeed heroism is determined by victory over the father, then the Semitic tribe, who purportedly murdered the great father imago in the person of Moses, would be the hero. But this would surely be an unlikely heroic scenario for someone convinced, as Freud seems to be, of "the personal influence of individual great men on world history"[128] and of the impossibility of the masses, who seek libidinal gratification, to implement the renunciations necessary for heroism. Indeed, Freud had to perform a rather cumbersome methodological shuffle to argue for the validity of the "great man" theory of history even though it was based solely on a single example, here that of Moses: "If, therefore, the investigation of a particular case demonstrates the superior influence of a single personality, then our conscience need not reproach us that by accepting it we have contradicted the doctrine of the significance of those general impersonal factors,"[129] which he identified as economic circumstances, food supply, technology, population, and climate.

In the segment "The Great Man" Freud indicates that "it is not so much the nature of the great man that interests us as the question of the means by which he affects his fellow human beings."[130] The mark of a great man is, then, the ability to influence others profoundly and therewith determine the course of history, which is accomplished in two ways: through the powers of his personality and through the ideas for which he stands. Thus, the greatness of Moses is to be found in his decisive qualities and the most fundamental characteristics of the religion he propagated; and these features share a territory and discourse in which authority, patriarchy, spirituality or intellectuality *(Geistigkeit),* archaic heritage, and tradition predominate.[131]

The areas of Moses' personality with which Freud is essentially concerned are his superiority, his individuality and uniqueness, and his power—to use Freud's terms—to lure, coerce, and subjugate the masses. These are the traits which enabled him to become the liberator and lawgiver of the Jewish people. Yet these very characteristics, which made it possible to create out of a primitive Semitic tribe a prominent religious people, set Moses apart from the people who were both his object and the medium through which he could fulfill his mission. The fact that he was an Egyptian and a nobleman merely reinforced his position as outsider. But although Moses as a superior individual is perceived as independent and apart, he is actually dependent on the people for both his personal and political fulfillment. He may be free to choose his people, but he must also—if he is to carry out his mission of keeping monotheism alive—adopt a people. By not addressing Moses' dependence on his followers and the interdependence of leader and people, Freud neglects that aspect of the biblical Moses which is particularly relevant for those Jews living dispersed in the modern world, many of whom could not reconcile personal fulfillment and communal demands. No matter how heavy the burden or difficult the struggle, the biblical Moses pursued a life in which he became the person he was by forming a nation of his own people, and his mission provided him with a profound personal and national identity. Freud's Moses, however, secures his identity by assuming a superior position and maintaining power over the very people he created into a nation. Because the leadership ability and superior status of Freud's Moses are traits appropriate to a father, Moses also appears as a father figure with unimpeachable male virtues: "The decisiveness of thought, the strength of will, the impetus of his deeds belong to the image of the father; above all, however, the self-reliance and independence, his divine unconcern, which may increase to ruthlessness. One must admire him, one may trust him, but one also cannot help fearing him."[132] Not only does Moses as the "powerful father prototype" present an overwhelming and menacing figure to his followers, the "children of Israel," but he also, in Freud's view, satisfies their "strong need for an authority which one can admire, to which one submits, and by which one is dominated and possibly even maltreated."[133] Thus, Moses appears as an individual with all power and authority, but no needs, while the group is completely needy and yearns for the protection an authority figure like the man and father Moses promises. Since within this understanding of the dynamics of leader and followers the forms of subjugation and domination satisfy the presumed essential features of each party involved, they are regarded as necessary and justified; and given the basic and apparently inviolable differences between leader and people, there would seem to be little need or likelihood for fundamental change. For Freud, such a relationship of independence for one person or group and subjugation for another merely recapitulates patriarchal structures that have existed from time immemorial or at least from the days of the primal horde, and is today permanently embedded in the Oedipus complex, in the biological and psychological makeup of the human being.[134]

Concerns with problems of "superiority" inform Freud's views of Moses, Mosaic ideas or beliefs, and the character traits that helped the Jewish people to resist extinction and survive. The man Moses was considered superior not only because he possessed qualities associated with greatness—decisive thought, strong will, and forceful actions—but also because he was perceived by the people as being extremely powerful. It was this perception of his superiority that was, in Freud's view, absolutely necessary for establishing Mosaic monotheism among the people. Moses' ability to liberate the Jews from Egypt helped to convince them that they too were privileged and superior to others, the chosen people of a great God who would protect and nurture them. Freud maintains that it was not God, whose existence he denies, but "the man Moses who imprinted this trait [of chosenness], significant for all time, on the Jewish people. He raised their self-esteem by assuring them that they were God's chosen people, he imposed holiness on them and constrained them to keep apart from others."[135]

Yet Freud found that superiority had such a substantive role in Mosaic religion not only because of the sense of superiority which its leader and lawgiver imparted to the people, but also because of the particular nature of the Mosaic God, a "unique, eternal and omnipotent" God which was so completely spiritual that it could not be seen or named, nor could an image of it be known or made.[136] According to Freud, this dematerialization of God, which established the ascendency of the spiritual over the material, marked an extraordinary step forward in culture, for "it meant a subordination of sense perception to what may be called an abstract idea, a triumph of spirituality [intellectuality] over sensuality, strictly speaking, a renunciation of instinct with its psychologically necessary consequences."[137] Abstract thinking, spirituality, and instinctual renunciation together create the foundation for the populace's sense of superiority, pride, and well-being: "All such progress in spirituality [intellectuality]," writes Freud, "results in increasing the individual's self-esteem, in making him proud, so that he feels superior to others who have remained under the spell of sensuality."[138]

Mosaic religion is, for Freud, essentially a male religion: its abstract thinking and spirituality are associated with masculine attributes and patriarchy, while a life of the senses that makes abstract thinking unlikely is considered feminine, weak, and characteristic of matriarchy.[139] Thus it comes as no surprise that circumcision is of such great importance in Freud's view of monotheism, for it is, for him, a mark of dedication and submission to the will of the father, whether God or Moses, and makes those who practice it feel proud and superior, while disdaining all others—including, of course, women—as unclean and unworthy. But, contrary to the biblical account, which holds that circumcision was part of God's covenant with Abraham, Freud insists that it was Moses who instituted this Egyptian custom as an external sign of the superiority of the Jewish people. Not only did it contribute to the insulation and exclusivity of the people who were devotees of Mosaic monotheism, it provided a tangible reminder of the instinctual renunciation required of them to enforce the prohibition of incest. There is what Freud called "a deeper meaning" to circumcision which is related to castration, under the threat of which Oedipal aggression is repressed: "Circumcision is the symbolic substitute for castration, which the primal father out of the fullness of his omnipotence once inflicted upon his sons; and whoever accepted this symbol thereby demonstrated that he was ready to submit to the father's will, even if it imposed the most painful sacrifice on him."[140] The practice of circumcision essentially established Judaism as a religion for men, a religion in which the circumcised have demonstrated their superior ability to repress and overcome their most powerful instincts.

Freud recognized that both the spiritual nature of Moses' ideas and the implementation of those ideas required instinctual restriction and renunciation by members of the group. And he knew such action could precipitate serious ambivalence in a people who sought both to be protected and enhanced by a great leader and a great God, and to be free to seek gratification where and when they desired. Thus, the nature of Moses' ideas and his attempts to realize them created the conditions for his own demise; that is, their dissatisfaction with stringent demands provoked the people to rebel and murder him. In Freud's view, however, the reverberations of Moses' murder—the repression of the murder as well as the unconscious remorse and guilt—along with the power of his ideas were ultimately positive, for they secured the future of monotheism, therewith accomplishing what neither Moses in his lifetime nor Ikhnaton in his could.

Authority Internalized and Intensified: Repression and the Return of the Repressed

Noting significant differences in the biblical narrative between the young Moses who led the Jews out of Egypt and his later appearance in Kadesh and Midian, Freud surmised that these were actually two different individuals: the Moses who liberated a semitic tribe from Egypt and proclaimed a spiritual God and religion, and the Midianite priest's son-in-law of later years who was a follower of the volcano God Yahweh and served as "mediator between God and people at this founding of a religion."[141] The Bible concealed this fact and presented them as a single Moses. The new religion, which came about as a compromise between the descendents of those Jews liberated from Egypt and the Yahweh worshipers, eventually evolved into the Mosaic religion. Freud claims that distortions in Scripture and the interpretations of a few biblical scholars led him to conclude that the Moses who directed the exodus from Egypt was actually murdered by his people, the crime repressed, and his religion resurrected only many years later. After Moses' death some of his followers—especially the Levites who, Freud maintains, were actually Egyptians and part of the nobleman Moses' retinue—kept alive his memory and beliefs and "also succeeded in accommodating the fact as well as the man in the new presentation of prehistory, in retaining at least the external sign of the Moses religion, circumcision, and perhaps in achieving certain restrictions in the use of the new divine name."[142] For their part, the Yahwists were eager to deny the newness and alien nature of their god Yahweh in order to heighten that god's claim to the people's devotion. A compromise resulted in a new religion that merged the Egyptian hero and the Midian mediator into one Moses and their two gods into one called Yahweh. In Freud's estimation, however, the priests who wrote and edited the biblical accounts had a vested interest in denying both the murder of Moses and the existence of two religions and in presenting an uncomplicated linear history of Mosaic religion beginning with Moses of Egypt. Therefore, they credited Moses with too much—with institutions, ritualistic regulation, and laws belonging to a later period; and their profound desire for continuity motivated them to deny the "gap between the lawgiving of Moses and the later Jewish religion, a gap which was first filled by the worship of Yahweh and only later slowly covered over."[143]

Given this interpretation of Moses' life and death, a compelling question which occupied Freud was how it happened that after the early demise of Moses and the elimination for decades of his religion, the Jewish people regained this Mosaic religion and finally adhered to it so adamantly. Freud offers explanations which draw—some by analogy, others by identity—on several of his major psychological theories. He outlines four major areas which are vital to the resurgence and preservation of Mosaic religion after its virtual extinction following the murder of Moses: repression of the murder; archaic heritage; renunciation, the superego, and ethics; and the return of the repressed.

Repression of the murder. Although subsequent to the murder of Moses the perpetrators dismissed his teachings and denied the deed and even Moses' existence, the repression of the crime did not eliminate the event, but in fact preserved it in the recesses of the group's unconscious. Some of Moses' followers overtly kept alive the memory of their liberator and leader, but conscious oral transmission was not sufficient to produce the obsessive devotion necessary for religious tradition. Referring to the same ascetic religon which he believed freed one from bondage to the senses, Freud acknowledges the thralldom of religious tradition as follows:

> [Tradition based on oral transmission] would be listened to, weighed, perhaps rejected like any other news from outside, would

never attain *the privilege of being liberated from the coercion of logical thinking.* It must first have undergone the fate of repression, the condition of lingering in the unconscious, before it was able to develop such mighty effects on its return, to *force the masses under its spell,* as we have seen with astonishment and hitherto without understanding in the case of religious tradition [emphasis added].[144]

Thus Mosaic monotheism, if it was to become an entrenched religious tradition, had to free itself from bondage not only to the senses, but also to logical thinking. Freud maintains that this religion "opened the way to the high regard for intellectual work,"[145] but it is difficult to imagine the nature of intellectual work produced within a tradition that necessitates subjugation of both the senses and logical thinking.[146]

Archaic heritage. One reason that the murder of Moses was important for the fate of monotheism and the Jewish people was that it repeated a crime which aeons earlier had brought into being the beginning of civilization. Without remembering the murder of the primal horde's father by his sons, Moses' murderers repeated this original crime. Although there is no evidence of such a prehistoric event, Freud asserts that he has "no misgivings about saying that people have always known—in that particular way [through memory traces of their archaic heritage]—that they once possessed a primeval father and killed him."[147] The remorse and guilt that resulted from the murder of Moses was only increased or intensified by the knowledge of the primal patricide in the unconscious. Although the murder of Moses may merely share a paradigm of father-son relationships with the primeval father and his sons, Freud claims that the knowledge of the primal crime had become part of an inherited human unconscious which contains among other things memory traces of actual experiences of generations long past. This Lamarckian notion of an archaic heritage provided him with a bridge between individual and mass psychology, for, given this heritage, an entire people can repress an event, and for millennia this repressed material can affect the behavior of a group, a nation, or civilization in the same way that repression affects an individual. But while the repressed content in an individual's unconscious was once actually experienced by the person, the content of the archaic unconscious was never experienced or even necessarily known by the affected person or group, but is reputed to have been the actual experience of people in times immemorial. Thus, all people inherit guilt for a crime they did not commit and pass on to their heirs psychical characteristics which are acquired as a result of the crime. By murdering their leader and father figure, the slayers of Moses repeated an unremembered, indeed unknown, event which, preserved as archaic inheritance in the psyche, apparently weighs heavily on the unconscious lives of all civilized people. And because of this the murder of Moses only increased their already existing unconscious sense of guilt. Neither conscious nor unconscious denial of the deed could eliminate the presence in the psyche of the act or guilt, but would merely intensify the unconscious store of guilt and anxiety; indeed Freud maintains that the obsession with this unrecognized remorse drove the perpetrators and their heirs to compensate for their sin and that of their primeval forefathers by becoming increasingly more devoted to the God and religion of Moses.

　　Renunciation, the superego, and ethics. Freud draws on his theory of the superego in individual psychology—the theory is summarized in *Moses and Monotheism*[148]—to explain, by analogy, how it is possible for a group of people to strive for increased renunciation of instinctual drives and to be proud of it. The internalized representative of authority figures, principally the father, comprises that part of the ego known as the superego, which in adult life monitors and regulates behavior that in childhood was regulated by the authority figures. Thus the superego demands "instinctual renunciation through the pressure of authority which replaces and continues the father."[149] Just as the child sought the approval of its parents, the adult continues to seek approbation, but now from an internalized authority: "The ego is concerned, just as it was in childhood, about risking the love of its master; it feels his recognition as liberation and satisfaction, his reproaches as pangs of conscience."[150] Those who make sacrifices in order to obey and please the superego feel a special sense of pride in their own renunciatory abilities, a pride made possible "after the authority itself has become part of the ego."[151] In Freud's cosmography, "the great man is precisely the authority for whose sake the achievement is accomplished, and since the great man is effective because of his similarity to the father, one need not be surprised if in mass psychology the role of superego devolves on him. That would, therefore, hold good for the man Moses in relation to the Jewish people."[152] Like the father in the formation of the superego, the man Moses must also be "spiritualized" and internalized, as it were, before others can feel proud and uplifted through fulfilling his commandments. Thus the firm foundation for the institutionalization of monotheistic religion was created by the murder of Moses, just as the superego with its obsessive expression of invisible but powerful authority was created in childhood by the abandonment (Freud uses the term *Untergang*, which carries a suggestion of destruction[153]) of the Oedipal situation, that is, of the actual hostile, competitive struggle between the father and son, followed by the internalization of parental authority.

While ethics may not be necessary for either the formation or the foundation of religion, it is, according to Freud, closely related to religion, particularly to one that demands considerable restriction of gratification, for ethics "is a curtailment of instinct."[154] Only when instinctual renunciation is demanded not by an actual father, but by some internalized authority or a deified omnipotent spiritual father, can one speak of ethics or a system of absolute moral precepts. In order to assuage the enormous unconscious guilt that resulted from the unacknowledged murders of the primeval father and their own leader Moses, the Jewish people pursued a life of increasing restriction and asceticism. "The religion that began with the prohibition against making an image of God developed more and more in the course of centuries into a religion of instinctual renunciations";[155] and difficult times as well as the exhortations of the prophets moved the people to seek ever greater and more intense renunciations. As the ethical proscriptions increased, so too did the sense of the power of the invisible God; and the more powerful the omnipresent deified father loomed, the greater was the necessity for enhanced subservience. While many Jews regarded these ethical feats as creative achievements second only to the Mosaic conception of one God, Freud thought that ethics originated with "consciousness of guilt due to the repressed hostility to God."[156] Exalted, overt devotion to God concealed the roots of the devotees' enormous unconscious guilt about both the murder of the father (be he the primeval one or Moses) and their enormous hostility that culminated in patricide. Thus, heinous, violent acts can serve as a source not only of spirituality and intellectual achievement, but also of ethical codes for a just and virtuous life.

Only once in *Moses and Monotheism* does Freud suggest that a people might be justified in overthrowing a powerful figure who, because he desires (as did Freud's Moses) only to fulfill his own idea, forces a people to follow a course of action not of their own choosing or making. In a passage comparing the fate of Ikhnaton and Moses, Moses is identified as a tyrant; but even there his tyranny is justified by the wild and savage nature of the Semites: "But while the tame Egyptians waited until fate had removed the sanctified person of their Pharoah, the wild Semites took their fate into their own hands and did away with the tyrant."[157] Yet in the case of Moses the tyrant is not rendered powerless or eliminated; on the contrary, he returns as the invisible tyrannical superego, or God the father, to rule with a vengeance. Indeed, Freud contends, some of the more noteworthy products of civilization—spirituality, intellectual activity, and ethical behavior—came into being in the wake of Moses' return as superego and the people's increased submission to its uncompromising demands.

Return of the repressed. Since in Freud's cosmography religious tradition apparently requires repression in order to produce in people an unrelenting and overwhelming adherence to God and religion, the transformation of Yahweh into the Mosaic God and the return of repressed Mosaic monotheism assured the survival of a living, active Mosaic tradition. The reappearance of monotheism signaled not only the restoration of patriarchal rights to the great father, who had returned in the form of the omnipotent, omnipresent, invisible God the father, but also the return of his children with their infantile need for his protection and guidance. Thus, with the return of the repressed in Freud's story of Moses, the people reverted to the state of subjection and dependence that they had experienced before they took liberation into their own hands and rid themselves of their "tyrant." In Freud's eyes, however, the rebellion of the people was not a sign of their strength, but of weakness, of their inability to carry out the renunciations required of them.[158] Yet it is curious and perhaps ironic that for Freud, who neither believed in the existence of God nor approved of a people so weak or childishly needy that they required a God for a sense of well-being, "reinstatement of the primal father's historic rights was a great step forward."[159]

Freud's Moses and Freud's Monotheism, the Bible Notwithstanding

Not unlike the menacing Moses in "The Moses of Michelangelo" who by essay's end was transformed into a controlled and benign protector, the feet of clay that imperiled Freud's mammoth construction have, by the conclusion of *Moses and Monotheism*, virtually vanished along with the insecurities that had threatened his initial interpretive objectives. The work's final essay reveals such a bracing confidence that Freud's new "discoveries" are used to corroborate his earlier theories (some, like those in *Totem and Taboo*, highly questionable), while his previous writings are cited to support his current views about Judaism. Yet there linger disturbing questions about the relationship of Freud's conceptions of Moses and Mosaic religion to those of the Bible, the adequacy of assertions he makes, and the validity of his interpretations. A comparison of Freud's understanding of Mosaic tradition with that in the Bible in at least two significant areas—the character of liberation and liberator, and the relationship of Moses and Jewish monotheism to conceptions of the individual and society—may provide a foundation for assessing Freud's reconstruction of Moses' life and his insights into the origins and development of Jewish monotheism.

The nature of liberation and liberator. Although Freud denies the existence and therefore the inherent significance of God, he does accept the biblical tradition that Moses freed the Jews from Egyptian bondage. But his presentation of the nature of this liberation and Moses' participation raises serious doubts about whether Freud's conception coincides with the biblical view. Freud's Moses is completely responsible for the exodus from Egypt, but he is far less concerned about liberation from actual enslavement than he is about release from bondage to the senses and total devotion to spiritual endeavors. The Moses of the Bible was so repelled by the brutal physical and political subjugation of his brethren that he murdered an Egyptian who beat a Jew and later returned to Egypt for the sole purpose of liberating the Jewish people from their oppressors. Freud's Moses, however, acts in his own interest and in that of his religious vision when he pursues a plan "of establishing a new empire, of finding a new people, to whom he wanted to give for veneration the religion that Egypt disdained."[160] This Moses led his adopted Semitic tribe out of Egypt in order to implement his grandiose scheme of forging an empire, albeit a spiritual one, by refashioning a people for his own ends. In this saga there is no suggestion that Moses wants his chosen people to be free of a repressive master; in fact, instinctual repression and restriction are requirements for his new spiritual and ethical religion. This liberator does not promise to prepare his flock for any kind of democratic life or self-determination, but requires instead total submission to his demands and complete devotion to a God accessible solely as an abstraction. Indeed, Freud maintains that in this instance, but also generally, societies of quality are grounded in inequality and distance between a vastly superior leader and his subaltern followers.[161]

Commanding the vigorous spirituality so vitally important to

Freud's Moses, the God of the Bible who guides both Moses and the Jewish people is also pragmatic and concerned with concrete human behavior. In the Decalogue, as elsewhere in Scriptures, God is the ineffable creator of the universe, but is also, as he reminds his people, the one "who brought thee out of the land of Egypt, from the house of slaves" (Deuteronomy 5:6). He is the God both of nature and history. And there are indications that during the long period of wandering in the wilderness the people were being readied for a life among equals and for a society of equitable laws and institutions.

Let me cite just two conspicuous examples. The fourth commandment enjoins the people to keep and make holy the Sabbath, a day of respite for all who work, Jew and gentile, even animals used for toil. It is worth noting that the reason for keeping the Sabbath differs in the Exodus and Deuteronomy versions of the Decalogue. In the former, God identifies himself as a laborer, as creator of the universe, God of nature; he too worked six days to create the universe and on the seventh rested. In the latter text, God speaks as the God of history when he exhorts the people, because they were once slaves in Egypt, to value liberation and the liberator. Another example is provided in Numbers 11:26–30. There Eldad and Medad, two members of the Council of Elders— one of the earliest institutions for participatory government among the liberated Jews—were rumored to be prophesying; Moses' response to a report about their activities reveals the democratic aspirations he had for the people: "Enviest thou for my sake? would God that all the Lord's people were prophets, and that the Lord would put his spirit upon them" (Numbers 11:29). Indeed, one purpose of the long and arduous sojourn in the desert was to educate the people for the permanent practice of the freedom which accompanied their release from slavery. It is this endeavor to educate which is absent from Freud's Moses story.

The character of liberation also bespeaks the character of the liberator. Whereas Freud believes that Moses was an Egyptian nobleman who adopted the Jewish people in order to implement his religious ideas, the Bible presents Moses as a Jew by birth who, despite being raised as an Egyptian prince, ultimately sought to liberate the Jews. Although a Jew assimilated into the most privileged stratum of the dominant society, this Moses seems nevertheless to have maintained ties to divergent groups: Egyptians and Jews, nobility and commoners, oppressors and oppressed. And when he murdered the Egyptian who beat a Jew, Moses demonstrated his sympathy with the enslaved people, even though he did not leave the palace until he realized that public knowledge of his act had endangered him. What becomes apparent from Moses' youthful behavior is that slavery is not eradicated by individual acts against particular targets. Only after going into exile and leaving his Egyptian life and the Jewish people is he called to take on the arduous task of liberating an entire people. As an insider and outsider of two divergent groups and one who had experienced both freedom and oppression, the biblical Moses liberates the oppressed Jews and in the process frees himself from his past among the enslavers. In his subsequent roles of mediator between God and the people, leader, lawgiver, and teacher, the biblical Moses maintains the status of insider and outsider. Referring to Deuteronomy, Robert Polzin points out that "Moses alternates his point of view between one who presents himself as above his hearers in special knowledge and one who emphasizes shared experiences with his fellow Israelites."[162] His dual position is apparent even in the ways he addresses the people: Deuteronomy 6, for example, opens with Moses speaking to the people about "the Lord *your* God," "the Lord *thy* God," and "the Lord God of *thy* fathers" (verses 1–3, emphases mine) and concludes with remarks about "the Lord *our* God" and the land which God "swore unto *our* fathers" (verses 23–25, emphases mine). Unlike Freud's liberator—an Egyptian nobleman who is a "great stranger" to the people he leads out of Egypt—the biblical Moses comes to the Jewish people as one of them, as one who will himself benefit from liberation, who even as leader and teacher remains an integral part of the group. Freud's Moses, member of the ruling caste, seeks to free a Semitic tribe from Egyptian slavery while he alone continues to rule, demanding total submission.

In the biblical narrative there are striking parallels between the development of Moses and that of the Jewish people. Both are separated from their usual habitats before they embark on the project of liberation: Moses leaves the Egyptian palace and goes into exile, and the Jewish people too must first be removed from Egyptian rule before they are educated for freedom. Through his efforts to liberate his people the biblical Moses is also liberated, himself becoming a model for others. Freud's Moses, however, presents no example for others to follow, but delivers orders they are to obey. He seems to conform to Freud's requirements for any effective ruler, that is, to be superior to his flock and to remain apart from them; thus, his Moses is the prototype of the powerful father and the Jews "his dear children." In fact, this conception of group dynamics was not new to Freud; he had already developed this model of the relationship between ruler and followers in *Totem and Taboo* and *Mass Psychology and the Analysis of the Ego*. Freud spells out his position in the latter work:

> Now let us not forget that the demand for equality in a group holds good only for the members themselves, not for the leader. All members should be equal to one another, but they all want to be ruled by one person. Many equals, who can identify themselves with one another, and a single person superior to them all—that is the situation that we find realized in the viable masses.[163]

The depiction of Moses and his chosen people in *Moses and Monotheism* provides but another affirmation—this time from the most significant epoch of Jewish national history—for Freud's conception of the necessary superiority of the individual leader ("the great man") and inferiority of the members of the group. I find it disturbing that from the late 1920s until his death in 1939 Freud should adhere so assiduously to a model of group dynamics that juxtaposes the absolute authority of a powerful leader with a group subjected to his rule. This was, after all, the period in which Hitler not only articulated the theory of his *Führerprinzip* (Führer principle), but also put it into practice with such barbarity against Freud's own people, be they Jews or psychoanalysts.

Moses and Jewish monotheism: conceptions of individual and society. In *Moses and Monotheism,* Moses' principal contribution to the religious culture of the Jewish people, apart from the imposition of circumcision, is grounded in the first three commandments of the Decalogue, the covenant between God and the Jewish people in which God speaks directly to them. Although the commandments are not specifically mentioned in the text, it is clear that Freud was largely concerned with the three prohibitions against having other gods, making graven images of God, and using the name of God for unworthy purposes. Because sustaining these prohibitions required "subordination of sense perception to what may be called an abstract idea," Freud regarded them as instrumental for what he called progress in spirituality (or intellectuality), that is, for the "triumph of spirituality [intellectuality] over sensuality, strictly speaking, a renunciation of instinct."[164] In addition to insisting on the preeminence of the spiritual and intellectual, this progress in spirituality accounted for the Jewish people's self-confidence and sense of superiority as well as for their strong inclination toward increased renunciation. While Freud clearly regarded spirituality—in his understanding, a dominant, masculine attribute—as the province of men, he identified sensuality with the feminine and material, with the inability to renounce instinct. Thus, Mosaic monotheism was considered a male religion sanctified by circumcision, a "symbolic substitute for the castration which the father out of the fullness of his absolute power inflicted on his sons, and whoever accepted this symbol showed that he was ready to submit to the will of the father, even if it imposed the most painful sacrifice on him."[165] According to Freud, it took centuries for Jewish monotheism, which began with the dematerialization of God and the prohibition against making an image of God, to develop into an ethical religion, that is, a religion of renunciation of instinct. Although cognizant of the importance of ethics, Freud did not regard it as an original or indispensible part of any religion (including the

Mosaic), but as a secondary development grounded in renunciation and guilt.[166]

Spiritual and abstract characteristics comprise only one aspect of the Mosaic God and religion in the Bible. The remaining portions of the Decalogue, for example, suggest that ethical and moral considerations are as integral and indissoluble a part of Mosaic God and religion as is the ineffability of the deity. In *Moses and Monotheism* Freud seems to be principally concerned with those commandments that address the uniqueness and non-representability of the deity, but essentially ignores those which articulate norms for human behavior necessary for a just society. In the final seven commandments God appears as a moral being for whom righteous human conduct is obligatory. Ethics are thus not a secondary development of Mosaic religion, but as fundamental to it as are the attributes of its deity. Indeed, divine spirit and human social ethics are coupled in the God of the Decalogue and in Jewish monotheism, and accordingly adherents are asked to lead a life in which the commitment to God demands the maintenance of an ethical society.

It may at first seem incongruous that Freud, for whom God is not a fact but a development of emotional obsession, should find the completely abstract and spiritual character of the Jewish God so culturally vital. But this incongruity may be elucidated by focusing on his understanding of the intersection of human authority figures and the evolution of the deity. On the one hand, Freud recognized that strong human need and longing for authority may result in idolization when "the figure of the great man has grown into the divine."[167] Therefore, God exhibits the authoritative and threatening attributes which a child or an otherwise insecure person perceives in an awesome father or powerful individual, namely, the autonomy and superiority of an omnipotent father.[168] On the other hand, the God created by human need reaffirms and eternalizes the power of the father, thereby validating both the superiority and the authority of the male individual and the inferiority of all others. And it is only when a people have invested all power in one supreme God that "the magnificence of

the father of the primal horde [is] restored."[169] The abstract
nature of God, it seems, is essential for restoring complete power
to the father; or, in Freud's terms, only with "progress in spirituality" is the father "elevated into an authority."[170] Thus, like
Freud's Mosaic God, who is absolutely superior and independent
and whose ethical teachings are, at most, of secondary significance, the father gains power not from his parental care or moral
position, but from his role as abstract authority figure. Also like
that God in whom invisibility and spirit are synonymous, the
father becomes sovereign and ubiquitous when he too is replaced
by an invisible, internal, anonymous superego. The murder of
Freud's Moses by his followers, its repression by the slayers, and
his persistent presence in their unconscious reproduce the conditions for their compelling attachment not only to an invisible,
omnipotent God, but to autocratic father figures as well. Thus,
although the conceptions of a Mosaic God and religion may be,
for Freud, manifestations of infantile wishes or desires, they vali-
date both the preeminent authority of the father (or father imago)
and his power over all his "dear children," those "poor Jewish
laborers," the "masses."[171] And this power, while regarded by
Freud as essential for the civilizing process, is by no means benign,
but necessarily coercive and repressive, especially in its invisible
form as the internalized superego of an individual or group.[172]

Spiritual exclusivity, however, does more than characterize
Freud's Mosaic God, the great man, and the father; it also identifies, by negation, those considered inferior, namely, the powerless, dependent, or ordinary masses. In doing so, Jewish monotheism functions as a model that affirms the power structure and
value system of Freud's conceptions of society and history. For
him, civilized society seems largely to consist of a small minority
of superior individuals, those great men who by virtue of gender,
status derived from birth or idea, ability to renounce instinctual
life, and the possession of power have attained autonomy, control,
and command; and the multitudes who by virtue of birth or sloth,
inability to master instinctual wishes, and weak wills remain dependent on authoritative guidance. If society is to remain civi-

lized, it must be organized, on the one hand, "to control the forces of nature and obtain its wealth for the satisfaction of human needs, on the other hand, . . . to regulate the relations of people to one another and especially the distribution of the available wealth."[173] And because workers who extract wealth for others do not do so willingly, "every civilization must be built upon coercion and renunciation of instinct."[174] Thus, ways must be found to harness the energy of the masses for toil, to inhibit their subsequent destructive and aggressive impulses, and to allow for the expression of intellectual and artistic creativity among the small minority of superior people who control and regulate the society. While Freud applauded the efforts of a benevolent despot like his Moses to elevate people spiritually, there is every indication in his works that the masses can never be elevated sufficiently to rule themselves and will therefore always require and even desire the coercive authority of a "great man."

In *Moses and Monotheism* the relationship between the Jewish minority and the Christian majority of Freud's own times seems to mirror that between Moses, viewed as a culturally superior or civilized individual (Freud did not distinguish between culture and civilization),[175] and his chosen Semitic tribe, perceived as a mob or mass. Because of their increased libidinal renunciation and resultant intellectuality, Jews in Western Christendom are perceived as possessing or seeking a position of superiority not unlike that originally occupied by Moses, the Egyptian nobleman turned Jewish liberator. Speaking about the grounds for antisemitism, Freud cites as an example "the circumstance that they [the Jews] live for the most part as minorities among other peoples, for the sense of community among the masses needs, for its completion, hostility to an external minority, and the numerical weakness of this excluded minority invites its suppression."[176] This minority may be numerically weak, but is in fact generally regarded, even by the majority, as culturally superior because it has survived oppression, been successful in practical life, and made valuable cultural contributions when circumstances allowed.

Presumably what the antisemitic masses of the majority society find offensive are not only the claims by Jews to be the chosen people, the "first-born, favorite children of God the father," but also the practice of circumcision, which reputedly "exalted, ennobled," and functioned as a manifest sign of sanctification.[177] Thus, the masses regarded the Jews as a privileged minority which was superior because of intellectual prowess, exalted ethical standards, and the power it attained from being most favored by the deity. In contrast to this view of the Jews, Freud presents the antisemitic masses as sharing characteristics of inferiority similar to those Moses encountered in the Semitic tribe in Egypt: "One might say they are all 'badly christened'; under a thin veneer of Christianity they have remained what their ancestors [i.e., ancient Semites and pagans] were, who payed homage to a barbaric polytheism. They have not overcome their grudge against the new religion imposed upon them, but they have displaced it onto the source from which Christianity came to them."[178] Because the relationship between Christians and Jews parallels that in ancient times between the Jewish people and Moses, the hostility of antisemitic Christians would then be comparable to the reaction that prompted the murder of Moses. Not unlike the understanding, in the Rome-phobia segment of *The Interpretation of Dreams*, of the origins of antisemitism in an individual's unconscious, distant past, in *Moses and Monotheism* Freud finds its origins in a people's unconscious, very distant past: "The deeper motives of hatred of the Jews [*des Judenhasses*] are rooted in long forgotten times, they operate out of the unconscious of peoples."[179]

The repetition of paradigmatic confrontations suggests that Freud conceived of history as the persistent recurrence of a cycle: the rise of powerful authority figures, reaction against them, and the increasingly powerful reinstatement of that authority as an unforgiving, invisible, internal presence.[180] This internalized authority, be it individual or national superego, relentlessly restricts activity and monitors behavior. Transgressions then produce guilt, which becomes the source of the authority figure's great power and his vulnerability to extreme reaction. Thus, abstract patriarchal authoritarianism, which functions as the foundation of religion and society, is compulsively retained because of the enormous guilt of the people and thereby undermines liberation, substantive change, and development.

But even if one accepts the principle of primal and subsequent patricide, scenarios other than the investiture of paternal power would be possible. A social arrangement could include women in governance; a compact among the brothers of the primal horde could, for example, regulate the equitable distribution of power and responsibility among the many; or the ethical portion of the biblical covenant might become the regulative basis of society, thereby rendering unnecessary the overwhelming coercive power of the father or "great man" for the future of society or history. In fact, Freud's views of society and history do not, and perhaps cannot, account for the significant developments that the biblical Moses and the Jewish people underwent while they struggled through the wilderness en route from slavery to nationhood, struggled not only to accept the reality of one ineffable God, but also to create a nation that was spiritual because it was ethical. Acting like a father assured of his own right and power, the Moses of *Moses and Monotheism* pursued the realization of his idea, and nowhere in his saga is there an indication that he sought to construct a society other than one based on coercion, renunciation, and guilt. His murder and the subsequent survival of monotheism are merely consequences of a coercive mission; indeed, they may be viewed as instrumental for fulfilling his dream. For as a consequence of their obsessive guilt because they murdered their leader, Moses' followers for millennia have adhered ever more tenaciously to the Mosaic idea, accepted—even desired—subservience, and demanded increasingly severe restrictions that bound them to their religion. They continue to affirm gladly what they do not have or perhaps only what they have as an idea, that is, the greatness and power that resides principally in an invisible and abstract God.

Freud's Two Moses Figures: Liberators or Enslavers?

On first consideration it would seem that the Moses of "The Moses of Michelangelo" and that of *Moses and Monotheism* have little in common; why should they? After all, more than two decades separate their appearance, decades of great upheavals: World War I, the demise of both Austria's millennium-old Hapsburg Empire and Germany's Second Reich, Hitler's rise to power, Nazi Germany's annexation of Austria, and the flight of European Jews—among them members of the Freud family—in the face of intensified virulent and perilous antisemitism. Freud's interest in the same biblical hero notwithstanding, the two Moses figures do seem significantly different. In "The Moses of Michelangelo," he constructed a Moses figure through an interpretation of Michelangelo's statue, which is, of course, itself an interpretation of the biblical Moses and how he was perceived in Western Christendom; in *Moses and Monotheism* Freud is concerned with both a construction (although he considered it merely a corrected and accurate representation) of the biblical hero and the development of Jewish monotheism. Unlike his idea of the biblical prophet, Freud's earlier Moses had mastered his great rage and in doing so preserved the Decalogue; his later protagonist, however, exhibits no great emotions to master, but instead coerces his adopted people to master their instinctual life for the sake of an invisible, ineffable God. The Moses Freud found in Michelangelo's statue would forever sit controlled, stony, and silent on the monument to a pope, even while Freud deciphered the drama of its gestures and stature in the pages of an essay; the Moses of the later work, because of his tyrannical demands on his followers, was murdered and virtually forgotten by them, only years later to have his ideas revived and securely institutionalized in Mosaic monotheism.

Despite obvious differences between the texts, questions arise about resemblances, which nonetheless haunt these Moses figures. Had Freud late in his life actually abandoned and replaced the "new and different Moses" whom he had once discovered and eulogized in the heart of Western Christendom? And in his waning years did Freud, forced like his ancestors to seek refuge in yet another country, finally uncover the historical Moses whom he deemed responsible for religious and national Jewish identity? Or do these two Moses figures, despite their obvious differences, share characteristics which their dissimilar external features and discourses obscure? Though answers are difficult to find, there are indications that these Moses figures are perhaps more intimately related than is at first evident.

Of paramount importance in the "new and different" hero Freud found in Michelangelo's Moses was the necessity to suppress his great rage in order to preserve the Decalogue, which in this instance consisted largely of restrictive legislation.[181] Such restriction may indeed liberate one from compelling passions so that one can maintain external control, as Freud imagined the stony figure to have done; it may also, like someone who has gained independence by renouncing Oedipal attachments and aggression, enable one to forge ahead in life, as do both the narrator at the text's conclusion and Freud himself on his return to Vienna. Yet such liberation, grounded not only in the repression of desire and need, but in submission to an ineffable higher authority, may also be understood as coercion and thralldom.

Although the Moses of *Moses and Monotheism* seems not to be concerned with mastering his own feelings, he accomplishes his mission of establishing the authority of his God by coercing the populace into mastering their impulses and renouncing instinctual gratification, which Freud considers absolutely necessary for progress in spirituality and the people's sense of superiority, indeed for civilization. Thus, the obsessive and coercive nature of Mosaic religion—"Such an idea [of one great God] has a compulsive character, it must be believed"[182]—certainly suggests that liberation from sensuality and from the fleshpots of Egypt necessitates forms of enslavement which may make one feel spiritually superior, though not liberated. The murderers of this Moses could certainly testify to that.

In "The Moses of Michelangelo" Freud's "new and different" Moses adopts constraints on his own behavior that result in compelling inactivity and are akin to those which the Moses of *Moses and Monotheism* demands of the people. Thus, restraint and control, which proved so successful in taming and immobilizing the earlier Moses while allowing him to attain "the highest possible mental achievement," function similarly in the later text: ultimately they tame an unruly Semitic tribe and dampen its revolutionary, emancipatory fervor, while allowing its members to make great advances in spirituality. The conception of liberation grounded in renunciation that informs the Moses of the earlier text is extended in *Moses and Monotheism* to a whole people; and whereas formerly one person's behavior and achievement were at stake, now it is the destiny for millennia of an entire people. This transference of assumptions about behavior from the individual to society is not new in Freud's work. Witness the transition from his self-analysis and individual case histories to a universal theory of the psyche, from the obsessional neurosis of the individual to that of groups who found and practice religions, from the mechanism of repression in individual psychology to its function in history and society. Thus, the two Moses figures together reveal the nexus between Freud's psychology of the individual and his later social theory. Whether the liberation of individual or nation is at stake, the same underlying tensions persist. And given the magnitude of these tensions—between restraint and liberation, instinctual renunciation and greater spirituality, suppression of the senses and development of abstract intellect—one wonders whether either of Freud's Moses figures can be expected to deliver a people from oppression and enslavement.

Though doubts surface in the pages of *Moses and Monotheism,* it is clear that Freud thought he had found in Moses the liberator he had sought. But it may just be that, enclosed in his study, his theories, and the depths of his psyche, Freud had not yet ventured out to search for an explanation of the character of Jews and antisemitism. Since, as he claims, it was current attacks on Jews that once again aroused his interest in Moses, it would seem especially important to devote at least a portion of his attention to the social and political significance of antisemitism and to the period of his own lifetime when Jews began to experience the possibility of a liberated life in Europe. Yet, as with many other of his psychological and cultural pursuits, Freud's inquiry into antisemitism, though apparently motivated by prevailing Nazi persecution, reaches into the remotest past and the most inaccessible regions of the psyche, indeed into the psyche of the victim: "The deeper motives of the hatred of the Jews," Freud remarks in *Moses and Monotheism,* "are rooted in times long gone, they operate out of the unconscious of the peoples."[183] There is an echo here of the Rome-phobia segment of *The Interpretation of Dreams,* where his preoccupation with antisemitism all but disappeared from his final insight into how heroes are chosen and constructed. At the end of that segment the interpreter Freud moved from the hostile social context of his father's and his own life into speculations about an unremembered past in his earliest childhood. In this work, written at the turn of the century, the transition from the dynamics of the social world to the remote recesses of the psyche and the past concerned only an individual. By the late 1930s, however, this transition seems to have gained the status of a general theory about the psychic foundation for political society. In *Moses and Monotheism* the victims of persecution are asked to explore their own unconscious for traces of a prehistoric repressed murder and to seek liberation in the recesses of their psyche, while antisemitic perpetrators, be they individuals or the state, are spared the full moral responsibility for their acts. Freud wants the individual to be liberated from society; yet he continues to plead for a more restrictive society to protect great individuals from a barbaric and anarchic rabble. In his last major work, Freud once again sought solutions to social and cultural conditions in the psyche of the isolated individual or archaic heritage of a people, thereby undercutting the social and communal context for the freedom of the individual.[184] I am not concerned, as many of his critics and interpreters are,[185] that Freud, as he says in the opening sentence of *Moses and*

Monotheism, has deprived a people of the man considered "the greatest of their sons." Even if the orgins of Moses and monotheism are to be found in Egypt, that does not make the Mosaic religion, to which Jews have adhered for millennia, any less Jewish, unless of course one subscribes to theories of genetic racial purity. Freud may not have destroyed the foundations of Mosaic monotheism; but he may very well have undermined Moses' exemplary, even radical, activity of liberating a people from brutal social and political oppression and preparing them for life in a principled and just society.

5

Word, Image, Idea: Schoenberg and Moses—A Tragic Coexistence?

Like Freud's parents, who left the territories of the Austro-Hungarian Empire for the capital, Arnold Schoenberg's parents came to Vienna in the middle of the nineteenth century, his father, Samuel, in the early 1850s from Pressburg (today Bratislava, Czechoslovakia),[1] his mother, Pauline Nachod, from Prague. His father apprenticed as a salesperson and finally bought a shoe shop, which earned him a meager living until his death in 1889. Although the forebears of both parents were apparently religious Jews, Schoenberg's uncle Fritz Nachod maintained that Samuel was an "idealistic freethinker,"[2] probably a euphemism for a nonpracticing or secular Jew. Nevertheless, Arnold Schoenberg's birth on September 13, 1874, and his circumcision eight days later were registered with the Viennese Jewish community, though no information exists about any religious education or affiliation during his youth.[3] The sixteen-year-old Schoenberg did write a cousin in whom he was romantically interested that he was an "unbeliever,"[4] but it is difficult to know—especially given the circumstances of adolescent correspondence—whether this was a considered philosophical or religious position. Less than a decade later, however, in 1898, Schoenberg was baptized in the Lutheran church.

Although Vienna at the turn of the century had the greatest number of conversions compared to other European Jewish communities,[5] it does not seem likely, as Lucy S. Dawidowicz suggests, that Schoenberg, like Gustav Mahler (who was baptized in the Catholic church), converted "in order to have easier access to important musical institutions and influential musicians";[6] being a Protestant in Catholic Austria was not an asset. Schoenberg's conversion could have been motivated by a number of reasons: by the religious fervor of his Protestant friend Walter Pieau, a singer who is inscribed as Schoenberg's godfather in the baptismal record;[7] by cultural considerations, as his wife Gertrud maintained;[8] perhaps, as Alexander L. Ringer conjectures, by his close association with workers' choral groups during a time of animosity between labor and the Catholic church.[9] Whatever his attachment to Christianity or a particular denomination may have been, Schoenberg was married to his first wife, Mathilde von Zemlinsky, in the church in which he was baptized; and even five decades later, in his last work, *Modern Psalms (Moderne Psalmen)*, long after returning to Judaism, he hailed Jesus as a redeemer who was "without a doubt the purest, the most innocent, selfless and idealistic being who ever wandered the earth."[10]

Schoenberg and Judaism

Despite his newly chosen religion, Schoenberg was not immune to antisemitism and other Jewish issues. In the summer of 1921 at the Mattsee in Austria an antisemitic incident—he was refused a hotel room because he was a Jew—terminated his working vacation. That experience proved so traumatic that two years later he turned down a very desirable invitation from his friend Wassily Kandinsky to join the Bauhaus cultural center in Weimar because of reports of antisemitism. In a letter to Kandinsky, Schoenberg wrote that he had heard that "even a Kandinsky sees only what is evil in the activities of Jews and in their evil activities only what is Jewish"[11] and that he did not care to be singled out as an exception. Alluding to the earlier antisemitic incident, he explained: "For what I was forced to learn in the course of last year I have finally understood and shall not again forget. Specifically that I am no German, no European, indeed perhaps hardly a human being (at least the Europeans prefer the worst of their race to me), but that I am a Jew."[12] Schoenberg demonstrates both an abhorrence of prejudice and injustice and a somber recognition that, despite emancipation and assimilation, a Jew converted to Christianity is only and always a Jew.

The prevalence of the seemingly oxymoronic appellation "baptized Jew" in nineteenth- and early twentieth-century Austria and Germany indicates that religion may no longer be the characterizing feature of a Jew, as it had been in the Middle Ages. In an observation about Germany also applicable to Austria, Reinhard Rürup notes that "the very definition of a Jew became problematical towards the end of the period of emancipation, and it is remarkable that even liberals and socialists began to speak of 'race', although they had no idea of superiority or inferiority or of any laws of nature in mind when using that term. Yet it cannot be overlooked that here were starting points for the posing of a 'Jewish question' with antisemitic intent."[13]

Antisemitism in Germany and Austria had accompanied the erratic and humiliating process of emancipation over eight decades as well as the period of incomplete assimilation following legal emancipation.[14] But in the last decades of the nineteenth century and the early years of the twentieth it was exacerbated by indigenous social and economic conditions—the devastating stock-market crash of 1873, the lingering deep depression that followed, the decline of liberalism, growing nationalistic fervor, and political instability. What Schoenberg realized at the Mattsee was that adopting Christianity would not bring about assimilation; for in the twentieth century a Christian could be characterized as not just German or Austrian, but even—and indelibly—Jewish. The insult he experienced at the Mattsee precipitated a profound change in Schoenberg's understanding of himself and his world, as documented in a second long letter to Kandinsky, written just two weeks after the first one mentioned above.

This second letter, in which Schoenberg speaks about Hitler and antisemitism, contains a passionate account of the effects of prejudice on Jew and gentile alike. It conveys his despair about the effects of antisemitism as well as his admiration for a people who have survived two thousand years of persecution:

> Where, however, should antisemitism lead if not to acts of violence? Is that so difficult to imagine? For them it is perhaps enough to deny Jews their rights. Then Einstein, Mahler, I, and many others will certainly be done away with. But one thing is certain: those far more tenacious elements, because of whose ability to resist, Jewry has maintained itself without protection for twenty centuries against all humanity, these they will not be able to extirpate. For these are apparently organized in such a way that they can fulfill the task which their God has assigned them: in exile to maintain themselves, unmixed and unbroken, until the hour of redemption comes![15]

The effects of an antisemitism that is inimical to humankind and seems impossible to overcome brought Schoenberg, as it did Freud, to an appreciation of the tenacity of the Jewish people. While for Freud survival was a psycho-social phenomenon, for Schoenberg it was a religious undertaking. Hans Keller observed that "Freud, the unwavering atheist, and Schoenberg, the consistent theist, met at Mount Sinai."[16] In fact, Schoenberg's return to Judaism, which seems to have been precipitated by the antisemitism he encountered in the early 1920s, is prefigured and fully articulated in his works about Moses and Mosaic tradition.

From exile in Paris in 1933, shortly after formally converting back to Judaism, Schoenberg wrote Alban Berg that what was now official—that is, his conversion—had in fact taken place years before: "As you surely have noticed, my return to Jewish religion took place long ago and can be recognized in my work, even in the published portions ('Thou shalt not . . . thou must . . .' ['Du sollst nicht . . . du mußt . . .']) and in *Moses and Aaron* [*Moses und Aron*], about which you have known since 1928, but which goes back at least five years before that; but especially in my drama, 'The Biblical Way' ['Der Biblische Weg'],[17] which was conceived at the latest in 1922 or 1923, though completed only in '26–'27."[18] Schoenberg's letters, pronouncements, and religious works leave little doubt that his conversion to Christianity was motivated by deep religious conviction, though clearly the political climate in Germany and Austria played an important role as well. The confluence of Schoenberg's personal experience, strong religious sentiments, and an uncompromising ethical stance seems to have provoked his return to Judaism; and an abiding preoccupation with Judaism, Moses, and the salvation of the Jewish people is central to many of his important works dating from the 1920s until his death in 1951.

It is surely significant that in the letter to Berg the three works cited as documenting his personal if not formal conversion are all concerned with certain aspects of the Mosaic tradition and with an unassimilable Moses. Composed in 1925, "Thou shalt not, thou must," the second of "Four Pieces for Mixed Chorus" ("Vier Stücke für gemischten Chor"), op. 27, refers to the second commandment of the Decalogue, which prohibits the making of images of God. The song also stresses the absolute centrality of divine spirit and the importance of those chosen to affirm it:

Du sollst nicht, du mußt

Du sollst dir kein Bild machen!
Denn ein Bild schränkt ein,
begrenzt, faßt,
was unbegrenzt und unvorstellbar bleiben soll.

Ein Bild will Namen haben:
Du kannst ihn nur vom Kleinen nehmen:
Du sollst das Kleine nicht verehren!

Du mußt an den Geist glauben!
Unmittelbar, gefühllos
und selbstlos.
Du mußt, Auserwählter, mußt, willst du's bleiben![19]

Thou shalt not, thou must

Thou shalt make no image!
For an image restricts,

limits, grasps,
what should remain unlimited and inconceivable.

An image wants a name:
You can only take it from what is small:
Thou shalt not revere what is small!

Thou must believe in the spirit!
without mediation, without emotion
and without self.
Thou must, chosen one, must, if you want to remain that!

The structure of this text calls to mind a statement repeatedly made in "The Biblical Way," "From a good idea everything flows of itself."[20] "Thou shalt not, thou must" presents several ideas in progression, each of which derives from the first. The song opens with a prohibition against making an image of something limitless and beyond conceptualization; proceeds to a prohibition against revering what is limited and confined; affirms the hegemony of the spirit; and concludes with a command to the chosen one to believe unconditionally in the spirit. The confluence of an ineffable and spiritual divinity and the obligation of those chosen to comprehend and live with that divinity informs Schoenberg's conception of Moses and Mosaic tradition, Judaism, and the moral obligation of Jews, whether expressed in song, drama, opera, or political program. The similarities as well as the differences between his conception and the biblical or traditional representation, his unique formulations, and his almost obsessive repetition offer insight into Schoenberg's struggle with the role of Judaism in a modern society rife with antisemitism.

"The Biblical Way"

The prohibition against making an image of boundless and unrepresentable spirit and the chosen person's absolute devotion to that spirit in "Thou shalt not, thou must" are prominent ideas in "The Biblical Way" and *Moses and Aaron,* the other texts mentioned in Schoenberg's letter to Berg. Indeed, the incompatibility of the ineffable with any concrete form that purports to express it, articulated in the first two verses of the song, is a dominant theme in the unpublished play "The Biblical Way." Here, the contradiction between subject and form appears in a play with a contemporary political setting and a biblical subtext. In a May 1933 letter asking the renowned theatrical director Max Reinhardt to produce the play, Schoenberg indicated that even in the 1920s he had had political aspirations for "The Biblical Way," a work intended "for the inauguration of a propaganda campaign."[21] Because of the desperate situation in 1933 Schoenberg thought his play could mobilize the Jewish people to work vigorously for their own salvation, as he himself planned to do on a tour through America and perhaps the world for "the Jewish national cause."[22]

"The Biblical Way" probes the limits and malleability of Jewish law and tradition as well as the politics involved in unifying a diverse Jewish population living in the diaspora for the purpose of establishing a modern, independent Jewish state governed by Mosaic law. Europe and the fictitious African country Ammongäa are the setting; the time contemporaneous with the writing of the work (1926–27); and the protagonist, Max Aruns, both a utopian Zionist and practical *homo faber* (man the worker), seeks to establish in Africa a modern Jewish nation, a "new Palestine." Although a large part of the play focuses on internal Jewish affairs, especially on the promotion of unity among Jews, I cannot agree that this is the exclusive focus of this work, as Michael Mäckelmann argues;[23] the impetus for the relocation project must also be attributed to the massive antisemitism suffered in the diaspora.[24] However, no consideration is given to fighting antisemitism, changing perceptions about Jews, or reforming society, all of which correspond to Schoenberg's view that fighting antisemitism is a "waste, a fatal waste of energy."[25] Indeed, the first point of his "Four-Point Program for Jewry," completed more than a decade later in 1938, states: "The fight against antisemitism must be stopped."[26] Accepting a seemingly unalterable hostility to Jews in the diaspora, "The Biblical Way" explores the possibility of constructing on the foundations of biblical tradition and Mosaic law an independent Jewish homeland that would include a diverse and contentious population of socialists, capitalists, intellectuals, Zionists, assimilationists, and orthodox Jews.

Allusions to the Bible—to Moses and Aaron, the exodus from Egypt, the sojourn in the wilderness *(Wüstenwanderung)*, the settlement in Canaan, and Joshua's destruction of the walls of Jericho—are numerous and prominent throughout the text. Max Aruns likens his "new Palestine" venture to the biblical wandering in the wilderness, a period of education and preparation necessary for those who will inhabit the promised land they are to build. He is even regarded as a coalescence of Moses and Aaron, as the name Max Aruns suggests. However, according to David Asseino, an orthodox Jew solicited to modernize Jewish law for the new state, aspiring to be both Moses and Aaron is a transgression of the biblical order:

> Max Aruns, you want to be Moses and Aaron in one person: Moses, to whom God granted the idea, but denied the power of speech; and Aaron, who could not grasp the idea, but could communicate and move the masses. Max Aruns, you who have understood how to interpret God's word in such a modern way, have you not understood why God did not unite both powers in one person?[27]

But Aruns has a more forgiving interpretation: "If I may juxtapose my view to yours, then the problem is resolved in the following manner: Moses and Aaron signify to me two activities of *one* person: of a *statesman*."[28] This recalls the struggle of Goethe's Faust: "His two souls know nothing of one another; the purity of his idea is not marred by his public actions, which are not weakened by taking into account the still unresolved problems posed, at times, by the idea."[29] Aruns insists that he had wanted at most to be a kind of Aaron, but exigencies of the times would not allow him to "wait for those with the gifts of a Moses to agree upon one, upon the one to lead."[30] Only grave necessity, the dire needs of the people, motivated him to undertake such an enormous burden alone.

There are profound differences separating Aruns and orthodox Jewry. To the deeply religious Aruns, the social conditions of the Jews, modern politics, and technological developments require that biblical interpretations be adapted to contemporary circumstances and needs. To the orthodox, however, no interpretation or reform that deviates from biblical law as authorized in the rabbinic tradition is permissible; new interpretations must conform to accepted, though perhaps archaic, exegeses. The following interchange between Aruns and Asseino reveals not only the nature of their differences, but also the social and political ramifications of their positions:

> *Asseino:* If I were a mouthpiece of God, then it would be only in order to lift my voice in all eternity for the eternity of his word.
> *Aruns:* What is eternal in God's word is its spirit! The letter [*Wortlaut*, literally 'word sound', generally means 'wording' or 'text'; here the meaning is closer to *Wortlaut des Gesetzes*, that is, 'letter of the law'] is merely phenomenal form, adapted to the moment, to the demands of wandering in the wilderness [*Wüstenwanderung*]. But a nation today cannot turn off the blast furnaces or close down the electrical plants every Friday.
> *Asseino:* Here your materialism has again betrayed the idea.
> *Aruns:* You refer to me as a man of action. Man of idea: as a man of action I demand of you the new law.
> *Asseino:* What you demand of me is akin to Aaron demanding of Moses consent and assistance for creating the golden calf.
> *Aruns:* No, I demand only your consent so that our people shall not be forced to live according to the letter of the law, but may maintain the spirit of the law.[31]

Aruns' distinction between spirit and letter of the word, which reappears in *Moses and Aaron*, is crucial because it also underscores the difference between Moses and Aaron and the possibility of their fundamental qualities merging in a single person. Just as the separation of letter *(Wortlaut)* and spirit allows for the extension, or "adaptation," of the letter without necessarily destroying the spirit of the word, so too may it be possible for Max Aruns, as a "merely phenomenal form," to represent Moses and Aaron without the loss of their biblical significance and difference. Aruns' interest in the locus of the power of the word is thus integrally connected to his concern for necessary dynamic change within a context of authoritative law associated with an "eternal, invisible, inconceivable God."[32] And his argument with orthodox Jewry does not merely take the form of abstract disputation, but more practically seeks justification for a modern Jewish state in which the basic tenets of Judaism can coexist with advanced technological and social developments. "The Biblical Way" suggests that this state might be established, although in another biblical parallel Aruns' successor Guido, the play's Joshua, will witness the success or failure of the project.

The conclusion of the play affirms the validity of Aruns' religious-political position even as the protagonist is destroyed. Not unlike Freud's Moses in *Moses and Monotheism,* Aruns is murdered by disgruntled and dissatisfied followers who believe themselves betrayed by him.[33] But the conclusion is also reminiscent of Christ's betrayal: Aruns' work has in fact been undermined by the government of Ammongäa, which secretly withheld food transports, and by Jewish opponents, who conspired against him. As he dies, Aruns concedes that Asseino was right after all: God has punished Aruns, on the one hand, for his arrogance in trying to be both Moses and Aaron and, on the other, for relying on a war machine, not merely God, to protect the state. Nonetheless he sees himself as a good Jew who died for the continuation of the idea of God, and his final words affirm this God: "I die gladly, for I know you will always give our people men [males, *Männer*] who will gladly die for the idea of the one, eternal, invisible and inconceivable God."[34] No sooner does Aruns die, however, than Guido arrives, brings in the war machine to protect the state, and takes over the reins of government with a pronouncement about Aruns that once again emphasizes the biblical analogy: "This destiny [the death of Aruns] was determined by divine providence. As Moses was not permitted to enter the promised land, as it was his task merely to lead his people there, as he had to die when his task was completed, so had this man completed his life when New Palestine had become a reality. What he has left behind is a different and easier task. For that a Joshua is enough, for it I shall perhaps suffice."[35] The orthodox Asseino also returns, this time with new insight, and at the bier celebrates Aruns' work, for he now understands that although Aruns had to die in order to realize his idea, others will benefit from his martyrdom. The play ends with an affirmation of Aruns' mission and of the spiritual destiny of the people and state (an anticipation of Moses' vision in *Moses and Aaron*):

As with every old people so it is also our destiny: to SPIRITUALIZE ourselves. To release ourselves from all that is material. We have one other goal: We must learn to think the idea of the one, eternal, inconceivable God . . . We want to perfect ourselves spiritually, want to be allowed to dream our dream of God—like all old peoples who have matter [*Materie*] behind them.[36]

What echoes throughout "The Biblical Way" is the ghost of Theodor Herzl, the founder of modern Zionism, and his plan to establish a Jewish state in Uganda. Although nowhere did Schoenberg discuss the Uganda proposal during the years he was writing this play and although there is no record of a work by Herzl in Schoenberg's library, there are indications that Herzl's plan was not unknown to Schoenberg. First, Herzl's program was presented to the Sixth Zionist Congress at Basel, Switzerland, in 1903 by the renowned publicist Max Nordau (which may account for Max Aruns' given name); the incident caused great turmoil among European Jews and received wide publicity. Second, some years later Schoenberg wrote about Herzl. In "A Four-Point Program," completed in 1938, Schoenberg noted, "Theodore Herzl dies when the Uganda Project was rejected by the Zionist Congress: his heart committed harakiri."[37] In an unpublished and undated document written in English after emigrating to the

United States in 1933, Schoenberg discusses at some length the probable reasons for Herzl's failure to "erect an independent colony in Uganda"; among them is Herzl's soft and humanitarian disposition, which rendered him unable to break the resistance of his opponents or to enlist inspired participants. According to Schoenberg, Herzl relied too heavily on the generosity of others instead of on his own powers or those of his followers; he did not himself go to Uganda with his few hundred followers and create the state.[38] Although Max Aruns does go abroad to create a state, he exhibits other weaknesses which Schoenberg later attributes to Herzl. Finally, parallelisms between the projects of Herzl and Aruns suggest that Schoenberg had Herzl in mind when he wrote his play. To mention just a few similarities: Herzl and Aruns had both been writers; they responded to a seemingly unalterable antisemitism by seeking to establish a Jewish state; since Palestine was unattainable at a time of dire necessity, both opted for a substitute African country which was to be technologically and politically modern; in both instances the "New Palestine" was viewed as a stepping stone to the historical Promised Land; neither was enamored of inexpedient democracy or opposed to more efficient authoritarian rule; for both, the unity of the Jewish people was paramount; and, finally, neither lived to enjoy the establishment of their proposed state.

There are also, of course, differences, primary among them Aruns' profoundly religious basis for his state as well as the unity of the people. While Aruns believed that the cohesion of the Jews as a people was deteriorating in contemporary Europe, Herzl was concerned about the increasing threat to assimilation. Aruns and Herzl viewed their corrective undertakings as latter-day liberating ventures akin to the biblical Moses' sojourn to the Promised Land. However, Herzl was largely uninterested in Mosaic law and tradition and sought unity through social and legal contracts; he was especially concerned with making room for "the immortal band of our Freethinkers, who are continually making new conquests for humanity."[39] In contrast, Aruns in "The Biblical Way" assumes that the Jewish state will be grounded in Mosaic law, possibly modernized, and in a people united by their complete devotion to an invisible, inconceivable God. In this work Mosaic law, which is the foundation for a Jewish people, is not concerned with ethical precepts and rules for ritual observance, but is concerned almost exclusively with the abstract God of the Decalogue's first three commandments, who demands total obedience. Given this view, there can be no separation of the theology and the politics of a Jewish state, though their relationship is still open to interpretation. At the play's end, Aruns and Asseino concur that, for a modern Moses or Moses-and-Aaron and for the Jewish people, the old biblical path can exist only if it and the wilderness it traverses are interpreted anew. It may be that with "The Biblical Way" and the later *Moses and Aaron* Schoenberg was recreating that way through the wilderness leading from the Mattsee to his return to Judaism, interpreting his way to emancipation. It is ironic then that both works remained unpublished, unfinished, and never performed during his lifetime, leaving him to hope that at least their spirit would survive.

Moses and Aaron

In October 1928, about a year after he wrote "The Biblical Way," Schoenberg completed the libretto to *Moses and Aaron,* which was largely based on the text of an unpublished oratorio of the same name written between 1927 and 1928.[40] Schoenberg did not compose music for the oratorio, but turned instead to the opera, the text of which he continued to revise while composing its music. The completed portions of the opera were written during the period of the increasing political success of National Socialism and growing antisemitism, both of which endangered Schoenberg's position at the Berlin Academy of the Arts. Thus, just as his strong ties to German and Austrian culture were being sundered, his own work turned to the profound religious foundations that underlie national Jewish identity. By August 1931 the score for act 1 of *Moses and Aaron* was completed, and in March of the following year the score of act 2. Act 3 remained incomplete: textual revisions were made in 1934 and 1935 after Schoenberg emigrated to the United States, but only sketches for a few measures of music were composed in 1937. There are indications, however, that Schoenberg intended to finish the work. Throughout the 1940s and almost to his death in 1951, letters and remarks reveal that he still planned to complete the opera.[41] René Leibowitz noted that difficulties with the composition caused Schoenberg to recommend in 1950 that the opera be presented without the third act.[42] But in November of that year Schoenberg wrote to the Artistic Director of the Maggio Musicale in Florence, suggesting that the opera could be performed with act 3 spoken. He explained that act 3 is "a dialogue between Moses and Aaron, which, after Aaron's death, is followed by Moses' long monologue."[43] The following year he wrote to Hermann Scherchen that he would permit the publication and performance of the first two acts only, but indicated that if "one performs the third act without music,—as an extra piece or just reads out the text, this reproduces the main content of the work."[44] Scherchen in fact performed the entire opera, accompanying the third act with the music from act 1, scene 1.[45] Schoenberg's wife, Gertrud, also reported that in 1951 Schoenberg agreed "that the third act may simply be spoken, in case I cannot complete the composition."[46] Although it is clear that Schoenberg intended to complete *Moses and Aaron,* it is certainly curious that he composed no music for it after 1937. And while most interpreters consider the opera to be a fragment, one may, it seems to me, also regard the final act without music as providing the necessary closure to the text, perhaps as a kind of coda appropriate, in its spoken form, to the general problems and specific ideas raised in the text.

It is not difficult to understand the preoccupation of so many critics with the fact that the opera is a fragment. They may be responding to two interrelated aspects: an audience's traditional visual and auditory expectations of opera; and this opera's principal concern with the problem of communicating what is ineffable through linguistic and visual means generally used to transmit insights about the phenomenal world. Theodor Adorno, for example, assumes that the subject matter rendered completion virtually impossible; in this work Schoenberg had encountered the "threshold of self-consciousness in his own venture, of the impossibility of aesthetic totality that it becomes by virtue of an absolute metaphysical content."[47] Winfried Zillig observes that "the problem taken on was insoluble."[48] And George Steiner makes the sweeping statement that "events that were now come to pass in Europe were, quite literally, beyond words . . . that art can neither stem barbarism nor convey experience when experience becomes unspeakable."[49] More recently Mäckelmann has maintained that, in *Moses and Aaron,* Schoenberg attempted to find a solution to the problem left unresolved in "The Biblical Way." Because in the earlier work Max Aruns is an inseparable coalescence of Moses and Aaron, the failure of his activist "Aaron" aspect results in Aruns' destruction and with him the unfulfilled spiritual Mosaic claims. According to Mäckelmann, *Moses and Aaron* could not be completed because Schoenberg "had not found the way which would make plausible Moses' victory over Aaron's falsification"; nor had he discovered "how, upon comprehension of the idea of God, unity of the people could be attained."[50] Daniel Albright considers the major concern of the opera to have been resolved in the first two acts: "the commandment against graven images was itself a graven image and has annulled itself"; the third act he, therefore, regards as superfluous.[51] And Monika Lichtenfeld enumerates various ways in which the third act was performed; and, in support of her thematic understanding of the opera as the irresolvable tension between abstract idea and sensuous presence, concludes that these different performances "fulfill the original conception of the opera—the triumph of the idea over the reality." But she also adds that there are good reasons for concluding the opera with the second act, for "the open ending of the second act stands for the truth of the work itself, for the irresolution of the conflict which Schoenberg neither could nor wanted to resolve musically."[52]

Such speculation on broad aesthetic and metaphysical possibilities is interesting but, in my view, not sufficient to explain or justify either the fragmentary text or the composer's failure to compose the music over a period of almost two decades. My own inclination is to explore the aesthetic implications of the opera as one whose third act is spoken and to resist speculating about the philosophical implications of an opera whose conclusion is without music.

The overall structure of *Moses and Aaron* suggests the significant concerns of the work as well as ways in which they are addressed and explored. Its central focus is the possibility of communicating the idea of an ineffable deity through language which can only falsify what is essentially unrepresentable *(unvorstellbar)*. The opera opens with a humble and insecure Moses who, after announcing the characteristics of his God, enters into a dialogue with a voice emanating from the thornbush; it directs him to liberate God's chosen people from bondage to what is transitory, thereby leading them to the one and eternal God. But apart from a few remarks interspersed with Aaron's in act 1, scene 4, Moses does not speak with this people until the concluding moments of the opera. There Moses for the first time addresses the people at some length, enjoining them to pursue only spirituality, that is, to reject the transitory and fight for the idea of God *(Gottesgedanke)*. The central episode of the work—Aaron's creation of the golden calf as a representation of a God whose true being cannot be represented—mediates between the opera's beginning and end, between the articulation of Moses' mission and its fulfillment. The episode of the golden calf precipitates the major conflict of the work, namely, what means are appropriate for communicating, without falsification and distortion, an inconceivable, unrepresentable deity. This critical issue is further elaborated in the opera through a consideration of how word, image, and idea function and interrelate. Indeed this complex of aesthetic, religious, and philosophical concerns within the context of the dramatic opera underscores Schoenberg's conceptions of Moses and Aaron, Mosaic doctrine, and the identity of the Jewish people as a nation.

The opening line of *Moses and Aaron* introduces Moses' overriding concern, the foundation of his cosmic vision: "Unique, eternal, omnipresent, invisible and unrepresentable [*unvorstellbarer*] God!"[53] Moses articulates this line slowly and cautiously in the "Sprechstimme"—a type of artificial vocal enunciation between speech and song—which, except for a single sentence that is sung and addressed to Aaron, he uses throughout the first two acts. Whether this initial statement is a declaration of theme or a cry to the Almighty and whether or not it elicits the subsequent response from the voice emanating from the thornbush, it surely calls attention to Moses' uncompromising conception of God.

The qualities of invisibility and unrepresentability are, it seems to me, substantiated by the disembodied voice which Moses attributes to God.[54] The voice that emanates from the thornbush consists of two choruses: one speaks, associated with Moses; the other sings, later associated with Aaron. David Lewin has suggested that these are the two aspects associated with God; and later, when this same kind of vocal mass appears as the people *(das Volk)*, a crucial link is established between them and God.[55] It is not surprising, then, that the voice from the thornbush speaks not solely in the abstract discourse one might anticipate from an ineffable being, but often in unexpectedly quotidian terms. Its first utterance concerns Moses' concrete human as well as spiritual aspects, and also the connection between the mundane and abstract, the phenomenal and the spiritual: "Take your shoes off: / you have walked far enough," God tells Moses, adding, with the inclusion of this second clause, a quality of caring mother to the biblical text's voice of authority; "you are standing on holy ground; / now proclaim!" (112). Whereas the biblical text—"put off thy shoes from off thy feet, for the place whereon thy standest is holy ground" (Exodus 3:5)—stresses the separation of the mundane from the holy, the opera's added phrase, "you have walked far enough," softens God's biblical command by the friendly regard for Moses' comfort. The pronouncements in the opera suggest that the sacredness of the place may not require divesting oneself of worldly paraphernalia, even though until the last act Moses remains adamant about the absolute and essential otherness of the divine. The ambiguity of this text, in which it is not clear why Moses is to remove his shoes, calls into question the absolute separation of the sacred from the worldly and allows for the possibility that holiness as a way of thinking and being may not be opposed to commonplace living, but an integral part of it.[56]

The interchange between Moses and God indicates that Moses may have a far more austere and rigid conception of the divine mission than this God intended, which could account for Moses' inability to communicate with common people until he has reconsidered his views, as I believe he does in the final act. While at the opening of the opera the voice of God enjoins Moses to liberate the oppressed Jews, not until the concluding speech to an assembly of people does Moses find the appropriate means of delivering the divine message and fulfilling his duty without falsification; not until then does he communicate to them how a liberated people behaves in the world. Finally, using metaphorical language he had earlier disdained, he speaks to the goal of liberation from the transitory; and he does not echo Aaron's promise of inhabiting an actual land of milk and honey, but articulates the spiritual reality of a wilderness which is also their actual location.

Moses' final words with which the work also concludes— "But in the wilderness you are unconquerable / and will reach the goal: / United with God" (204)—announce the profound coalescence of metaphysical and social issues raised in the text. Clearly here "wilderness" no longer refers to the absolute spirituality he enunciated in the first act (150); here is an image which mediates between the phenomenal and noumenal realms, between the locus of concrete activity and the attainment of a spiritual goal.[57] Moses apparently has discovered a means of articulating, within the capacity of human thought and activity, the idea of a God that defies definition and description, and of communicating this to a people whose freedom depends on understanding and affirming that idea. However, from Moses' first words detailing the characteristics of his God until his final public address, the trajectory of his message reveals overwhelming obstacles—the nature of the message, the limitations of language, and the needs and expectations of the populace—that make revelation, communication, and understanding treacherously uncertain.

Although aspects of *Moses and Aaron* correspond to particular segments of the Bible—Exodus 3, 4, and 7 in act 1; Exodus 32 and 40 and Numbers 14 in act 2; and Exodus 17 and Numbers 20 in act 3—Schoenberg uses these texts freely, exploring a wide range of philosophic, religious, and cultural issues that are often peripheral to them. It is clear from a letter of 1933 that Schoenberg's interest in Moses was circumscribed: "Of this tremendous subject," he wrote, "I myself have placed in the foreground these elements: the idea of an unrepresentable God, of the Chosen People, and of the leader of the people."[58] The emphasis here on the basic elements of the communicative act (message, addressee, and addressor) highlights Schoenberg's concern with problems of communication and accounts for the absence of those aspects of the biblical story which have little to do with revelation and communication—for example, Moses' birth, his confrontation with the Pharoah, and Mosaic legislation.[59]

A critical problem of revelation is charted in the relationship between Moses and Aaron. Moses, to and through whom God speaks, feels himself inadequate to the task of transmitting God's word, while Aaron is to be the means of delivering the message that can liberate the people "so that they no longer serve the transitory" (114) and transform them into "the people of the One God" (116). Unlike Moses, for whom speaking is very difficult, Aaron has a gift of fluency, which is readily apparent in his agile bel canto singing style. Since, as God indicates, Aaron is to be for Moses what Moses is for God (116), that is, the voice that each needs to complete his mission, they should share the same ideas and discourse. But from the initial encounter of the brothers, who at first seemed to complement one another, differences between them quickly develop into irreconcilable opposition.[60] Moses' religious convictions seem unshakable and his ideas uncompromising, while Aaron's are subject to the exigencies of the moment and the demands of the populace. While for Moses God is and remains invisible and ineffable, an idea that cannot be represented ("Unrepresentable God! / Unspeakable, ambiguous idea!" [194]), Aaron, occupied with formulating expressive means sure to please, insists on the efficacy of constructing familiar and attractive images of the deity.

The divergent positions of Moses and Aaron are revealed in their differing concepts of freedom and liberation. In the opera's opening scene the voice from the thornbush articulates two views of freedom. In the first instance, the voice, clearly referring to the oppression of slavery, tells Moses: "You have seen the horror, recognized / the truth: so you can no longer do otherwise: / you must free your people from that!" (112). In the second, freedom has a broader, more metaphysical significance, namely, freedom from what is transitory: "The Eternal One wants to liberate them [the people], so that they no / longer serve the transitory" (114). Throughout acts 1 and 2 Moses adheres adamantly to this second view of freedom, Aaron almost exclusively to the first. While these views are not mutually antagonistic, Moses' fixation on the most abstract and absolute formulation as well as his apparent lack of concern for the people's social oppression supports his uncompromising assessment of the inadequacy of language to communicate what is absolutely spiritual, to liberate them. And Aaron's persistent attraction to a concrete formulation of freedom from enslavement permits him to advocate and create images that promise only tangible well-being. Arguing that the people will only accept a God who punishes, rewards, and responds in recognizable ways to their pleas and sacrifices, namely, a God they can perceive, fear, and love, Aaron seeks a representation of God tailored to the people's needs and to the religious and social conventions known to them. In doing so he suppresses the idea of freedom as release from service to the transitory and as unwavering devotion to the eternal and opts instead for freedom from physical bondage.

In the initial fraternal encounter in act 1 Moses tries to explain his position to Aaron, but Aaron dominates the exchange and makes it difficult for Moses' message to be heard distinctly. While Moses speaks, Aaron sings, virtually obscuring Moses' pronouncements. The one brief time in the opera when Moses does not use "Sprechstimme" and sings occurs during this exchange, and his solo voice rings clear. His song comes at the conclusion of an unusual dialogue in which each brother addresses God— Aaron telling God how much he appreciates the deity's virtues, Moses questioning God about Aaron's views. Seemingly in despair and making an enormous effort to direct Aaron to the righteous path, Moses adopts Aaron's communicative medium and sings a pained and very brief aria which can be heard as both a command and a plea: "Purify your thinking, / free it from what is worthless, / dedicate it to what is true: / no other reward is given for your sacrifice" (122).

Neither the power of Moses' song nor the clarity of the words seems to reach Aaron, whose mind remains preoccupied with the anticipated success of fulfilling the expectations of the people. The more Aaron focuses on the expectations of the people and the art of pacification, the less attention he devotes to the demands of God; and the divine mission fades into obscurity or becomes identical with his own victories. Thus, when Aaron performs the miracles that God had granted Moses, the significance shifts from a demonstration of divine power to the glorification of both audience and performer, whom God has seemingly graced. Success seems to be Aaron's. But just as the people rally to the God Aaron proffers and prepare to follow him into the wilderness, Moses intervenes and admonishes them to purify their thoughts, just as he had earlier admonished Aaron. And when they ask about nourishment in the wilderness, Moses replies: "In the wilderness purity / of thought will nourish, sustain, / and develop you" (150). Aaron, however, quickly interrupts Moses and subverts his message by directing the people to pending riches and worldly rewards: "and the eternal will let you see," he sings, "an image of your physical good fortune / in every spiritual miracle" (150). The magnitude of this subversion of God's intention becomes clear when one compares Aaron's promises of tangible rewards from spiritual endeavors with God's message of the spiritual significance in all things mundane; the voice from the thornbush tells Moses:

> Just as out of this thornbush,
> dark, before the light
> of truth fell on it,
> so will you perceive my voice
> in every thing. (114)

Moses no longer responds and, although present, does not say another word in this act. Indeed he does not speak again until he returns with the Decalogue from Mount Sinai in the fourth scene of act 2. Aaron's success with the people is evident in the concluding chorus of the first act, when they sing of Aaron's promise, a life free of toil and struggle in a land where milk and honey flow.

From the beginning of the opera, Moses reveals an obstinacy appropriate to his commitment to an ineffable and unrepresentable God; and it is difficult to imagine that he could ever be brought to question this idea and mission. But in the second act, upon returning from Mount Sinai, a situation develops that threatens to undermine his beliefs. Moses discovers not only debauched revelers worshipping a golden calf, but also a recalcitrant Aaron who defiantly justifies his image-making activity. Aaron even contends that the miracle by which Moses destroyed the golden calf was but an image ("And yet the miracle was no more than an image: / when your word destroyed my image" [186]), implying that the event of word banishing image is also merely a representation of spiritual power. At the conclusion of this act Moses rejects as "graven images" the pillars of fire and cloud perceived by Aaron as divine signs and approaches to the Almighty. In Aaron's words:

> God's sign like the glowing thornbush.
> Therein the Eternal One shows not himself,
> but the way to him;
> and the way to the promised land! (194)

Without relinquishing their former polytheism, the people, who want primarily to affirm their illusions and gratify their desires, follow Aaron and the pillar of fire; they go off singing praises for a god who is only one among many, but one more useful than the others: "Almighty, / you are stronger than Egypt's gods!" (194).

When the people and Aaron exit the scene, only Moses remains. He questions God about Aaron's interpretation, but God does not speak; Moses is left to ponder the dilemma and seek a solution alone. If Aaron, who is after all Moses' God-appointed spokesperson, is correct about the signifying function of images, then he, Moses, may indeed be guilty of having created an image—albeit a false one—of God, an image of God as an ineffable idea. No answer is forthcoming. "O word, you word that I lack!" (194) are Moses' final words. He collapses in despair, and it is not clear whether the "word" he lacks is God's or his own, perhaps both.

The tremendous loneliness and uncertainty of Schoenberg's Moses—who lives with a God who has chosen only him as an agent, a God present only in physical absence—are vividly portrayed in the final moments of act 2. But his situation is best understood in relation to what happened just before this, that is, the creation of the golden calf. The people are cognizant of the fact that their wealth and devotion comprise the substance of their gods and idols. In a joyous encomium to their gods, they sing also of their complicity:

> Gods, images of our eye,
> gods, masters of our senses!
> Your physical visibility,
> presence, assures our security;
> . . . . .
> To your gods you gave as content
> your inner being,
> your feeling of life.
> The appearance of your gods
> safeguards your gold:

Part with it!
Make yourself poor, make them rich!
They will not let you starve! (164)

Aaron, the artist-magician, knows too that for the people any external evidence indicating the existence of powerful protectors is well worth the economic and mental impoverishment they suffer. Even the tentative security gained from the illusory presence and familiarity of their gods as well as the sense of community resulting from worshipping common idols stand in sharp contrast to the terrible loneliness of Moses.[61] His God and divine mission bind him to a people from whom he could only be estranged since his idea of God precludes any means for communicating that idea, and therefore also precludes the means for organizing a community. Aaron's alternative to this incommunicability only exacerbates Moses' despair, and Moses' cry for the word he lacks is surely a plea for the word that could deliver the idea and, in doing so, create the community God seeks.

Schoenberg's conception of Moses as someone convinced that the word is grounded in "the origin, the idea" (198)—that images can only falsify the idea—may be responsible for the opera's curious distortion of the biblical text. In Numbers 20:7–12, God tells Moses to speak to the rock in order to obtain water from it, but instead he smites it. Because of this infraction Moses and the entire congregation are condemned never to enter the promised land. If the issue here simply involved the power of the word to create a miracle, then the rock, when struck, could have remained dry; but the water did flow. Yet, although the word and the rod could apparently cause the water to flow, the word's overwhelming significance is readily apparent in the enormous punishment meted out to an entire generation and its leader, who was chosen to be closer to God than was any other person. In *Moses and Aaron,* unlike the biblical text, the infraction is not committed by Moses, but by Aaron, whose solidarity with the people gives rise to celebration of the image. Indeed Moses reprimands Aaron for relying on an image, the rod, and not the word, and for disparaging the spiritual by promises to inhabit physically an "unreal land where milk and honey flows" (198). How could Schoenberg's Moses, who holds such inflexible ideas of God and God's unrepresentability, disobey a divine command?[62] A transgressor with such poor judgment and human frailty could hardly remain the zealous titan of *Moses and Aaron* who struggles so doggedly for the purity of the word.

Before Moses finally communicates directly with the people in the third act, he first reconsiders a critical issue—the nature and relationship of idea, word, and image—which had surfaced previously when Moses attributed the destruction of the golden calf to the power of the word. Moses' explanation reflects his belief in the divine basis of the word: "God's eternity annihilates the presence of gods! / That is no image, no miracle. / That is the law!" (186). Until act 3, "image"—be it "Bild," "Abbild," or "Sinnbild"—was, for Moses, a construct as antithetic to both word and idea as the mundane is to the spiritual. Since treachery lay not in the use or abuse of images but rather in any gesture that purports to express a spiritual idea, any image is "false, as an image only can be" (194). In effect Moses was imprisoned in a conception of the absolute exclusivity of word and image, idea and image, and because of this he remained insulated from the people he was called upon to liberate. Apart from Aaron's intercession, which in its betrayal of the idea proved disastrous, Moses found no way to enter the society within which he was to fulfill his mission.

In the final act Moses reappraises his ideas, assumes direct control, and becomes more than a distant leader who speaks through another; he begins to resolve the dilemma of the relationship between word and image. With Aaron in chains, Moses now takes direct charge of his mission with the people. The dialogue between Moses and Aaron in act 3 speaks to the nature of Moses' distinction between word and image and reflects his revaluation of the status of the image. The word continues to be associated with the idea of God and divine origin; but since all images originate in the word, Moses now admits their validity if they retain the idea and obey the word (202). Images that appropriately represent the ways in which the divine "appears" to human beings may then be free of serving what is transitory. Moses' fear that the image would obliterate or lose its connection with the idea underlies his attack on Aaron for creating the golden calf and for using the rod:

> You, for whom the word flees with the image,
> you yourself linger, you yourself live
> in the images which you pretend
> to generate for the people.
> Alienated from the origin, the idea,
> then neither word nor image suffices for you. (196–8)

Aaron stands accused of neglecting the word and constructing images that were estranged from idea; and when finally the image did not suffice and the people demanded a tangible deity, Aaron transformed the image into a concrete object that represented nothing other than itself. In response to Aaron's defense that the word must be interpreted for the people and that the rod was merely the communicative means people could understand, Moses contends that images—he names three: the rock, the wilderness, and the burning bush—cannot provide what the spirit needs, namely, "that freedom from craving which / is sufficient for eternal life" (200). Moses recognizes Aaron's self-interest: "Thus, you won the people not for the Eternal One, / but for you" (200), but Aaron's last words reiterate his compelling concern for the people, for "its freedom, that it become a people!" (200). Since for Moses freedom can mean only devotion to the idea of God, it is not Aaron's images, but his *false* images of human self-sufficiency and divine contingency that have led the people back into the "slavery of godlessness and pleasures" (202). Only after this last interchange, after he has distinguished between appropriate and false images, does Moses finally address the seventy Elders directly and, through them, the people by consciously using images.

Apart from an initial doubt about his ability to carry out God's mission, Schoenberg's Moses uncompromisingly pursues his metaphysical goal. The "eternal unrepresentable God" of this Moses is projected as an "unrepresentable idea," not a God intimately concerned with the ethical and social condition of the people or one with whom a biblical Abraham or Moses would argue, at times even successfully. In *Moses and Aaron* the chosen people is enjoined to free itself from the transitory and devote itself solely to the eternal, but nowhere in the text is there any indication that this people is expected to create an exemplary nation through obedience to commandments and law that regulate the conduct of everyday life. For this Moses, like the one in Freud's *Moses and Monotheism,* the second commandment, which prohibits images of God, is not merely a fundamental condition of Jewish monotheism and a meaningful life, it is virtually the only condition.[63]

At the end of the opera Moses recognizes the wilderness as an image, but an image only of the soul, of the absence of worldly desire, that is, an image of divine idea or "of the soul, whose very freedom from craving is sufficient for eternal life" (200). He then speaks to the Elders and, after reminding them that they were chosen to fight for the divine idea, he turns to the language best understood by the people, the language of images. He refers to the wilderness—here functioning as both an image and their present physical environment—in order to address the idea of spirituality, the "wilderness' freedom from craving" ("Wunschlosigkeit der Wüste" [202–04]), an idea which this people was chosen to know and share. Now at opera's end the image of the wilderness not only mediates between quotidian experience and transcendent reality, between the people and Moses, but even delivers the liberating message as it liberates the messenger to fulfill his duty.

Moses' success at delivering the message is evident in Aaron's reaction. At the end of his speech, Moses orders the soldiers to remove Aaron: "'Set him free, / and if he is able, / he shall live.' (Aaron free, stands up and falls down dead)" (204). Moses'

message—that any "success" from the abuse of divine gifts will
be rewarded only by a return to the wilderness, to that place
which is also the image of freedom from the transitory, from
desire—functions as a summary of Aaron's errors and as guide
and warning for the chosen people:

> Always when you mix among peoples
> and use your gifts,
> which you were chosen to possess,
> in order to fight for the idea of God,
> and you use your gifts for false
> and vain purposes, in order to compete
> with alien peoples for their lowly pleasures,
> always, when you leave
> the wilderness' freedom from craving
> and your gifts have led you to the highest heights,
> always will you again
> be thrown down from the success of the
> abuse, back into the wilderness. (202–204)

Aaron—magician, rhetorician, and creator of fantasies—has no
role left to play. And now in an environment without music and
song, he can fall back on neither the ornamentation of his images
nor the seductive beauty and overpowering effect of the bel canto
tenor. The victory of Moses is complete and fully apparent in this
final act in which music and its seductions are but a memory,
where only the spoken word rules.

Although just a month before his death in 1951 Schoenberg
referred to *Moses and Aaron,* noting that its "subject matter and
treatment are purely religious-philosophical."[64] This of course
does not dismiss the possibility that the work had a broader
cultural agenda (there is evidence that cultural, historical, and
political factors contributed to his elaboration of the work's religious perspective). With this work in mind, Adorno speculated
that Schoenberg, although reared in a relatively emancipated secular environment, had acquired by some mysterious process a
"subterranean, mystical tradition" once prominent among the

Jews of Pressburg, the home of his parents, and that "the experiences of German pre-Fascism, under which he rediscovered his Judaism, must have liberated that undercurrent: *Moses and Aaron* was composed just before the Third Reich erupted, perhaps as a defense against what was dawning."[65] It is difficult to ascertain whether the religious ideas derive from subterranean mystical strains, but there are indications that "The Biblical Way," *Moses and Aaron,* and Schoenberg's return to Judaism are responses to his experiences of growing antisemitism and the rise of National Socialism. Indeed Schoenberg's prominent concern in the work with a *Volk* (people) and *Führer* (leader) who are to be united in a spiritual mission suggests an alternative to the *Volk-Führer* ideology used to promote a "thousand-year Reich" controlled absolutely by a dictator.

Unlike Freud's Moses in *Moses and Monotheism,* who demands a people dedicated to his leadership and compliant with his austere demands, Schoenberg's Moses wants not to lead, but through his agency to have the people devote themselves entirely to the one eternal, unrepresentable God. The prohibition against making images is especially important not merely for a person returning to Judaism from an earlier conversion to Christianity, but for those who had everything to fear from the Nazis and their preoccupation with symbols, ritual, and worship of heroes and idols. The idea of a people chosen for a spiritual mission that offers no worldly gain may best be interpreted, as it is in the opera, as a means of uniting a people in opposition to an exploitative situation and to an oppressor, be it Pharoah or Hitler.

A letter Schoenberg sent in 1933 from Paris to several prominent Jews speaks of his own austere religious views and recognizes the severe demands his view places on others. It was, however, the current mortal danger facing Jews as individuals and as a nation that justified these demands. Schoenberg addressed this letter to musicians, including Ernst Toch and Joachim Stutschewsky, intending to organize and rally all Jews, in the face of imminent destruction, for self-defense. It must have struck others as unrealistic and even bizarre, for apparently no one responded.

Its text contained the kind of archaic language and austerity of idea that may have been appropriate to the biblical environment of *Moses and Aaron,* but seems incongruous in Schoenberg's contemporary world. In the letter Schoenberg expressed alarm about the inadequacy of Jewish organizations, faced with a perilous situation, to activate the Jewish people to unite in a "state on their own territory." "For this," he continued, "it will be necessary to use all means known to history, without taking into consideration the conventional ideas which Jews and others have about the essence of the Jewish people. But with consideration, on the other hand, of the duties imposed on the Jewish people by virtue of its status as God's Chosen People; as the people destined to preserve an idea of the unrepresentable God."[66] He added that he was willing and ready to assume the leadership of this movement, a job for which he is well suited because of his hardheadedness, his obduracy. Schoenberg, who perceived of himself as inflexible and inexorably devoted to the idea, seemed ready to take upon himself the burdens of his operatic Moses—or had he merely created Moses in his own image?—and apparently hoped to surpass even his Moses' success.

While it is clear that Schoenberg conceived of himself as someone compelled to pursue Moses' path, the letter suggests instead a closer affinity with Max Aruns, another Moses who strayed onto Aaron's territory. It is worthwhile to consider that Moses' promises in *Moses and Aaron,* which are presented as completely metaphysical, are taken very literally in this letter; here the land promised is a state, a particular territory in which a nation can insulate itself from external danger. Reminding others and perhaps himself that the Jews have been chosen to preserve the idea of God, Schoenberg does not wait for a disembodied voice to solicit his assistance; instead he appoints himself to lead the people, a task for which he feels qualified merely because he is a stubborn and inflexible visionary. It may be that in this perilous twentieth century, Aaron, the pragmatist and *Realpolitiker,* is a necessity; otherwise Schoenberg surely would have noticed that the Moses he himself proposed to become was an Aaron in disguise ready to perform miracles. The letter's message speaks painfully and forcefully to hard choices imposed upon a people threatened with extermination in the midst of an ostensibly enlightened and humanistic society that prided itself on its egalitarian and just ways. For centuries in a European diaspora, the Jewish people had sought the means to survive as Jews, as Europeans, as human beings. Schoenberg was no exception. But confronted with fascism and dangerous antisemitism, and facing the prospect of obliteration, Schoenberg turned once again to Moses the liberator and lawgiver, this time seeking the way out of a deadly wilderness. He made his own way out of Europe, but could not bring his people with him. Like Moses, Schoenberg's entire life was formed in the context of the diaspora. He never took the opportunity to emigrate to Israel, but—perhaps emulating the biblical hero—remained in the diaspora, continuing his personal and artistic struggle with Moses until the end of his days.

Notes

All translations from the German are my own. Where possible I cite comparable texts in English translation; these follow the citation of the German text.

1. Moses in a European Wilderness

1. The term *emancipation* technically applies to the granting of legal civil rights. After the enactment of emancipatory legislation, however, the problems of civil rights shifted from the legal to the social arena. During the almost eight decades it took for full legal emancipation to be enacted and for almost a century thereafter, Jews were neither regarded nor treated as fully enfranchised citizens. Social and political discrimination remained a serious problem until the end of World War II, during which a large part of European Jewry was destroyed. The age of emancipation in this work refers to the period beginning with the introduction of the Napoleonic Code into French-occupied Germany after the defeat of Prussia in 1806, through the legal enfranchisement of Jews in Austria and Germany in 1867 and 1871, respectively, and the intermittent and ongoing threats to the lives and rights of the Jewish people until at least 1945.

2. Hans Mayer, "Das Gedächtnis und die Geschichte: Gedanken beim Aufschreiben von Erinnerungen," *Juden in der deutschen Literatur: Ein deutsch-israelitisches Symposium,* ed. Stéphane Moses and Albrecht Schöne (Frankfurt am Main: Suhrkamp, 1986) 13.

3. Joseph Roth, *Briefe, 1911–1939,* ed. Hermann Kesten (Cologne: Kiepenheuer, 1970) 257.

4. Roth 257.

5. Ahad Ha'Am, "Moses," *Selected Essays,* trans. Leon Simon (Philadelphia: Jewish Publication Society of America, 1912) 311.

6. Jacob Katz, *Emancipation and Assimilation: Studies in Modern Jewish History* (Westmead, Eng.: Gregg International, 1972) x.

7. Stephen M. Poppel, "New Views on Jewish Integration in Germany," *Central European History* 9 (1976): 86–87, makes a useful distinction between "acculturation" as an activity undertaken *by* Jews (also, assimilation *by* Jews) and "integration" as a process dependent on attitudes of the dominant society and its citizens (assimilation *of* the Jews).

8. See Reinhard Rürup, "Jewish Emancipation and Bourgeois Society," *Leo Baeck Yearbook* 14 (1969): 67–70; Reinhard Rürup, "Die Emanzipation der Juden in Baden," *Emanzipation und Antisemitismus* (Göttingen: Vandenhoeck, 1975) 37–73, which provides an excellent overview, using the instance of Baden, of the uneven and difficult course of emancipation from the late eighteenth century to 1862; Hans-Joachim Bieber, "Anti-Semitism as a Reflection of Social, Economic and Political Tension in Germany: 1880–1914," *Jews and Germans from 1860 to 1933: The Problematic Symbiosis,* ed. David Bronsen (Heidelberg: Winter, 1979) 33–39.

9. Katz, *Emancipation and Assimilation* xi, 5–6; Rürup, "Jewish Emancipation" 68.

10. Jacob Katz, *Out of the Ghetto: The Social Background of Jewish Emancipation, 1770–1870* (New York: Schocken, 1973) 204–7.

11. Reinhard Rürup, "Emancipation and Crisis: The 'Jewish Question' in Germany 1850–1890," *Leo Baeck Yearbook* 20 (1975): 18.

12. Katz, *Out of the Ghetto* 176–90.

13. Peter Pulzer, *The Rise of Political Anti-Semitism in Germany and Austria* (Cambridge: Harvard University Press, 1988) 122–30; Jacob Katz, *From Prejudice to Destruction: Anti-Semitism, 1700–1933* (Cambridge: Harvard University Press, 1980) 245–59, 281–91; Detlev Claussen, *Vom Judenhaß zum Antisemitismus Materalien einer verleugneten Geschichte* (Darmstadt: Luchterhand, 1987), "Introductory Essay," 7–46; Zygmunt Bauman, *Modernity and the Holocaust* (Ithaca: Cornell University Press, 1989), especially chapter 2, "Modernity, Racism, Extermination I."

14. Peter Gay, *Freud, Jews and Other Germans: Masters and Victims in Modernist Culture* (Oxford: Oxford University Press, 1978) 99, maintains that the ways in which German Jews constructed their creative works "were indistinguishable from the ways of other Germans." He insists that "there would have been no way of deducing their religious affiliation from the quality or character of their work" (95). Whereas Gay may be correct in many instances, this study of Moses figures, in some small way, calls into question his thesis. It is interesting that in this work Gay does not discuss either of Freud's Moses figures; and

although he notes "how deeply antisemitism had penetrated his [Freud's] consciousness in his late years" (91), he does not remark on Freud's preoccupation with antisemitism and Judaism as early as *The Interpretation of Dreams (Die Traumdeutung)*. See my introduction to the Freud chapter below.

15. Rürup, "Jewish Emancipation" 86–88.

16. Hereafter this text will be referred to as *Moses and Monotheism*, the title it bears in the standard English translation of Freud's works. Sigmund Freud, *The Standard Edition of the Complete Psychological Works of Sigmund Freud*, vol. 23, trans. James Strachey (London: Hogarth, 1959).

17. Schoenberg capitalized "Biblische" on the title page of the typescript.

18. Exod. 2:22.

19. See Lawrence W. Levine, *Black Culture and Black Consciousness: Afro-American Folk Thought from Slavery to Freedom* (Oxford: Oxford University Press, 1977) 23, 50–51. Levine writes that spirituals were largely concerned with deliverance in *this* world. He quotes Thomas Wentworth Higginson's view that in the songs of black soldiers "most great events of the past, down to the period of the American Revolution, they instinctively attributed to Moses"; and Levine further notes that "a northern army chaplain wrote of the slaves, 'Moses is their *ideal* of all that is high, and noble, and perfect, in man,' while Christ was regarded 'not so much in the light of a *spiritual* Deliverer, as that of a second Moses'" (50). Also see, for example, Zora Neale Hurston's novel *Moses, Man of the Mountain* (Urbana: University of Illinois Press, 1984).

20. See the Decalogue in Exod. 20 and Deut. 5.

21. "Moses," *Encyclopedia Judaica*, 1972 ed., vol. 12: 373.

22. Rürup, "Jewish Emancipation" 85–86, correctly attributes the difficulties with Jewish emancipation to three factors: (1) gradual phased emancipation, (2) many differing attempts at resolutions in various German states, and (3) attempts to emancipate Jews in an unemancipated or partially emancipated society. Indeed, the emancipation processes in Austria and Germany reveal a history of continuing failures that did not abate even after legal emancipation was instituted in the late 1860s.

2. Heinrich Heine

1. Katz, *Out of the Ghetto* 54–79. For a more thorough discussion of Mendelssohn's role, see Michael A. Meyer, *The Origins of the*

Modern Jew: Jewish Identity and European Culture in Germany, 1749–1824 (Detroit: Wayne State University Press, 1967) 29–56.

2. Heinz Mosche Graupe, *The Rise of Modern Judaism: An Intellectual History of German Jewry 1650–1942*, trans. John Robinson (Huntington, NY: Krieger, 1978) 123–29.

3. Rürup, "Jewish Emancipation" 74–75.

4. Rürup, "Jewish Emancipation" 76–77.

5. Eleonore O. Sterling, "Anti-Jewish Riots in Germany in 1819: A Displacement of Social Protest," *Historia Judaica* 12 (1950): 105–42, concentrates on the social, political, and economic foundations of the Hep-Hep riots, concluding that they were essentially a displaced reaction to an oppressive government in a time of economic crisis. However, Katz, *From Prejudice to Destruction* 97–104, finds little evidence to support Sterling's contention that rioters were actually motivated by ideals of social change, but misdirected their protest. "The ground for the riots was prepared," Katz maintains, "by prolonged anti-Jewish propaganda whose purpose was to tilt the balance against the Jews on the question of full citizenship" (102).

6. Jeffrey L. Sammons, *Heinrich Heine: A Modern Biography* (Princeton: Princeton University Press, 1979) 108.

7. For comprehensive discussions of Heine's involvement with Judaism and Jewish issues, see S. S. Prawer, *Heine's Jewish Comedy: A Study of his Portraits of Jews and Judaism* (Oxford: Clarendon, 1983); Ruth L. Jacobi, *Heinrich Heines jüdisches Erbe* (Bonn: Bouvier, 1978); Hartmut Kircher, *Heinrich Heine und das Judentum* (Bonn: Bouvier, 1973); Ludwig Rosenthal, *Heinrich Heine als Jude* (Frankfurt am Main: Ullstein, 1973); Israel Tabak, *Judaic Lore in Heine: The Heritage of a Poet* (Baltimore: Johns Hopkins University Press, 1948).

8. Jacobi 46; Tabak 12–13; Kircher 95.

9. Sammons 16.

10. Heinrich Heine, *Sämtliche Schriften,* ed. Klaus Briegleb et al., vol. 6/1 (Munich: Hanser, 1975) 495–96.

11. According to Sammons 37, 39, Heine attended the Hebrew school for about two years; according to Jacobi 46, for five years.

12. For discussion of the Society, its members, and Heine's participation, see Rosenthal 118–46; Kircher 53–62; Sammons 89–94; Jacobi 48–53; Meyer 165–72.

13. See, for example, Heine's laudatory remarks about the Society in "Ludwig Marcus: Recollections" ("Ludwig Marcus. Denkworte"), *Sämtliche Schriften,* vol. 5, 179–84.

14. According to Sammons (93), Heine had apparently been reading in the fifteen-volume Jacques Basnage de Beauval, *Histoire et*

la religion des Juifs depuis Jésus-Christ jusqu'à présent (Rotterdam: Leers, 1706–1707). In a footnote, Rosenthal (356) indicates that Heine was interested in Basnage's discussion of Gentiles placing corpses into Jewish homes at Easter, a motif that is central to *The Rabbi of Bacharach*. See also Jacobi 53.

15. Letters he wrote for the *Augsburger Allgemeine Zeitung* in 1840 about the Damascus blood libel incident appear in Book 1 of *Lutetia, Sämtliche Schriften*, vol. 5, 267–71, 273–77, 280–90, 299–304, 307–10. See also Prawer 297–309; Sammons 242–44.

16. See, for example, Heine's letter of 27 September 1923 to Moser in Heinrich Heine, *Briefe*, vol. 1, ed. Friedrich Hirth (Mainz: Florian Kupferberg Verlag, 1950) 108.

17. *Sämtliche Schriften*, vol. 6/1, 622.

18. *Briefe*, vol. 1, 101.

19. See, for example, Heine's comments in *The Romantic School (Die Romantische Schule), Sämtliche Schriften*, vol. 3, 381–82; *Confessions (Geständnisse), Sämtliche Schriften*, vol. 6/1, 483–84. Also Jacobi 111, 114; Kircher 150–51.

20. *Briefe*, vol. 1, 242.

21. *Briefe*, vol. 1, 250.

22. *Sämtliche Schriften*, vol. 3, 570.

23. *Sämtliche Schriften*, vol. 6/1, 184.

24. For a thorough discussion of Heine's interest in Hellenism, see Robert C. Holub, *Heinrich Heine's Reception of Graecophilia* (Heidelberg: Winter, 1981). See also Manfred Schneider, "Die Angst des Revolutionärs vor der Revolution: Zur Genese und Struktur des politischen Diskurses bei Heine," *Heine Jahrbuch* 19 (1980) especially 10–12, for commentary on the political and cultural complexities of this Venus de Milo passage.

25. *Sämtliche Schriften*, vol. 3, 685.

26. *Sämtliche Schriften*, vol. 3, 570.

27. *Sämtliche Schriften*, vol. 6/1, 182

28. *Sämtliche Schriften*, vol. 6/1, 182–83.

29. *Sämtliche Schriften*, vol. 6/1, 183.

30. *Sämtliche Schriften*, vol. 6/1, 480.

31. *Sämtliche Schriften*, vol. 4, 39.

32. *Sämtliche Schriften*, vol. 4, 40.

33. *Sämtliche Schriften*, vol. 4, 40.

34. *Sämtliche Schriften*, vol. 3, 518; also 519–22, 566–67; *Sämtliche Schriften*, vol. 4, 41.

35. *Sämtliche Schriften*, vol. 4, 41.

36. *Sämtliche Schriften*, vol. 4, 45.

37. Heb. 3:4–6.
38. *Sämtliche Schriften*, vol. 4, 45.
39. *Sämtliche Schriften*, vol. 4, 45.
40. *Sämtliche Schriften*, vol. 4, 44.
41. *Sämtliche Schriften*, vol. 4, 45.
42. *Sämtliche Schriften*, vol. 4, 45.
43. *Sämtliche Schriften*, vol. 6/1, 483–86.
44. *Sämtliche Schriften*, vol. 6/1, 481.
45. *Sämtliche Schriften*, vol. 6/1, 481.
46. *Sämtliche Schriften*, vol. 6/1, 486.
47. *Sämtliche Schriften*, vol. 6/1, 488.
48. *Sämtliche Schriften*, vol. 2, 382.
49. *Sämtliche Schriften*, vol. 4, 41.
50. *Sämtliche Schriften*, vol. 6/1, 471–76.
51. *Briefe*, vol. 3, 194–95.
52. See, for example, in *Sämtliche Schriften*, the discussion of Shylock's daughter Jessica in *Shakespeare's Girls and Women (Shakespeares Mädchen und Frauen)*, vol. 4, 251–61; "Ludwig Marcus: Recollections," vol. 5, 185–86, 189; *Confessions*, vol. 6/1, 286–88.
53. *Sämtliche Schriften*, vol. 5, 186.
54. *Sämtliche Schriften*, vol. 4, 257–58.
55. *Sämtliche Schriften*, vol. 5, 186.
56. *Sämtliche Schriften*, vol. 4, 258.
57. *Sämtliche Schriften*, vol. 4, 258.
58. *Sämtliche Schriften*, vol. 6/1, 486.
59. *Sämtliche Schriften*, vol. 6/1, 487.
60. *Sämtliche Schriften*, vol. 6/1, 486.
61. *Sämtliche Schriften*, vol. 5, 189.
62. *Sämtliche Schriften*, vol. 6/1, 488.
63. "Correction" ("Berichtigung"), *Sämtliche Schriften*, vol. 5, 108.
64. *Sämtliche Schriften*, vol. 6/1, 483–85.
65. *Sämtliche Schriften*, vol. 4, 40.
66. *Sämtliche Schriften*, vol. 6/1, 483–85 passim.
67. *Sämtliche Schriften*, vol. 6/1, 485.
68. *Sämtliche Schriften*, vol. 6/1, 478.
69. *Sämtliche Schriften*, vol. 6/1, 481.

3. Between Bondage and Liberation

1. For details of Kafka's forebears, parents, and early life, see Klaus Wagenbach, *Franz Kafka: Eine Biographie seiner Jugend, 1883–*

1912 (Bern: Francke, 1958); Ronald Hayman, *Kafka: A Biography* (New York: Oxford University Press, 1981); Ernst Pawel, *The Nightmare of Reason: A Life of Franz Kafka* (New York: Farrar, 1984); Christoph Stölzl, *Kafkas böses Böhmen: Zur Sozialgeschichte eines Prager Juden* (Munich: Text und Kritik, 1975); Max Brod, "Franz Kafka: Eine Biographie," *Über Franz Kafka* (Frankfurt am Main: Fischer Bücherei, 1966); Anthony Northey, *Kafkas Mischpoche* (Berlin: Wagenbach, 1988).

2. Simon Dubnow, *From the Congress of Vienna to the Emergence of Hitler,* vol. 5 of *History of the Jews,* trans. Moshe Spiegel (New York: Yoseloff, 1973) 291; Katz, *Out of the Ghetto* 183–4; William O. McCagg, Jr., *A History of Hapsburg Jews, 1670–1918* (Bloomington: Indiana University Press, 1989) 11–12.

3. Klaus Wagenbach, "Wo liegt Kafkas Schloß," *Kafka-Symposium,* ed. Jürgen Born, Ludwig Dietz, Malcolm Pasley, Paul Raabe, Klaus Wagenbach (Berlin: Wagenbach, 1965) 167.

4. Ruth Kestenberg-Gladstein, "The Jews Between Czechs and Germans, 1848–1914," *The Jews of Czechoslovakia: Historical Studies and Surveys* (Philadelphia: Jewish Publication Society of America, 1968) 27–37, and Marsha L. Rozenblit, *The Jews of Vienna, 1867–1914: Assimilation and Identity* (Albany: State University of New York Press, 1983) 15–16, indicate that migrations in Austria, unlike those in Russia mandated by the government, were the result of the elimination of restrictions on Jews. Kestenberg-Gladstein also distinguishes between two waves of immigration: the first to emigrate, when permitted, moved close to home, leaving intact the dominant Jewish settlement areas; their children later moved into the larger urban areas, following the general shift of European population during the second half of the nineteenth century from agrarian to industrial and commercial areas. The fathers of Freud and Kafka participated in this latter migration. Arieh Tartakower, "Jewish Migratory Movements in Austria in Recent Generations," *The Jews of Austria: Essays on their Life, History and Destruction,* ed. Josef Fraenkel (London: Vallentine, 1967) 285–310, is largely concerned with the demographics and conditions of the migrations in Austria from 1850 to 1960. Oscar Handlin's brief but interesting discussion of the migrations in "Jews in the Culture of Middle Europe," *Leo Baeck Memorial Lecture 7* (New York: Leo Baeck Institute, 1964) 9–11 underlines the social and economic opportunities that became available to Jews as a result of the deteriorating corporate structure of the towns.

5. Stölzl 32. Note the spelling "Herrmann," which Kafka's father retained until the founding of the Czechoslovak Republic in 1918;

thereafter he dropped an *r* and added a haček over the remaining *r* (Stölzl 103).

6. Stölzl 21–34; Gary Cohen, "Jews in German Society: Prague, 1860–1914," *Jews and Germans from 1860 to 1933: The Problematic Symbiosis,* ed. David Bronsen (Heidelberg: Winter, 1979) 309–13.

7. Stölzl 38–40.

8. Stölzl 39–43, 59–71; for a detailed account of antisemitic activity in the 1890s, see Michael A. Riff, "Czech Antisemitism and the Jewish Response before 1914," *The Wiener Library Bulletin* 29, no. 39/40 (1976): 8–16.

9. Stölzl 76.

10. Ezra Mendelsohn, *The Jews of East Central Europe: Between the World Wars* (Bloomington: Indiana University Press, 1983) 136.

11. For the political and social significance of Liberalism and its failure in the Hapsburg Empire, see Robert A. Kann, *Empire and Nationalities,* vol. 1 of *The Multinational Empire: Nationalism and National Reform in the Hapsburg Monarchy 1848–1918* (New York: Columbia University Press, 1950) 90–97; Carl E. Schorske, *Fin-de-Siècle Vienna: Politics and Culture* (New York: Knopf, 1980) 116–19; Allan Janik and Stephen Toulmin, *Wittgenstein's Vienna* (New York: Simon, 1973) 48–53; Howard Morley Sachar, *The Course of Jewish History* (New York: Dell, 1958) 110–13; and Stölzl 49, 55–56.

12. Among those who have argued that in his later years Kafka was a committed or militant Zionist are Max Brod, in *Über Franz Kafka* 270–71; Felix Weltsch, in "The Rise and Fall of German-Jewish Symbiosis: The Case of Franz Kafka," *Leo Baeck Yearbook* 1 (1956): 274–76; Felix Weltsch, in *Religion und Humor im Leben und Werk Franz Kafkas* (Berlin-Grunewald: Herbig, 1957) 36–38; and, more recently, Clara Pomeranz Carmely, in *Das Identitätsproblem jüdischer Autoren im deutschen Sprachraum: Von der Jahrhundertwende bis zu Hitler* (Königstein: Scriptor, 1981) 152–66. Kafka's writings, however, indicate that, while interested in the Zionist movement, he had reservations about it and about commitment to it. Giuliano Baioni, "Zionism, Literature and the Yiddish Theater," trans. Mark Anderson, *Reading Kafka: Prague, Politics and the "Fin de Siècle",* ed. Mark Anderson (New York: Schocken, 1989) 95–114, perceptively and convincingly assesses Kafka's interest in Zionism, not unlike his deep attachment to Eastern European Jewry, as being largely motivated by his anxiety over assimilation (and, I would add, antisemitism in the midst of emancipation) and by his desire, as a writer, to reconcile "his Jewish consciousness with his consciousness as a writer" (113). See also Marthe Robert, *As Lonely as Franz Kafka,* trans. Ralph Manheim (New York: Harcourt, 1979)

87–92; and Ritchie Robertson, *Kafka: Judaism, Politics and Literature* (Oxford: Clarendon, 1985) 12–13, 156–61, 171–72.

13. Franz Kafka, Letter to Else Bergmann, July 1923, *Briefe 1902–1924*, ed. Max Brod (Frankfurt am Main: Fischer, 1958) 437–38; *Letters to Friends, Family, and Editors*, trans. Richard and Clara Winston (New York: Schocken, 1977) 374.

14. Franz Kafka, *Briefe an Milena*, ed. Willy Haas (Frankfurt am Main: Fischer, 1965) 268; *Letters to Milena*, trans. Tania and James Stern, ed. Willi Haas (New York: Schocken, 1962) 236.

15. Letter to Max Brod, June 1921, *Briefe, 1902–1924* 337; *Letters to Friends* 289.

16. Kol Nidre, said on the eve of Yom Kippur, the Day of Atonement, is the prayer asking God to undo all oaths with God taken during the previous year and not fulfilled. Yom Kippur is the one day when many nonobservant and assimilated Jews would go to the synagogue to maintain their connection with Judaism.

17. Franz Kafka, *Tagebücher*, ed. Hans-Gerd Koch, Michael Müller, Malcolm Pasley (Frankfurt am Main: Fischer, 1990) 47–48; *The Diaries of Franz Kafka, 1910–1913*, trans. Joseph Kresh, ed. Max Brod (New York: Schocken, 1965) 72.

18. *Tagebücher* 753; *The Diaries of Franz Kafka, 1914–1923*, trans. Martin Greenberg with Hannah Arendt, ed. Max Brod (New York: Schocken, 1965) 130.

19. *Briefe an Milena* 220–21; *Letters to Milena* 196.

20. See, for example, Kafka's discussion of nondominant literatures, referring specifically to Jewish literature in Warsaw and contemporary Czech literature, in *Tagebücher* 312–15; *Diaries, 1910–1913* 191–94.

21. *Tagebücher* 59; *Diaries, 1910–1913* 80–81.

22. *Briefe an Milena* 221; *Letters to Milena* 196.

23. *Tagebücher* 698; *Diaries, 1914–1923* 97.

24. Franz Kafka, *Tagebücher: Kommentarband*, ed. Hans-Gerd Koch, Michael Müller, Malcolm Pasley (Frankfurt am Main: Fischer, 1990) 169.

25. *Tagebücher* 699; *Diaries, 1914–1923* 98.

26. *Tagebücher* 311; *Diaries, 1910–1913* 190–91.

27. Franz Kafka, *"Hochzeitsvorbereitungen auf dem Lande" und andere Prosa aus dem Nachlaß*, ed. Max Brod (Frankfurt am Main: Fischer, 1953) 120; *Dearest Father*, trans. Ernst Kaiser and Eithne Wilkins (New York: Schocken, 1954) 99.

28. *Briefe an Milena* 247; *Letters to Milena* 219.

29. "Brief an den Vater," *Hochzeitsvorbereitungen* 200; *Dearest*

Father 174. Kafka wrote this letter, some sixty printed pages, in November 1919. According to Max Brod, he had hoped that this letter would prepare the ground for some kind of rapprochement with his father. He gave the letter to his mother to deliver to his father, but she thought the better of it and did not pass it on.

30. *Hochzeitsvorbereitungen* 199–200; *Dearest Father* 173–74.

31. *Hochzeitsvorbereitungen* 201; *Dearest Father* 175–76.

32. *Hochzeitsvorbereitungen* 120–21; *Dearest Father* 99–100.

33. *Briefe an Milena* 247; *Letters to Milena* 219.

34. *Tagebücher* 871; *Diaries, 1914–1923* 198.

35. The series "Er" is in Franz Kafka, *Beschreibung eines Kampfes: Novellen, Skizzen, Aphorismen aus dem Nachlaß* (Frankfurt am Main: Fischer, 1936); the "Paralipomena (zu der Reihe 'Er')" in *Hochzeitsvorbereitungen*.

36. *Hochzeitsvorbereitungen* 418; *Dearest Father* 378.

37. *Briefe an Milena* 240–41; *Letters to Milena* 213.

38. *Beschreibung eines Kampfes* 295; *Great Wall of China*, trans. Willa and Edwin Muir (New York: Schocken, 1946) 269.

39. Letter to Max Brod, June 1921, *Briefe, 1902–1924* 336; *Letters to Friends* 288.

40. Letter to Max Brod, June 1921, *Briefe, 1902–1924* 337; *Letters to Friends* 288.

41. Letter to Max Brod, June 1921, *Briefe, 1902–1924* 337; *Letter to Friends* 288–89.

42. Letter to Max Brod, June 1921, *Briefe, 1902–1923* 336; *Letters to Friends* 288.

43. Sander L. Gilman, *Jewish Self-Hatred: Anti-Semitism and the Hidden Language of the Jews* (Baltimore: Johns Hopkins University Press, 1986) 139–42, 270–86.

44. Letter to Max Brod, June 1921, *Briefe, 1902–1924* 337; *Letters to Friends* 288.

45. Letter to Max Brod, June 1921, *Briefe, 1902–1924* 336; *Letters to Friends* 288. Gilman 284, translates "*Papierdeutsch*" in Kafka's text as "paper German" because, in his view, it refers to "the official language of the state." Gerhard Wahrig, *Deutsches Wörterbuch*, 1968 ed. (Berlin: Bertelsmann Lexikon-Verlag, 1968) 2745, defines "*Papierdeutsch*" as "*trockenes, unlebendiges, unanschaul. Deutsch*" (dry, dull, vapid German). "Bookish German" seems to me a more accurate rendering. Census polls taken in Bohemia in the nineteenth century inquired about a person's "*Umgangssprache*" (colloquial language) and distinguished that from her/his written or cultural language. I agree with Gilman that here the opposition of "*Papierdeutsch*" and "*Gebär-*

densprache" (language of gesture) is associated with Western and Eastern Jewry respectively. But, it seems to me, the cultivated, learned language rather than the use of "official state language" is thought to distinguish Western Jews from their Eastern compatriots.

46. Letter to Max Brod, June 1921, *Briefe, 1902–1924* 337; *Letters to Friends* 289.

47. Letter to Max Brod, June 1921, *Briefe, 1902–1924* 337–38; *Letters to Friends* 289.

48. *Hochzeitsvorbereitungen* 348; *Dearest Father* 312.

49. Gustav Janouch, *Gespräche mit Kafka: Aufzeichnungen und Erinnerungen* (Frankfurt am Main: Fischer, 1968); Gustav Janouch, *Conversations with Kafka*, trans. Goronwy Rees, 2nd. revised and enlarged ed. (New York: New Directions, 1971). While the reliability of Janouch's reports of his discussions with Kafka have been questioned, and rightly so, the texts I have selected are in general agreement with Kafka's diary entries. The Janouch-Kafka conversations often explore issues in a more concrete social or political context.

50. See *Briefe, 1902–1924* 333–34; *Letters to Friends* 285–86; "Das vierte Oktavheft," *Hochzeitsvorbereitungen* 125; *Dearest Father* 102–3.

51. *Tagebücher* 867; *Diaries, 1914–1923* 195–96.

52. Janouch, *Gespräche* 149–50; *Conversations* 107.

53. Janouch, *Gespräche* 153–54; *Conversations* 110–11.

54. Samuel Hugo Bergmann, "Can Transgression Have an Agent? The Law of the State and the Conscience of the Individual," *The Quality of Faith: Essays on Judaism and Morality* (Jerusalem: World Zionist Organization, 1970) 22.

55. Janouch, *Gespräche* 231–32 passim; *Conversations* 172–73 passim.

56. Janouch, *Gespräche* 145; *Conversations* 104.

57. Janouch, *Gespräche* 231–32; *Conversations* 172–73.

58. *Tagebücher* 312–15; *Diaries, 1910–1913* 191–94.

59. Janouch, *Gespräche* 59–60; *Conversations* 35.

60. Janouch, *Gespräche* 60; *Conversations* 35.

61. *Tagebücher* 894; *Diaries, 1914–1923* 214.

62. *Tagebücher* 893–94; *Diaries, 1914–1923* 213–14.

63. *Tagebücher* 894; *Diaries, 1914–1923* 214.

4. From Rome to Egypt

1. The explanation and interpretation of Freud's given name, Sigismund, and its change to Sigmund in 1878 provide some insight

into the role speculation plays in critical discussions of issues in Freud's life (here Jewish issues). According to David Bakan, *Sigmund Freud and the Jewish Mystical Tradition* (Princeton: Van Nostrand, 1958) 56, and Earl A. Grollman, *Judaism in Sigmund Freud's World* (New York: Appleton-Century, 1965) 47, Sigmund was named Sigismund (actually Sigismund Schlomo) because his parents admired Sigismund, the tolerant Polish king who lived between 1467 and 1548. Freud changed his name to Sigmund after he entered the University, presumably because he wanted a more Austro-German name, although Peter Gay, *Freud: A Life for Our Time* (New York: Doubleday, 1988) 5, indicates that Freud never commented on the reasons for the change. Dennis B. Klein, *Jewish Origins of the Psychoanalytic Movement* (New York: Praeger, 1981) 46, 49, claims, on the basis of very scant and problematic evidence, that Freud's decision to change his name was not only a "reaction to the increase in anti-Semitic sentiment at the end of the 1860s," but also a desire to sever an "important link with his Jewish background," meaning his roots in Eastern Europe. Marianne Krüll, *Freud and his Followers,* trans. Arnold J. Pomerans (New York: Norton, 1986) 253 n. 3, giving no reason, claims Bakan is "plainly incorrect" in the assertion that Sigismund was named for the Polish king. According to her, Sigismund "was a Germanization of Schlomo [the name of Freud's deceased paternal grandfather] and probably also an evocation of the German *Sieg* (victory)" (108). This reasoning seems problematic. One of many names beginning with an *S* could be considered as a Germanization of Schlomo; and if both a German name and one invoking "Sieg" were required, then Sigmund or Siegfried would seem a better choice.

2. Although Freud spoke only of one former marriage of his father, J. N. Isbister, *Freud: An Introduction to His Life and Work* (Cambridge, Eng.: Polity, 1985) 8–9, documents two former marriages.

3. Sigmund Freud, "Selbstdarstellung," *Gesammelte Werke,* vol. 14, ed. Anna Freud (Frankfurt am Main: Fischer, 1968) 34; "An Autobiographical Study," *The Standard Edition of the Complete Psychological Works of Sigmund Freud,* trans. James Strachey, vol. 20 (London: Hogarth, 1959) 7–8. Hereafter, all references to the *Gesammelte Werke* will appear as *G.W.* followed by the volume and page numbers, and all references to the English *Standard Edition* as *S.E.* followed by the volume and page numbers. Emanuel Rice, *Freud and Moses: The Long Journey Home* (Albany: State University of New York Press, 1990) 192, considers the location of the family's origins in Germany (Cologne) as Freud's "fantasy," a "family romance," through which Freud tries to dissociate himself from Eastern European Jewry and elevate "his geneology from the lower middle class to the high bourgeoisie." Freud may

have been trying to rewrite his origins, but one can hardly associate fifteenth century Jews, who were driven out of Germany, with the bourgeoisie; and Peter Gay, *Freud* 5, has noted: "The evidence for Freud's ancestry may be plausible, but it is slender." Freud may, however, be concerned about the alien status of the family and the Jewish people. Just a decade later in *Moses and Monotheism* Freud returned to the centuries-long persecution of Jews and called into question the accusation of their alien status by indicating that they were among the oldest inhabitants of Germany: "That applies, for example, to the city of *Cologne* to which the Jews came with the Romans before it was even occupied by the Germans" (*G.E.*, vol. 16, 197; *S.E.*, vol. 23, 90).

4. Sigmund Freud, letter to Ernst Freud, 12 May 1938, *Briefe 1873–1939*, ed. Ernst L. Freud, 2nd. expanded ed. (Frankfurt am Main: Fischer, 1968) 459; *The Letters of Sigmund Freud*, trans. Tania and James Stern, ed. Ernst L. Freud (New York: Basic Books, 1975) 297–98. For a discussion of the legend of Ahasuerus, the wandering Jew, see Eduard König, *Ahasver "der ewige Jude"* (Gütersloh: Bertelsmann, 1907). The story of the wandering Jew Ahasuerus, first printed in 1602, was a Christian story about a Jew who had verbally abused Christ when he was about to be crucified. Ahasuerus apparently regretted his words and lived his life as a wanderer, never returning to his home in Jerusalem. Many Christians have read in this story an eternal damnation of the Jews for not accepting Christ; for Jews, especially in the nineteenth century, the wandering Jew represented an innocent people which had been abused and maltreated everywhere. It is interesting that, in his letter, Freud responds as a persecuted and passive Jew (his children will take him to England) who will live out his life as his people have for thousands of years in a hostile diaspora (Egypt).

5. For a detailed discussion of the March Revolution of 1848 and its aftermath as well as the role of and effects on Jews, see Dubnow, *From the Congress of Vienna to the Emergence of Hitler* 289–314; Salo Baron, "The Impact of the Revolution of 1848 on Jewish Emancipation," *Jewish Social Studies* 11 (1949): 195–248; Katz, *From Prejudice to Destruction* 223–29; McCagg, Jr., *A History of Hapsburg Jews* 93–101. McCagg develops a thesis that in 1848 bourgeois Jews seeking to become modern citizens of the Austrian state had reason to be optimistic about assimilation and ultimately emancipation. Their hope lay in their becoming an integral part of the bourgeoisie whose security, however, had been undermined soon after the revolution when political gains first offered were rescinded or eroded.

6. Kestenberg-Gladstein 21–43 is concerned largely with social and economic conditions in Bohemia and Moravia after 1848; see also

Stölzl 20–43, the chapter "The Difficult World of Jakob and Herrmann Kafka" ("Die schwierige Welt des Jakob und Herrmann Kafka").

7. Some of the Viennese Jews prominent in the last decades of the nineteenth century and the first decades of the twentieth are: writers Arthur Schnitzler, Stefan Zweig, Joseph Roth, Karl Kraus, Theodor Herzl, Otto Weininger, Peter Altenberg, Hermann Broch; composers Gustav Mahler and Arnold Schoenberg; physicians and psychiatrists Josef Breuer, Sigmund Freud, and Otto Rank; philosophers of language Fritz Mauthner and Ludwig Wittgenstein; and political figure Viktor Adler. It should be noted that none of these—apart, perhaps, from Schoenberg, after he converted back to Judaism—were religious Jews; and several of them, including Kraus, Mahler, and Adler, converted to Christianity. Steven Beller, "Class, Culture and the Jews of Vienna, 1900," *Jews, Antisemitism and Culture in Vienna*, ed. Ivar Oxaal, Michael Pollak, Gerhard Botz (London: Routledge, 1987) 43, notes that "at strategic points of Viennese modernism . . . one might perhaps talk of a Jewish preponderance, and in certain fields of a Jewish predominance" of major and minor cultural figures. See also Steven Beller, *Vienna and the Jews, 1867–1938: A Cultural History* (Cambridge: Cambridge University Press, 1989), which offers in some detail a statistical perspective of the educational, professional, and class structure of Jews and non-Jews in Vienna as well as a discussion of their cultural interests and values. See also Robert S. Wistrich, *The Jews of Vienna in the Age of Franz Joseph* (Oxford: Oxford University Press, 1989), especially the chapter in Part IV, "Culture and Identity," and those on Kraus, Weininger, Freud, Schnitzler, Stefan Zweig, and Joseph Roth. Michael Pollak, "Cultural Innovation and Social Identity in Fin-de-Siècle Vienna," *Jews, Antisemitism and Culture in Vienna* 74, argues that, after 1867, access to new status for Jews, along with the end of liberalism, the threatening disintegration of the empire, and the resulting insecurity among Jews, created the conditions for burgeoning creativity, for that "'modernity' which characterized many of the attempts to restore a climate of security." See also Jacques Le Rider, *Das Ende der Illusion: Zur Kritik der Moderne*, trans. Robert Fleck (Vienna: Österreichischer Bundesverlag, 1990), especially chapter 10, "Die Situation der assimilierten Wiener jüdischen Intellektuellen," and the ensuing chapters on Freud, Herzl, Kraus, and Beer-Hofmann. Part One of *The Jews of Austria: Essays on Their Life, History and Destruction*, ed. Josef Fraenkel (London: Vallentine, 1967), contains a series of essays on the cultural contributions of Austrian Jews in the fields of music, jurisprudence, medicine, literature, and journalism. See also Frederic V. Grunfeld, *Prophets without Honour: A Background to Freud, Kafka, Einstein and Their World* (New York:

Holt, 1979), which explores the cultural milieu, lives, and work of German and Austrian Jews; among the latter are Kafka, Mahler, Freud, Schoenberg, and Broch.

8. *Die Traumdeutung* was actually published in November 1899, but 1900 was the date printed on the title page.

9. Pulzer, *The Rise of Anti-Semitism in Germany and Austria* focuses on political antisemitism from 1879; social and political results of failed liberalism; and the antisemitic agenda of political movements, organizations, and parties. Beller, *Vienna,* especially 188–206, treats at some length the effects of Christian Social antisemitism and the Jewish response to it. See Wistrich, *The Jews of Vienna* 205–343, on the incidence of antisemitism in Austria and the political, social, and cultural responses to it in Vienna. See also Dubnow, *From the Congress of Vienna to the Emergence of Hitler* 476–511. Schorske 116–80 treats three mass movements which arose as responses to failed liberalism: the antisemitic movements of Georg von Schönerer and Karl Lueger and the Zionist movement of Theodor Herzl. Menachem Z. Rosensaft, "Jews and Antisemites in Austria at the End of the Nineteenth Century," *Leo Baeck Yearbook* 21 (1976): 57–86, presents a complex picture of antisemitism in Austria (especially in Vienna) and Jewish responses to it.

10. Schorske 117–18.

11. In an interview with the American journalist George Sylvester Viereck in "Sigmund Freud Confronts the Sphinx," *Glimpses of the Great* (London: Duckworth, 1930) 34, Freud indicated that his response to antisemitism was to assert his Jewishness: "My language . . . is German. My culture, my attainments are German. I considered myself a German intellectually, until I noticed the growth of anti-Semitic prejudice in Germany and in German Austria. Since that time, I prefer to call myself a Jew."

12. In the first section, for example, Freud mentions the story of a poor Jew who, without a ticket, boards a train for Carlsbad and at each stop is treated more and more harshly for not having a ticket. When he meets a friend who asks where he is going, he replies: "If my constitution holds out—to Carlsbad," *G.W.,* vol. 2/3, 200–201; *S.E.,* vol. 4, 195. Schorske 190 rightly connects Carlsbad, as a "city of recreation (re-creation), of resurrection," with Rome. However, although the protagonist is a Jew, any poor, resourceful, and tenacious person might have experienced what he did; and nowhere in the story is it stated that he was evicted from the train because he was a Jew.

13. *G.W.,* vol. 2/3, 200; *S.E.,* vol. 4, 194.

14. See, for example, Marthe Robert, *From Oedipus to Moses: Freud's Jewish Identity,* trans. Ralph Manheim (Garden City, NY: An-

chor, 1976), chapter IV, especially 103–12; Schorske 190–93; William J. McGrath, "Freud as Hannibal: The Politics of the Brother Band," *Central European History* 7 (1974), especially 35–37, 56–57; and Sebastiano Timpanaro, "Freud's 'Rome Phobia'," *New Left Review* 147 (September/October, 1984): 4–31. Robert detects a strong love-hate ambivalence in Freud's Rome-phobia; Schorske 191–92 finds that, for Freud, Rome is "first an object of hate, an enemy to be conquered, the second [in later mature dreams] an object of desire, to be entered in love"; while Timpanaro, generally agreeing with Schorske about Freud's response to Rome in *The Interpretation of Dreams*, finds no expression of love at all, but a great antipathy that motivates Freud's desire to conquer Rome. The Schorske and Timpanaro readings are convincing.

15. See Alexander Grinstein, *Sigmund Freud's Dreams* (New York: International Universities Press, 1980) 70. Freud visited the tubercular fiancé of his sister-in-law Minna Bernays in Gleichenberg in 1883; in 1886 the fiancé, Ignaz Schönberg, died. This reference to Gleichenberg recalls Freud's earlier story about Carlsbad, another health spa, which Schorske 190 connects with Rome as a "city of recreation (re-creation), of resurrection." Also see note 12 above. Since his stay at Gleichenberg did not help Schönberg, Gleichenberg (and Rome) might be connected with failed resurrection.

16. Ernest Jones, *The Life and Work of Sigmund Freud,* vol. 1 (New York: Basic Books, 1953) 150; see also 132 and 352.

17. Salo Baron, *Die Judenfrage auf dem Wiener Kongreß: Auf Grund von zum Teil ungedruckten Quellen* (Vienna: Löwit, 1920) 39–42, 197–99.

18. *G.W.,* vol. 2/3, 202; *S.E.,* vol. 4, 196.

19. In the last five years of the century, when Freud was writing *The Interpretation of Dreams,* the presence of antisemitism was not only becoming more public, but had moved into political and governmental spheres: there were riots and open discrimination against Jews; public oratory denouncing Jews and German culture; newspaper reports of ritual murder cases, such as the Leopold Hilsner accusation in Bohemia and the Dreyfus affair in France; and antisemitic political movements and parties, including the Christian Social movement, whose candidate for Mayor of Vienna, Karl Lueger, had been elected four times before receiving the Kaiser's confirmation in 1897. See Wistrich, *The Jews of Vienna,* chapters 2 and 3; Pulzer 142–83; Beller, *Vienna and the Jews* 188–206. For a discussion of Freud's experience with antisemitism during his student days at the University and later in the *Gesellschaft der Ärzte* (Society of Physicans), see Klein 48–62.

20. See Peter Pulzer, "Spezifische Momente und Spielarten des Österreichischen und des Wiener Antisemitismus," *Eine zerstörte Kultur: Jüdisches Leben und Antisemitismus in Wien seit dem 19. Jahrhundert,* ed. Gerhard Botz, Ivar Oxaal, Michael Pollak (Buchloe: Obermayer, 1990) 128–34.

21. *G.W.,* vol. 2/3, 203; *S.E.,* vol. 4, 197.

22. Ernst Simon, "Sigmund Freud, The Jew," *Leo Baeck Yearbook* 2 (1957): 271, suggests that the fur hat may be what is called in Yiddish a *Streimel,* which Orthodox Jews wore on the Sabbath. Although Freud's father did come from a Hasidic family, he had left Orthodoxy as a young man; and it hardly seems logical that he would adopt Orthodox dress. Fur hats, however, a fashion worn by all kinds of nineteenth century Europeans who could afford the luxury, were more likely associated in the Crownlands with the bourgeoisie and "bourgeoisified" Jews. Rice, *Freud and Moses* 75, whose thesis is (all solid evidence to the contrary) that Jakob Freud remained an observant Orthodox Jew and that Sigmund and his family were not assimilated and in fact concealed the extent of their observance, of course accepts Simon's view (74). According to Rice, Sigmund's avowed atheism really concealed his yearning for the retention of Judaism "in its original Orthodox form" (117). Martin S. Bergmann, "Moses and the Evolution of Freud's Identity," *The Israel Annals of Psychiatry and Related Disciplines* 14 (1976): 11–12, also sees the hat as a *Streimel,* but criticizes Sigmund for not understanding that his father's reaction was "anything but undignified"; in Jakob's youth a Jew was expected to control his anger and maintain "his own spiritual superiority." David S. Blatt, "The Development of the Hero: Sigmund Freud and the Reformation of the Jewish Tradition," *Psychoanalysis and Contemporary Thought* 11 (1988): 644, augments the significance of the hat, creating his own pious fantasy about "the Shabbes [Sabbath] walks that Jacob Freud took as a young man after the synagogue."

23. *G.W.,* vol. 2/3, 203–4; *S.E.,* vol. 4, 198.

24. McGrath, "Freud as Hannibal" 36, notes that Freud here traces the politics of antisemitism to early childhood sibling rivalry; but McGrath adopts a far more sanguine view than I of Freud's "dissolution of history and politics into psychology" (56) and does not in fact address what the consequences—social or otherwise—of such a transformation might be.

25. Robert, *From Oedipus to Moses* 165.

26. Robert, *From Oedipus to Moses* 103–13.

27. Letter to Wilhelm Fliess, 1 February 1900, cited in Max

Schur, *Freud: Living and Dying* (New York: International Universities Press, 1972) 201.

28. Sigmund Freud, letter to Wilhelm Fliess, 11 March 1902, *Aus den Anfängen der Psychoanalyse: Briefe an Wilhelm Fließ, Abhandlungen und Notizen aus den Jahren 1887–1902,* ed. Marie Bonaparte, Anna Freud, Ernst Kris (Frankfurt am Main: Fischer, 1950) 194–96; *The Origins of Psychoanalysis: Letters to Wilhelm Fliess, Drafts and Notes: 1887–1902,* trans. Eric Mosbacher, James Strachey, ed. Marie Bonaparte, Anna Freud, Ernst Kris (New York: Basic Books, 1954) 342–45. Gay, *Freud* 136, notes that Freud's "visit was at once emblem and instrument of inner freedom, token of a new flexibility for social and political maneuver."

29. Letter to Wilhelm Fliess, 19 September 1901, *Aus den Anfängen* 288; *Origins* 335–36.

30. See pp. 27–28.

31. "Der Moses des Michelangelo," *G.W.,* vol. 10, 175; *S.E.,* vol. 13, 213.

32. Jones, vol. 2, 365.

33. Letter to Martha Bernays, 25 September 1912, *Briefe, 1873–1939* 308; *Letters of Sigmund Freud* 293.

34. Jones, vol. 2, 364–65.

35. Sigmund Freud and Karl Abraham, letter to Karl Abraham, 3 May 1908, *Briefe, 1907–1926,* ed. Hilde C. Abraham and Ernst L. Freud (Frankfurt am Main: Fischer, 1965) 47; *A Psycho-Analytic Dialogue: The Letters of Sigmund Freud and Karl Abraham, 1907–1926,* trans. Bernard Marsh and Hilda Abraham, ed. Hilda Abraham and Ernst L. Freud (London: Hogarth, 1965) 34.

36. Letter to Karl Abraham, 26 December 1908, *Briefe, 1907–1926* 73; *A Psycho-Analytic Dialogue* 64.

37. Sigmund Freud, C. G. Jung, letter to C. G. Jung, 17 January 1909, *Briefwechsel,* ed. William McGuire and Wolfgang Sauerländer (Frankfurt am Main: Fischer, 1974) 218; *The Freud/Jung Letters: The Correspondence between Sigmund Freud and C. G. Jung,* trans. Ralph Manheim and R. F. C. Hull, ed. William McGuire (Princeton: Princeton University Press, 1974) 196–97. William J. McGrath, *Freud's Discovery of Psychoanalysis: The Politics of Hysteria* (Ithaca: Cornell University Press, 1986) 299–302, connects this statement to Jung with Freud's dream—some ten years earlier—of dissecting his pelvis and legs in *The Interpretation of Dreams, G.W.,* vol. 2/3, 455–58, 481; *S.E.,* vol. 5, 452–55, 477–78. Although not explicitly stated by Freud, McGrath presents a convincing interpretation of the dreamer as a Moses figure whose children (here understood as Freud's psychoanalytic followers), but not he, will reach the promised land.

38. Letter to James Putnam, 8 July 1915, *James Putnam and Psychoanalysis: Letters between Putnam and Sigmund Freud, Ernest Jones, William James, Sandor Ferenczi, and Morton Prince, 1877–1917,* trans. of German texts Judith Bernays Heller, ed. Nathan G. Hale Jr. (Cambridge: Harvard University Press, 1971) 189.

39. Jones, vol. 3, 186–87.

40. Letter to Karl Abraham, 23 July 1908, *Briefe, 1907–1926* 57; *A Psycho-Analytic Dialogue* 46.

41. Letter to Sandor Ferenczi, 17 October 1912, reported in Jones, vol., 2, 367.

42. *G.W.,* vol. 10, 198; *S.E.,* vol. 13, 233.

43. *G.W.,* vol. 10, 181; *S.E.,* vol. 13, 219. Robert, *From Moses to Oedipus* 142–45, assumes that Freud "really became afraid" of Michelangelo's Moses and "really expected it to spring to its feet" because he experienced the figure as his own father, whom he had disavowed. Thus this confrontation is another episode in Freud's unconscious Oedipal struggle. Her insight may be correct, but it cannot be verified. After all, the sentiments communicated are part of the textual discourse and are to be understood within the overall context of the argument and structure of the essay. For Yosef Hayim Yerushalmi, in *Freud's Moses: Judaism Terminable and Interminable* (New Haven: Yale University Press, 1991) 76, "Jewish guilt"—the result of disobeying what Yerushalmi considers Freud's father's "mandate" that his son return to the Bible—was responsible for the "angry scorn" of Michelangelo's Moses, whom Freud experienced as "Moses-Jakob," and the containment of that anger. This kind of speculation about the unstated origins and significance of Freud's (or the narrator's) psychic life is interesting, but not particularly fruitful for an understanding of the essay. (I am also not convinced by Yerushalmi's contention that Jakob Freud's ornate and erudite Hebrew inscription in the Bible given Sigmund for his thirty-fifth birthday was a "mandate," nor whether the son interpreted it as such.) My own effort, at any rate, is to resist using Freud's psychoanalytic principles to expose the depths of his unconscious, but to explore as carefully as possible the text itself, its structure, methodology, and argument.

44. *G.W.,* vol. 10, 198; *S.E.,* vol. 13, 233.

45. *G.W.,* vol. 10, 173; *S.E.,* vol. 13, 212.

46. *G.W.,* vol. 10, 177; *S.E.,* vol. 13, 215.

47. *G.W.,* vol. 10, 177; *S.E.,* vol. 13, 215.

48. *G.W.,* vol. 10, 172; *S.E.,* vol. 13, 211.

49. *G.W.,* vol. 10, 185; *S.E.,* vol. 13, 222.

50. *G.W.,* vol. 10, 174–75; *S.E.,* vol. 13, 213.

51. *G.W.,* vol. 10, 198; *S.E.,* vol. 13, 233.

52. *G.W.*, vol. 10, 194; *S.E.*, vol. 13, 229.

53. *G.W.*, vol. 10, 194; *S.E.*, vol. 13, 230.

54. *G.W.*, vol. 10, 194; *S.E.*, vol. 13, 230.

55. *G.W.*, vol. 10, 198; *S.E.*, vol. 13, 233.

56. Bergmann 16–17 takes note of this possibility, but seems not to know whether to attribute Freud's oversight to "repression due to the special circumstances in Freud's life at the time" (as he does at other times) or merely to forgive it, or perhaps both. Krüll 186–87 adopts Bergmann's view of a Moses who has returned a second time with new tablets, but she also wants to account psychologically for Freud's oversight: "Freud overlooked the obvious interpretation—consciously or unconsciously—simply because the image of a composed Moses . . . did not lend itself to a projection of his own feelings." This is only one instance in Krüll's work in which insights into Freud's texts are marred by speculative efforts to psychoanalyze both Freud and his father, to find in Freud's writings verification not only of his own unarticulated sexual secrets, but those of his father as well.

57. *G.W.*, vol. 10, 198; *S.E.*, vol. 13, 233.

58. *G.W.*, vol. 10, 198; *S.E.*, vol. 13, 233.

59. *G.W.*, vol. 10, 195; *S.E.*, vol. 13, 230.

60. *G.W.*, vol. 10, 194; *S.E.*, vol. 13, 230.

61. Elias Auerbach, *Moses*, trans. and ed. Robert A. Barclay and Israel O. Lehman (Detroit: Wayne State University Press, 1975) 127.

62. *G.W.*, vol. 10, 198; *S.E.*, vol. 13, 233.

63. Le Rider 316 notes that, according to Freud, Michelangelo here is largely concerned with correcting Jewish tradition by rejecting the limitations of dogmatic scripture for a "humanistic universality." Le Rider finds that Freud identifies with Michelangelo's views, but I would question whether restraint and quiescence are necessarily humanistic or universal values.

64. *G.W.*, vol. 10, 198; *S.E.*, vol. 13, 233.

65. *G.W.*, vol. 10, 199; *S.E.*, vol. 13, 234.

66. *G.W.*, vol. 10, 199; *S.E.*, vol. 13, 234.

67. *G.W.*, vol. 10, 199; *S.E.*, vol. 13, 234.

68. Paul Roazen, *Freud: Political and Social Thought* (New York: Knopf, 1968) 169–70, notes the similarity between Freud's ambitions and those of the pope and Michelangelo, but doesn't note the irony in Freud's identification with these Christians within the context of a church in Rome.

69. Elliott Oring, *The Jokes of Sigmund Freud: A Study in Humor and Jewish Identity* (Philadelphia: University of Pennsylvania Press, 1984) 94, "is tempted to say" that Michelangelo's Moses is a "Christian

Moses" because he is forgiving. Nowhere in the essay does Freud indicate a concern for the virtue of forgiveness, which suggests a changed attitude to the unruly masses. Instead he is almost solely preoccupied with Moses' ability to control his own rage and hostile desires.

70. *G.W.,* vol. 10, 201; *S.E.,* vol. 13, 236.

71. *G.W.,* vol. 10, 199; *S.E.,* vol. 13, 234.

72. Gay, *Freud* 241.

73. Jones, vol. 2, 362–63, 366.

74. Jones, vol. 2, 366.

75. Letter to Karl Abraham, 6 April 1914, *Briefe 1907–1926* 166–67; *A Psycho-Analytic Dialogue* 171.

76. Oring 93 interprets this "joke" as a "representation of the opposite." Thus, Freud's concern is not about disgracing Moses, but actually about "disgrace for Freud," that is, "his antipathy toward his Jewish identity." This may be so, but it seems to me important to characterize the "Jewish identity" which Freud here attributes to the biblical Moses, namely, behavior which derives from and expresses volatile passions and hostile impulses. Freud's conception of "Jewish identity" is markedly different in *Moses and Monotheism.*

77. Yosef Haim Yerushalmi, "Freud on the 'Historical Novel': From the Manuscript Draft (1934) of *Moses and Monotheism," International Journal of Psycho-Analysis* 70 (1989): 379. This quotation is a translation from the introductory section to Freud's 1934 manuscript draft; the German text is quoted in the Appendix, 392–93. The subtitle, "A Historical Novel," did not appear when the first two parts of *Moses and Monotheism* were published separately in *Imago* in 1937, nor when the entire work appeared in book form in 1939.

78. Quoted in Yerushalmi, "Freud on the 'Historical Novel'" 379.

79. Sigmund Freud and Arnold Zweig, letter to Arnold Zweig, 16 December 1934, *Briefwechsel,* ed. Ernst L. Freud (Frankfurt am Main: Fischer, 1968) 109; *The Letters of Sigmund Freud and Arnold Zweig,* trans. Elaine and William Robson-Scott, ed. Ernst L. Freud (New York: Harcourt, 1970) 98.

80. Yerushalmi, "Freud on the 'Historical Novel'" 390, suggests that the original subtitle "was meant to indicate nothing more than Freud's awareness of the lack of corroborating facts for his thesis and so to disarm potential critics by anticipating such criticism." Later, insisting on the "historical truth" of his views, Freud deleted the subtitle because he feared that his work would be regarded as art rather than science.

81. *G.W.,* vol. 16, 114; *S.E.,* vol. 23, 17.

82. Letter to Arnold Zweig, 6 November 1934, *Briefwechsel* 108; *Letters of Freud and Zweig* 97. In an infelicitous rendering, the translators collapse Freud's "Montierung auf eine höhere Basis" (which I translate literally as "mounting on a higher foundation") with the statue's feet of clay ("founding it on a base of clay"). The connection between the "feet of clay" and a theoretical foundation which Freud found problematic is lost in the letter's figurative translation.

83. There are three prefaces in the third part, "Moses, His People, and the Monotheistic Religion" ("Moses, Sein Volk und die monotheistische Religion"), two prefaces at the beginning of the first section and one at the beginning of the second. The quotation that follows is from the second preface.

84. *G.W.,* vol. 16, 160; *S.E.,* vol. 23, 58.

85. Letter to Arnold Zweig, 16 December 1934, *Briefwechsel* 108; *Letters of Freud and Zweig* 98.

86. Philip Rieff, *Freud: The Mind of the Moralist,* 3rd ed. (Chicago: University of Chicago Press, 1979) and Paul Ricoeur, *Freud and Philosophy: An Essay on Interpretation,* trans. Denis Savage (New Haven: Yale University Press, 1970), both call attention to the fact that in *Moses and Monotheism* Freud intends something other than a discussion or exegesis of the Bible. Rieff notes the lack of Old Testament sensibility in Freud's text and indicates that it "is a study of the moral hero putting a higher civilization over on the rabble . . . Freud's *Moses and Monotheism* is a triumph of psychological romance" (283–84 passim). And Ricoeur observes: "There is hardly any need to state that *Moses and Monotheism* does not operate at the level of an exegesis of the Old Testament and in no way satisfies the most elementary requirements of a hermeneutics adapted to a text . . . The works of religion, the monuments of belief, are treated neither with the same sympathy nor with the same rigor; instead, we are presented with a vague relationship between religious themes and paternal prototype" (545). In an address to the B'nai B'rith a decade earlier, two indispensable characteristics which Freud attributed to "his Jewish nature" are also central aspects of his late Moses: "Because I am a Jew, I found myself free of many prejudices, which restricted others in the use of their intellect; as a Jew I was prepared to go into the opposition and to renounce consent with the 'compact majority'" (*G.E.,* vol. 17, 52; *S.E.,* vol. 20, 274).

87. Letter to Arnold Zweig, 30 September 1934, *Briefwechsel* 102; *The Letters of Freud and Zweig* 91.

88. Robert, *From Oedipus to Moses* 146, notes that, for Freud, the causes of Nazism were not to be found in social or political data which would be "accessible to analysis"; but she also finds that Jews who are

victims of antisemitism and persecution somehow regard their "singularity" as responsible for hostility toward them and, therefore, feel compelled to search their own psyches or Jewish history for an answer to it: "For where others can take sides with a clear conscience on the strength of their enlightened opinions, a Jew *must* first put himself to the test, *must* first look not among his persecutors but within himself and in the dense texture of his millennial history, for the explanation of the millennial hatred that his race has brought upon itself by the mere fact of its existence" (emphasis added). It seems to me, however, that it was not uncommon for Freud to seek causes, reasons, and motivations in the innermost recesses of an individual or group rather than in the social world. Robert may be correct about the direction that Freud's inquiry took, but her generalizations about the behavior of Jews do not coincide with positions taken by Jews generally, as the many studies of antisemitism written by Jews attest. Too often Robert undercuts sound observations about Freud by connecting them with sweeping generalizations about Jews and the absolute differences between Jews and other peoples, particularly Germans.

89. Letter to Lou Andreas-Salomé, 6 January 1935, *Briefwechsel,* ed. Ernst Pfeiffer (Frankfurt am Main: Fischer, 1966) 222; *Letters,* trans. William and Elaine Robson-Scott, ed. Ernst Pfeiffer (New York: Harcourt, 1972) 204.

90. *G.W.,* vol. 16, 213–14; *S.E.,* vol. 23, 106.

91. *G.W.,* vol. 16, 165; *S.E.,* vol. 23, 62.

92. *G.W.,* vol. 16, 142; *S.E.,* vol. 23, 41–42 and passim.

93. *G.W.,* vol. 16, 143–44; *S.E.,* vol. 23, 43.

94. *G.W.,* vol. 16, 143; *S.E.,* vol. 23, 43.

95. *G.W.,* vol. 16, 144; *S.E.,* vol. 23, 43.

96. *G.W.,* vol. 16, 144; *S.E.,* vol. 23, 43.

97. See Sigmund Freud, *Totem und Tabu, G.W.,* vol. 9; *Totem and Taboo, S.E.,* vol. 13.

98. In *Totem and Taboo* and throughout *Moses and Monotheism* Freud insists that the murders of the primal father and Moses, respectively, actually took place; otherwise it would not have been possible for the memory of it to have entered into archaic inheritance. Jones, vol. 2, 354, reports that when he spoke with Freud about *Totem and Taboo* and "asked him why he who wrote *The Interpretation of Dreams* could now have such doubts, he wisely replied: 'Then I described the wish to kill one's father, and now I am describing the actual killing; after all it is a big step from a wish to a deed.'" Rieff 194 and Ricoeur 208, 246, concur. Susan A. Handelman, *The Slayers of Moses: The Emergence of Rabbinic Interpretation in Modern Literary Theory* (Albany: State Uni-

versity of New York Press, 1982) 139 understands these murders not as actual, but as "interpretive construction of a text, not as actual deed; as Freud too forgets that there is no literal reality to the primal seductive father." It seems to me that since Freud clearly did not *forget* that there was no literal reality here, but maintains that these murders actually took place, the critic's task is to interpret the text as written, not to correct and ameliorate fundamental aspects of the text by seeking reasons (excuses) in Freud's psyche. Handelman continues: "Freud's parricide was a fantasy—interpretive, not actual—and interpretation was as much an attempt to identify with his father as to destroy him" (139).

99. Letter to Lou Andreas-Salomé, 6 January 1935, *Briefwechsel* 224; *Letters* 205 (Freud's emphasis).

100. *G.W.,* vol. 16, 33; *S.E.,* vol. 20, 72.

101. *G.W.,* vol. 16, 238; *S.E.,* vol. 23, 129.

102. *G.W.,* vol. 16, 115; *S.E.,* vol. 23, 17.

103. In the *Standard Edition* this title reads *Group Psychology and the Analysis of the Ego*.

104. Robert, *From Oedipus to Moses* 211 n. 11, finds "humanity and masculinity" stressed in the title; I read only masculinity in "der Mann Moses." Focusing closely on the title, Yerushalmi, *Freud's Moses* 55, 129 n. 58, makes the point that Freud did not use "Judaism" out of concern "that psychoanalysis not be viewed as a 'Jewish national affair'" and avoided "Monotheism" because it was too abstract, opting instead for "Monotheistic Religion," which in the text clearly signifies Judaism. Curiously, Yerushalmi makes no mention of what "The Man Moses" of the title might signify, nor does he broach the controversial issue of the opposition of "Geistigkeit" and "Sinnlichkeit" (intellectuality or spirituality and sensuality) or masculinity and femininity which is articulated throughout *Moses and Monotheism*.

105. *G.W.,* vol. 16, 108; *S.E.,* vol. 23, 12.

106. *G.W.,* vol 16, 113; *S.E.,* vol. 23, 16. Although Freud indicated that Moses' Egyptian heritage was not what was essential (letter to Arnold Zweig, 16 December 1934, *Briefwechsel* 109; *Letters* 98), many critics—many of them Jews offended by the change in ethnic origin and identity of the founder of the Jewish people as a nation—have understood this as the most significant aspect of *Moses and Monotheism*. See, for example, Robert, *From Oedipus to Moses*, especially 150–54, who insists that Freud's denials have only convinced her that Moses' Egyptian heritage is of primary importance. In her view, Freud declared a whole people illegitimate, rewrote Western history, and "turned the whole world upside down" only because he wanted to rewrite his own parental origins. This may be so, but is, for me, mere speculation. Ritchie

Robertson, "Freud's Testament: *Moses and Monotheism*," *Freud in Exile. Psychoanalysis and Its Vicissitudes*, ed. Edward Timms, Naomi Segal (New Haven: Yale University Press, 1988) 84, refutes Robert's view that Freud's identification with an Egyptian Moses implies "a fantasy in which Freud is no longer a Jew." He argues that Freud allows for the significance of being able to choose one's identity, one's religion, and one's destiny: "Rather it implies that Freud deliberately chooses to be a Jew." Bakan, *Freud and the Jewish Mystical Tradition* 145–61, is far less apologetic than Robert on this issue. He finds that the "idea of Moses as Gentile makes the Jews the buffoons of history." He attributes this view of Moses' origin to a "psychological act of apostasy" by "a modern product of the enlightenment" and to Freud's attempt to ward off antisemitism because Moses, the creator of the Jewish people, was a Gentile and he, not the Jews, is the rightful target of antisemitism. When discussing the murder of Moses, he notes that "[if] it is necessary to kill Moses, however, then the idea that Moses was an Egyptian serves to take some of the edge off the guilt" (167–68). In my view such positions—which insist on pure blood lines, which cannot imagine that a foreigner's influence or foreign religion can be so assimilated by a people that it becomes an integral, even fundamental identifying characteristic—border on a kind of biological racism. The danger of such a position may be seen in Bakan's remark about the lessening of guilt if a person of another ethnic group were murdered. Ricoeur 244 suggests that Moses' Egyptian origin "marks the renouncement on the part of Sigmund Freud the Jew of the value that his narcissism could still rightfully claim, the value of belonging to a race that engendered Moses and imparted ethical monotheism to the world." Freud had, it seems to me, nothing to renounce and everything to gain: he was a member of a group which was descended from a majority culture and from nobility, in addition to being a Jew and enjoying the superiority of minority status. I fully agree with Yerushalmi, *Freud's Moses* 53, that if "monotheism was genetically Egyptian, it has been historically Jewish."

107. *G.W.*, vol. 16, 104–5; *S.E.*, vol. 23, 8.

108. *G.W.*, vol. 16, 104; *S.E.*, vol. 23, 8.

109. *G.W.*, vol. 16, 108; *S.E.*, vol. 23, 12. In the segment on dreams of the *Introductory Lectures on Psycho-Analysis (Vorlesungen zur Einführung in die Psychoanalyse)*, written in 1915–1916, Freud connects Rank's views about birth myths of heroes—particularly their exposure in and rescue from water—with the possibility of Moses' Egyptian heritage, "in the myth a person, who has rescued a child from the water, acknowledges that she is the real mother. In a well-known joke, the intelligent Jewish boy is asked who was the mother of Moses. He

answers unhesitatingly: the princess. But no, he is reproached, she only pulled him out of the water. So she says, he replied and with that proves that he has discovered the correct interpretation of the myth." *G.W.,* vol. 11, 165; *S.E.,* vol. 15, 161.

110. *G.W.,* vol. 16, 104–5; *S.E.,* vol. 23, 8–9.

111. Ilana Pardes, "You Name It," unpublished manuscript, 3–4.

112. *G.W.,* vol. 16, 225; *S.E.,* vol. 23, 118. See also *G.W.,* vol. 16, 221–22; *S.E.,* vol. 23, 113–14.

113. *G.W.,* vol. 16, 219–25; *S.E.,* vol. 23, 111–18. Jonathan Culler, *On Deconstruction: Theory and Criticism after Structuralism* (Ithaca: Cornell University Press, 1982) 59–60, reinterprets Freud's position that the movement from matriarchal to patriarchal power, from sense perception to the primacy of thought, was an advance in intellectuality: "But when we consider that the invisible, omnipotent God is God the Father, not to say God of the Patriarchs, we may well wonder whether, on the contrary, the promotion of the invisible over the visible and of thought and inference over sense perception is not a consequence or effect of the establishment of paternal authority: a consequence of the fact that the paternal relation is invisible." And quoting Dorothy Dinnerstein's *The Mermaid and the Minotaur: Sexual Arrangements and Human Malaise* (New York: Harper, 1976), he notes that "men's powerful 'impulse to affirm and tighten by cultural inventions their unsatisfactorily loose mammalian connection with children' leads them to value highly cultural inventions of a symbolic nature."

114. Pardes, "You Name it" 8; also Ilana Pardes, *Countertraditions in the Bible: A Feminist Approach* (Cambridge: Harvard University Press, 1992) 82–83, 169 n. 18. "More often than not it is the mother or mother surrogate who names the child in biblical texts. Freud seems to ignore this fact . . . in the opening pages of *Moses and Monotheism,* where he robs Pharoah's daughter of her role as name-giver and attributes the naming of Moses to his Egyptian father" (169).

115. Pardes, "You Name It" 18.

116. Otto Rank, *Der Mythus von der Geburt des Helden: Versuch einer psychologischen Mythendeutung* (Leipzig: Deuticke, 1919).

117. *G.W.,* vol. 16, 109; *S.E.,* vol. 23, 13.

118. *G.W.,* vol. 16, 111–12; *S.E.,* vol. 23, 15.

119. See *G.W.,* vol. 16, 115; *S.E.,* vol. 23, 16; also the very revealing footnote, *G.E.,* vol. 16, 125; *S.E.,* vol. 23, 27 (note 2), in which Freud speaks about methodological difficulties and their consequences: "Whenever we deal with biblical tradition in such an autocratic and arbitrary way, drawing on it for confirmation where it serves us, and rejecting it unhesitatingly where it contradicts us, then we know

very well that we are exposing ourselves to serious methodological criticism and weakening the conclusiveness of our explanations. But this is the only way in which one can treat material about which one knows with certainty that its reliability has been damaged by the influence of distorting tendencies. One hopes at a later time to acquire a certain degree of justification, if one comes upon the trail of those secret motives. Certainty cannot be attained at all; and moreover it may be said that all other authors proceed in the same way."

120. See note 106 for a discussion of critics' commentary.

121. *G.W.,* vol. 16, 118–19; *S.E.,* vol. 23, 20–22.

122. *G.W.,* vol. 16, 127; *S.E.,* vol. 23, 28.

123. *G.W.,* vol. 16, 127; *S.E.,* vol. 23, 29.

124. *G.W.,* vol. 16, 115–16; *S.E.,* vol. 23, 18.

125. Michael Carroll, "'Moses and Monotheism' Revisited—Freud's 'Personal Myth?'" *American Imago* 44 (1989): 19, points out that traditionally Moses' birth parents were not considered to be of low status within the Israelite community: in Exodus 2, his parents are both Levites, thus "of noble birth"; in the Talmud, his father is described as "the greatest man of his generation"; and Josephus refers to Moses' father as a "Hebrew of noble birth." Freud was apparently interested in Moses' status within the dominant culture, not within an enslaved tribe or oppressed minority.

126. *G.W.,* vol. 16, 112; *S.E.,* vol. 23, 15.

127. *G.W.,* vol. 16, 217; *S.E.,* vol. 23, 110.

128. *G.W.,* vol. 16, 154; *S.E.,* vol. 23, 52.

129. *G.W.,* vol. 16, 215; *S.E.,* vol. 23, 108.

130. *G.W.,* vol. 16, 216; *S.E.,* vol. 23, 109.

131. See Judith Van Herik, *Freud on Femininity and Faith* (Berkeley: University of California Press, 1982), for a thorough discussion of important connections between Freud's assessments of gender and religion. The relationship between Mosaic monotheism and masculinity, Jewish tradition, and progress in spirituality or intellectuality is explored in chapter 11, "Renunciation in the Past: Moses' Monotheism" 170–90.

132. *G.W.,* vol. 16, 217; *S.E.,* vol. 23, 109–10.

133. *G.W.,* vol. 16, 217; *S.E.,* vol. 23, 109.

134. See Ricoeur 186–211 for an informative exploration of what he considers "genetic ways of interpreting" the Oedipus complex and its relationship to the primal father and horde in the prehistory of mankind; see Van Herik 41–47 for a discussion of the connection of psychoanalysis and biology.

135. *G.W.,* vol. 16, 213; *S.E.,* vol. 23, 106.

136. Ilana Pardes, *Countertraditions* 169 n. 18, refers to Freud's

Moses and Monotheism and notes that "the Mosaic prohibition against images does not imply that God is invisible. God's image may not be duplicated, nor can it be seen commonly, but it is nonetheless visible. The invisibility of the monotheistic God is but a Platonic misreading, which has become rooted in Western thought."

137. *G.W.*, vol. 16, 220; *S.E.*, vol. 23, 113.

138. *G.W.*, vol. 16, 222; *S.E.*, vol. 23, 115.

139. Van Herik 109–12.

140. *G.W.*, vol. 16, 230; *S.E.*, vol. 23, 122. It is interesting that Freud's comprehensive essay on the dissolution of the Oedipus complex was entitled "Der Untergang des Ödipuskomplexes" (translated as "The Dissolution of the Oedipus Complex"), which Freud—in a 14 March 1924 letter to Andreas-Salomé—hoped would sound "as tragic as the title of Oswald Spengler's book," *Untergang des Abendlandes (Decline of the West)* (*Briefwechsel* 146; *Letters* 133). This remark seems to imply that the repression of Oedipal aggression was a monumental moment in the decline or destruction of one culture and the beginning of another, the decline of an epoch of fulfilled wishes (at least for the primal father) and the rise of the masculine culture of renunciation and the superego.

141. *G.W.*, vol. 16, 133; *S.E.*, vol. 23, 34.

142. *G.W.*, vol. 16, 165; *S.E.*, vol. 23, 62.

143. *G.W.*, vol. 16, 169; *S.E.*, vol. 23, 65–66.

144. *G.W.*, vol. 16, 208–9; *S.E.*, vol. 23, 101.

145. *G.W.*, vol. 16, 231; *S.E.*, vol. 23, 123.

146. Robertson 87 maintains that Freud's conception of Jewish identity was associated with "lofty ethical and intellectual ideals" of the rational and enlightened Jew, but that these ideals are transmitted by irrational means. It seems to me that Freud's ethical and intellectual ideals themselves are products of psychological processes which are antithetic to rational thought and considered debate. Le Rider 340 argues that because Moses chose his people and, subsequent to his murder by them, they chose him, Judaism is presented as "the more progressive, here more rational religion which is more faithful to the right of the father [*Vaterrecht*]. The choice of the father by the son presupposes the superiority of reason to the senses . . ." What Le Rider omits, however, is the irrational motivation for this choice, that is, the guilt which drives the sons to submit, this time to an overpowering father imago.

147. *G.W.*, vol. 16, 208; *S.E.*, vol. 23, 101.

148. See the section "Triebverzicht," *G.W.*, vol. 16, 223–25; "Renunciation of Instinct," *S.E.*, vol. 23, 116–17.

149. *G.W.,* vol. 16, 228; *S.E.,* vol. 23, 120.
150. *G.W.,* vol. 16, 224; *S.E.,* vol. 23, 117.
151. *G.W.,* vol. 16, 225; *S.E.,* vol. 23, 117.
152. *G.W.,* vol. 16, 225; *S.E.,* vol. 23, 117.
153. See note 140.
154. *G.W.,* vol. 16, 226; *S.E.,* vol. 23, 118.
155. *G.W.,* vol. 16, 226; *S.E.,* vol. 23, 118.
156. *G.W.,* vol. 16, 243; *S.E.,* vol. 23, 134.
157. G.W., vol. 23, 148–49; S.E., vol. 23, 47.

158. Responding in 1883 to a letter in which his fiancée Martha Bernays had apparently described her experience at a fair, Freud expressed an assessment of the general populace that reappears later in, for example, *Mass Psychology and the Analysis of the Ego, Civilization and Its Discontents,* and *Moses and Monotheism.* I quote here extensively from the letter because it is clear that his ideas about the multitude *(das Volk)* and the elite—the communal folk and the individuals, those who live for pleasure and those who renounce instinctual gratification, those who live for the day or moment and those who "chain" themselves to lifelong tasks—were not merely acquired from such writers as the antidemocratic and racialist French sociologist Gustave Le Bon, from whose *Psychologie des Foules* (translated as *The Crowd: A Study of the Popular Mind*) Freud quoted very liberally in *Mass Psychology.* Although Freud indicated in the letter that he could understand the multitude's behavior as a response to the social, political, and physical privations they suffered, he nevertheless did not acknowledge their discipline or dignity at work or in the home: "The rabble lives out its desires and we do without," Freud wrote to Martha Bernays. "We do without to maintain our integrity, we economize with our health, our capacity for pleasure, our excitations, we save ourselves for something, we ourselves do not know for what— and this habit of constantly suppressing natural instincts gives us the character of refinement . . . Thus we strive more to avoid pain than to gain pleasure; and at the highest level there are people such as we two, who chain ourselves together with fetters of death and love, who for years do without and yearn in order not to become unfaithful to one another, who surely would not be able to overcome a stroke of fate which robbed us of our most beloved one . . . The poor, the populace, they could not exist without their thick hide and their slight sensibility . . . The poor are too impotent, too exposed, to behave like us . . . There is a psychology of the common man that is rather different from ours. They also have a greater sense of communality than we have, the only thing alive for them is that they each continue the life of another, whereas for each of us the world is extinguished with his death" (letter

to Martha Bernays, 29 August 1883, *Briefe, 1873–1939* 56–57; *Letters of Sigmund Freud* 50–51).

159. *G.W.*, vol. 16, 192; *S.E.*, vol. 23, 86.

160. *G.W.*, vol. 16, 127; *S.E.*, vol. 23, 28.

161. For an excellent discussion of Freud's understanding of the dynamics of leadership and the politics of culture, see Rieff 228–38.

162. Robert Polzin, Pt. 1, "Deuteronomy, Joshua, Judges," *Moses and the Deuteronomist: A Literary Study of the Deuteronomic History* (New York: Seabury, 1980) 45.

163. *G.W.*, vol. 13, 134–35; *S.W.*, vol. 18, 121.

164. *G.W.*, vol. 16, 220; *S.E.*, vol. 23, 113.

165. *G.W.*, vol. 16, 230; *S.E.*, vol. 23, 122.

166. See *G.W.*, vol. 16, 226–27, 230; *S.E.*, vol. 23, 118–19, 122.

167. *G.W.*, vol. 16, 217–18; *S.E.*, vol. 23, 109–10.

168. Letter to C. G. Jung, 12 May 1912, *Briefwechsel* 558–59; *The Freud/Jung Letters*, 504, including notes 1 and 2. In this letter to Jung, Freud pursued differences between himself and Jung about incest, apparently rejecting J. J. Bachofen's understanding of original human organization as matriarchal for Darwin's view that it was dominated by a strong, promiscuous male. Freud's definition of a father as "one who posseses a mother sexually (and the children as property)" reveals the absolute social and biological authority of the patriarch over the entire family, tribe, and society.

169. *G.W.*, vol. 16, 242; *S.E.*, vol. 23, 133.

170. *G.W.*, vol. 16, 226; *S.E.*, vol. 23, 118.

171. See *The Future of an Illusion* for Freud's view of the fundamental, seemingly unchangeable characteristics of the masses that make coercive authority absolutely necessary for a civilized society: "Just as one cannot dispense with coercion in the work of civilization [*Kulturarbeit*], one cannot dispense with domination of the mass by a minority; for the masses are lazy and without understanding, they do not love instinctual renunciation, are not to be convinced by argument of its inevitability, and their individuals strengthen one another in freely venting their licentiousness." *G.W.*, vol. 14, 328; *S.E.*, vol. 21, 7–8. See also note 158.

172. See, for example, *The Ego and the Id (Das Ich und das Es)*, *G.W.*, vol. 13, 264–66; *S.E.*, vol. 19, 36–38; and *The Future of an Illusion*, *G.W.*, vol. 14, 326–34; *S.E.*, vol. 21, 6–12.

173. *The Future of an Illusion*, *G.W.*, vol. 14, 326; *S.E.*, vol. 21, 6.

174. *The Future of an Illusion*, *G.W.*, vol. 14, 328; *S.E.*, vol. 21, 7.

175. "Human culture [*Kultur*]—I mean all that in which human

life has elevated itself above its animalistic conditions and distinguishes itself from the life of animals—I disdain separating culture [*Kultur*] and civilization [*Zivilisation*]." *G.W.*, vol. 14, 326; *S.E.*, vol. 21, 5–6. See also *Das Unbehagen in der Kultur* (translated in the *Standard Edition* as *Civilization and its Discontents*), *G.W.*, vol. 14, 448–49; *S.E.*, vol. 21, 89. In the *Standard Edition*, *Kultur* has been generally translated as 'civilization'. There are times, however, when a translation is not consistent and differences are implied; for example: "It is, of course, natural to assume that these difficulties are not inherent in the nature of civilization [*Kultur*] itself, but are determined by the imperfections of cultural forms [*Kulturformen*] which have so far been developed" (Strachey's translation). *S.E.*, vol. 21, 6.

176. *G.W.*, vol. 16, 197; *S.E.*, vol. 23, 90.

177. *G.W.*, vol. 16, 128; *S.E.*, vol. 23, 29–30.

178. *G.W.*, vol. 16, 198; *S.E.*, vol. 23, 91.

179. *G.W.*, vol. 16, 197; *S.E.*, vol. 23, 91. Freud does not seem to distinguish between *Judenhaß* and *Antisemitismus* (in English both terms are usually translated as 'antisemitism', although *Antisemitismus* is often referred to as 'modern antisemitism'); they are, for example, used interchangeably in the paragraph in which the last two quoted passages appear. The term *Antisemitismus* was apparently coined by Wilhelm Marr in 1879 to refer to his contemporary nonreligious prejudice. One of his most popular pamphlets, written in 1879, was "Der Sieg des Judentums über das Germanentum vom nicht konfessionellen Standpunkt aus betrachtet" ("The Conquest of Judaism over Germanism Regarded from a Nondenominational Perspective"), which considered the Jew as inherently materialistic and avaricious. *Judenhaß* is associated with an earlier prejudice against Jews, which is grounded in religious history and theology and legitimized by the Church; here, Jews who wished to reform themselves could accept Christ and convert. *Antisemitismus* is understood as a product of nineteenth- and twentieth-century bourgeois society in which, with emancipation, Jews were allowed relatively free rein in the economic and political spheres; Jews, now deemed inherently materialistic and exploitative or as radical socialists and revolutionaries, are perceived as a threat to Western culture. See, for example, Claussen, 7–46; Pulzer *The Rise of Political Anti-Semitism in Germany and Austria*, 47–57; Wistrich *The Jews of Vienna*, 33–37. Although Freud differs with the Church's reading of the significance of Christ and Christianity, his conception of antisemitism as having existed continuously from the advent of Christianity is essentially that of *Judenhaß*, not of *Antisemitismus*, which is best understood as a

development of a particular period, namely, nineteenth- and twentieth-century capitalism, industrialization, modernity, and a problematic emancipation. Yerushalmi, *Freud's Moses,* 50–53, raises issues about the connection Freud made between antisemitism and Christianity that seem to me fundamental and problematic, but does not then address the discrepancies in Freud's assessment of the differences between Judaism and Christianity and between Jews and Christians. Thus, for example, Yerushalmi writes of "the dialectic that Freud establishes between Judaism and Christianity, and the difference in his view of Judaism as a religion and the Jews as a people" and of the fact that antisemitism, for Freud, was "not incidental, but endemic to Christianity." But he does not indicate that (or why) Freud did not also distinguish between Christianity as a religion and the Christians as a people, which may account for Freud's identification of what he interpreted as Jung's antisemitism with being a Christian.

180. Rieff, chapter 6, "The Authority of the Past." Exploring Freud's psychological and cultural theory, Rieff is impressed by Freud's persistent interest in the "rehabilitation of constant nature" that underlies the history of the individual and society. "Thus, in Freud, change becomes constancy, history nature, development repetition . . . For Freud, the past that lives, that is so difficult to expunge, is that which is farthest from the present. It is the 'remotest of time' that is the 'really decisive factor' . . . His desire was always to find, in emergence, sameness; in the dynamic, the static; in the present, latent pasts" (215–16).

181. Of the Decalogue's ten commandments, eight legislate behavior by restricting what can be done. Only the fourth and the fifth command behavior that is not a negation (sanctification of the sabbath and honoring one's parents); yet even the fourth commands that no work be done on that day.

182. *G.W.,* vol. 16, 238; *S.E.,* vol. 23, 130.

183. *G.W.,* vol. 16, 197; *S.E.,* vol. 23, 91. See also P. C. Gordon Walker, "History and Psychology," *Sociological Review* 37 (1945): 37–48, who inquires into the historical relation (from the sixteenth century) of restriction and civilization, which may account for the preoccupation of psychoanalysis with self-control, internalization, and repression. In his introductory remarks, Walker notes that "Freud in nearly all his works assumes that there is no interval between modern man and primitive man—that psychoanalytic method might have been discovered at any time—that the psychic state of the individual has been for ages the same. Further, he always tends to lay stress on the isolated individual. He does not see that the essential problem is that at some recent stage the psychic state of modern man was *created* by historical factors—and that this radical transformation was essentially a social one" (37).

184. See Rieff 253–56 on inner freedom and individual freedom within the dynamics of a social context.

185. See note 106.

5. Word, Image, Idea

1. Willi Reich, *Schoenberg: A Critical Biography*, trans. Leo Black (New York: Praeger, 1971) 1.

2. H. H. Stückenschmidt, *Arnold Schoenberg: His Life, World and Work*, trans. Humphrey Searle (New York: Schirmer, 1977) 18.

3. Stückenschmidt 31.

4. Stückenschmidt 26; see also Pamela C. White, *Schoenberg and the God-Idea: The Opera "Moses und Aron"* (Ann Arbor: University of Michigan Research Press, 1985) 51–52.

5. Rozenblit, *The Jews of Vienna* 7.

6. Lucy S. Dawidowicz, "Arnold Schoenberg: A Search for Jewish Identity," *The Jewish Presence: Essays on Identity and History* (New York: Holt, Rinehart and Winston, 1977) 40.

7. White 53.

8. Dawidowicz 39.

9. Alexander L. Ringer, "Arnold Schoenberg and the Prophetic Image in Music," *Journal of the Arnold Schoenberg Institute* 1, no. 1 (1976): 30.

10. Arnold Schoenberg, "Moderner Psalm No. 9," *Moderne Psalmen* (Mainz: Schott's Söhne, 1956). Pages not numbered.

11. Arnold Schoenberg, letter to Wassily Kandinsky, 20 April 1923, *Ausgewählte Briefe*, ed. Erwin Stein (Mainz: B. Schott's Söhne, 1958) 90. Hereafter cited as *Briefe*; *Letters*, trans. Eithne Wilkins and Ernst Kaiser, ed. Erwin Stein (Berkeley: University of California Press, 1964) 88.

12. Letter to Wassily Kandinsky, 20 April 1923, *Briefe* 90; *Letters* 88.

13. Rürup, "Emancipation and Crisis" 19.

14. See Katz, *Emancipation and Assimilation* 8–9; also Rürup, "Jewish Emancipation" 84–86.

15. Letter to Wassily Kandinsky, 4 May 1923, *Briefe* 95; *Letters* 92–93.

16. Hans Keller, "Moses, Freud and Schoenberg—I," *The Monthly Musical Review* 88, no. 985 (1958): 15. The sequel to this, "Moses, Freud and Schoenberg—II," *The Monthly Musical Review* 88, no. 986 (1958): 63–67, was a disappointing attempt to show, on the basis of almost no textual evidence and with no consistent argument, that a "reasonable case could be made out for an *objective* identification

of Freud with Moses and of Schönberg with Moses, except that we don't know enough about Moses" (67).

17. Arnold Schönberg, DICH-33, ts., "Der Biblische Weg: Schauspiel in drei Akten," Arnold Schoenberg Institute, University of Southern California. In the typscript *Biblische* is capitalized.

18. Letter to Alban Berg, 16 October 1933, *Briefe* 200–201; *Letters* 184.

19. Arnold Schoenberg, "Vier Stücke für gemischten Chor" ("Four Pieces for Mixed Chorus"), op. 27.

20. "Der Biblische Weg" 24, 48, 57, 87, 101.

21. Letter to Max Reinhardt, H-48, ts.-Nachlass, Arnold Schoenberg Institute, University of Southern California, 10.

22. See letter to Anton Webern, 4 August 1933, quoted in Reich, *Schoenberg* 189–90.

23. Michael Mäckelmann, *Arnold Schönberg und das Judentum: Der Komponist und sein religiöses, nationales und politisches Selbstverständnis nach 1921* (Hamburg: Musikhandlung Wagner, 1984) 75, 98.

24. "Der Biblische Weg" 43–44; see Max Aruns' long speech to the public.

25. Arnold Schoenberg, "A Four-Point Program for Jewry," *Journal of the Arnold Schoenberg Institute* 3, no. 1 (1979): 53.

26. Schoenberg, "A Four-Point Program" 49.

27. "Der Biblische Weg" 87.

28. "Der Biblische Weg" 87. In an unpublished document written in English, Schoenberg identifies the primary characteristic of the statesman as complete devotion to his people: "A statesman has one ideal: His people; one ethics: His People; one thought: His People; one feeling: His People." "Two Fragments on Jewish Affairs," ms., Arnold Schoenberg Institute. Listed also as C. 62 in Josef Rufer, *Das Werk Arnold Schönberg* (Kassel: Bärenreiter, 1959) 151.

29. "Der Biblische Weg" 87–88.

30. "Der Biblische Weg" 88.

31. "Der Biblische Weg" 88–89.

32. "Der Biblische Weg" 24, 25, 96, 101, 102.

33. In *Moses and Monotheism,* because the repressed murder of Moses and the ensuing guilt account for his followers' obsessive adherence to Mosaic monotheism, the murder of Moses has psychological and historical significance. In "The Biblical Way," the death of Aruns fulfills the biblical prohibition that Moses not enter the promised land; Aruns' murder, it seems to me, emphasizes the significance of religious martyrdom.

34. "Der Biblische Weg" 96.

35. "Der Biblische Weg" 100.

36. "Der Biblische Weg" 102.

37. Schoenberg, "A Four-Point Program" 65. Schoenberg is in error when he says that the plan was rejected; it was in fact accepted on the first ballot, but by a very slim majority. The plan threatened to divide the Zionist movement, and was scuttled soon thereafter when the English expressed misgivings about the offer. Herzl died the following year of a heart condition, which some maintained was exacerbated by his struggles for a Jewish homeland.

38. Arnold Schoenberg, "Two Fragments on Jewish Affairs," ms., Arnold Schoenberg Institute, University of Southern California, 10–11; noted in Rufer, *Das Werk Arnold Schönbergs* 151 as C. 62.

39. Theodor Herzl, *The Jewish State: An Attempt at a Modern Solution to the Jewish Question* (New York: American Zionist Emergency Council, 1946) 133.

40. Arnold Schoenberg, "Moses und Aron: Oratorium," DICH-20, ts. Arnold Schoenberg Institute, University of Southern California.

41. See letter to Henry Allen Moe, General Secretary of the John Guggenheim Foundation, 22 January 1945, *Briefe* 243–45, in which Schoenberg applied for a grant to help complete *Moses and Aaron* and *Jacob's Ladder (Die Jakobsleiter)*.

42. René Leibowitz, "Das unmögliche Meisterwerk," *Österreichische Musikzeitschrift* 28 (1957): 217.

43. Letter to Franceso Siciliani, 27 November 1950, *Briefe* 295.

44. Letter to Hermann Scherchen, 29 June 1951, Stückenschmidt 519.

45. White 232.

46. Gertrud Schoenberg, note to act 3, libretto of *Moses and Aaron* accompanying recording, cond. Pierre Boulez, BBC Symphony Orchestra, Columbia Records M2 33594, 1975, 22.

47. Theodor W. Adorno, "Sakrales Fragment: Über Schönbergs *Moses und Aron*," in *Quasi Una Fantasia, Musikalische Schriften II* (Frankfurt am Main: Suhrkamp, 1963) 307.

48. Winfried Zillig, "Schönbergs *Moses und Aron*," *Melos, Zeitschrift für Neue Musik* 3, no. 24 (1957): 70.

49. George Steiner, "Schoenberg's *Moses and Aaron*," in *Language and Silence* (New York: Atheneum, 1967) 139.

50. Mäckelmann 189. See section "Zum dritten Akt" 167–90.

51. Daniel Albright, *Representation and the Imagination: Becket, Kafka, Nabokov, and Schoenberg* (Chicago: University of Chicago Press, 1981) 43–44. Albright presents a rather restricted, yet interesting read-

ing of the complex issues of the opera; he is largely concerned with the inadequacy of image and art to represent the divine and with this opera's attempt and failure to do just that. The failure at the end of act 2 is then, paradoxically, its success.

52. Monika Lichtenfeld, "Über Schoenbergs 'Moses und Aron,'" *Arnold Schoenberg: Gedankenausstellung 1974,* ed. Ernst Hilmar (Vienna: Universal Edition, 1974) 134.

53. Karl H. Wörner, *Schoenberg's 'Moses and Aaron'* trans. Paul Hamburger (London: Faber, 1963) 112. This volume contains the entire libretto in German with an English translation. Because the English version is problematic, I have translated all of the passages quoted here. References to this libretto will appear in parentheses in the text.

54. David Lewin, "*Moses und Aron:* Some General Remarks, and Analytic Notes for Act I, Scene 1," *Perspectives on Schoenberg and Stravinsky,* ed. Benjamin Boretz and Edward Cone (Westport, CT: Greenwood, 1972) 61, has noted that the "row" (the twelve tones) or the "musical idea" is "an abstraction that manifests itself everywhere" in the text and is thus well suited to the idea of a God that is an unrepresentable *(unvorstellbar)* presence that nevertheless demands to be represented *(vorgestellt)*.

55. Lewin 62–63; also see Michael Cherlin, "Schoenberg's Representation of the Divine in *Moses und Aron,*" *Journal of the Arnold Schoenberg Institute* 9.2 (1986): 210–13.

56. The opposition between divine idea and worldly or sensuous being—most often associated with Moses, on the one hand, and Aaron, on the other—is regarded by most critics to be the underlying theme of *Moses and Aaron.* For readings of the opera that depart from such polarization, see Lewin 60–64; White (note 57 below); and Hans Mayer, "Die Oper als Endspiel: *Moses und Aron,*" *Versuche über die Oper* (Frankfurt am Main: Suhrkamp, 1981) 208–11, whose views of the polarization between Moses and Aaron depart from those of other critics. He finds that Aaron's primary interest in the "Volk" coincides with God's proclamations at the opening of the opera, while Moses is concerned only for his own idea of a God as a "deus absconditus, who continually remains hidden." Mayer's view of Moses' tendency to "tyranny" and "terroristic ecstasy" (210–11) is the result of a provocative reading that does not account for significant portions of the text, including the episode of the golden calf.

57. White 110 misunderstands the significance of the wilderness. She writes that the wilderness "represents a state of mind, that of the renunciation of the truth of God, desolation due to a separation from

God," whereas Schoenberg's text states that the wilderness is associated with "purity of thought [that] will nourish, sustain and develop you" (150) and with liberation, with "freedom from craving" (202–4).

58. Letter to Walter Eidlitz, 15 March 1933, *Briefe* 188; *Letters* 172. The ordering of these elements—God, people, leader—suggests the importance of the people, an idea substantiated by the text, particularly its conclusion. Too many interpretations overlook their significance. For example, since Albright 38–44 is fundamentally interested in the aesthetics of representation and not of communication, he ignores the people and dismisses act 3 as unnecessary. Lewin, however, notes the prominence of the "Volk" in the opera; and his summary of the dramatic relationships, for example, coincides with the order in the Eidlitz letter noted above: "God loves the Volk (more than He loves Moses, as we gather from Act I, Scene 1) but cannot communicate with them directly" (162). See also Mayer 209–11.

59. It is clear from a number of Schoenberg's statements that he thought it appropriate, even necessary, to adapt biblical texts for his own contemporary purposes. See his letter to Richard Dehmel, 13 December 1912, *Briefe* 31; *Letters* 35–36: "For those in the Bible quarrel with God, express themselves also as people of their time, speak of their affairs, maintain their social and spiritual level. Therefore, they are artistically strong, but nevertheless cannot be composed by a contemporary musician who fulfills his task"; also an April 1951 unpublished letter to his friend, Dr. G. Wolfsohn, quoted in Peter Gradenwitz, "The Religious Works of Arnold Schönberg," *The Music Review* 21.1 (1960): 19: "But I believe that the forms of the ancient Biblical language are no more convincing in our present use of language. One has to talk to the people of our time in our own style and of our own problems."

60. When God informs Moses that Aaron will assist him, he does not refer to them as brothers; and their first interchange, which notes the differences in character, implies that they are siblings, but leaves open a doubt. Aaron says to Moses, "You son of my fathers, / did the great God send you?", to which Moses replies: "You son of my father, brother in spirit, / through whom the unique One wants to speak" (116). For Aaron they are brothers because they share the same forefathers, while in Moses' response the "father" is ambiguous, possibly referring to the birth father, but more likely to God the father. Even when Aaron calls Moses "My brother" (118), it is not clear whether he is speaking literally or metaphorically.

61. An interesting parallel between Moses' loneliness and the condition of contemporary society and art is discussed in Adorno 318–20. He speaks of the collectivization of the "atomized" individuals

("Vereinzelte") and the loneliness that arises in the late phase of individualistic society. These are expressed in Expressionist art as well as in Schoenberg's music and are associated with transcendence: "The shrill expressionistic visions of solitude . . . are already at the same time phantasms of transcendence; the figures, developed into spirits, resemble frightening messengers from beyond" (320).

62. Letter to Walter Eidlitz, 15 March 1933, *Briefe* 188; *Letters* 172. It is clear from this letter that Schoenberg was puzzled by two instances in the Bible that seemed to him almost incomprehensibly contradictory: in Exodus 17:1–7 Moses is told to smite the rock, and in Numbers 20:1–13 he is told to speak to the rock, but smites it instead. Schoenberg indicates that he has been revising act 3 for the fourth time; and while he does not need to resolve the contradiction for his own work, he is nonetheless troubled by it.

63. Adorno 312 cites Schoenberg's interest in the Decalogue's prohibition of images *(Bilderverbot)*, but also notes that music "is the imageless art and excluded from that prohibition; that is indeed the key to the relationship of music and Judaism . . . Schoenberg must have involuntarily, with inscrutable irony, wanted to pay tribute to [the prohibition of images]."

64. Letter to Josef Rufer, 13 June 1951, *Briefe* 298; *Letters* 288.

65. Adorno 315–16; see also Steiner 139 and Mäckelmann 169–70.

66. Schoenberg, H-48, ts., Arnold Schoenberg Institute. See also Mäckelmann 227–28; for an English translation see Stückenschmidt 541–42.

Acknowledgments

This book took shape over a number of years, and I am certain that my indebtedness surpasses my ability to remember all of the people who provided important contributions. There were those who responded with valuable insights and questions to papers I gave on related subjects at the World Congress for Jewish Studies in Jerusalem and at a conference on Kafka at the University of Southern California. There is the help of a number of research assistants, whose remuneration could not begin to compensate them for the invaluable work they did. Rosemary Delia, Judith Hilman, and Gail Wise tracked down documents that were difficult to find, checked references, and made many useful suggestions. Others made available their expertise: Linda von Hoene brought her knowledge of Freud; Larry Vaughan, an excellent grasp of German history; and Eric Zakim, a comprehensive knowledge of Schoenberg's work.

There were discussions with friends and colleagues that changed and refined my ideas and my perspective. Comments by my University of California, Berkeley, colleagues Robert Alter and Robert Holub, who read portions of the manuscript, were critical, helpful, and supportive. Discussions with Ilana Pardes, now at Hebrew University, Jerusalem, went on for a number of months; and although we had differences of opinion, her insights into the Bible and Freud's work were very informative and helped me to clarify my own views. I am grateful also for the permission to cite her unpublished essay, "You Name It." If my colleague Chana Kronfeld were only the friend she has been for many years now, I would not be able to find the words to express my deep gratitude for her care and consideration—Brecht called it "Freundlichkeit," a rare combination of friendship and humanity. But having read and reread portions of this work, she continuously challenged the ideas, the arguments, and the methodology in ways that caused me to redefine and reshape my thinking. For all that I cannot thank her enough.

The University of California supported my project with research funds and a sabbatical leave that allowed me to complete it. Permission for all of the citations from Schoenberg's works was granted by Belmont Music Publishers, Pacific Palisades, California.

While working on this study of Moses figures in German and Austrian letters, a long-forgotten conversation came to mind. When I was still in graduate school my mother phoned to ask whether I would be interested in a set of Nietzsche's works in German; a neighbor wanted to dispose of the volumes, which dated from the early years of this century. My mother had never heard of Nietzsche and wanted to know who he was. She was an immigrant from a small Eastern European village who was generally unschooled in elite Western culture, and a very large part of her family—parents, her siblings and their children, many relatives—had been murdered by the Nazis. I explained that Nietzsche was a very important nineteenth-century German philosopher; but she could not hear about "good" Germans or "important" German thinkers. Clearly disappointed with my response, she continued to pursue the issue of Nietzsche's value: Was he really a good philosopher? Just how good a philosopher was he? When I repeated my earlier assessment, she had one more question, and in her voice I now detected anger and irritation as well as a certain amount of desperation. She asked: Was this

Nietzsche as good as Moyshe Rabeynu? "Moyshe Rabeynu," Moses our teacher, was how Yiddish-speaking Jews referred to Moses. I had no answer. Though both touching and amusing, the comparison seemed to me largely idiosyncratic.

Later, when reflecting on the interest in Moses and Mosaic tradition of the four writers with whom this study is concerned, it occurred to me that my mother's remark may not have been as idiosyncratic as I had originally thought. There was perhaps more to our conversation than I had once perceived. Like many impoverished immigrants, my mother had lionized Western culture and wanted her daughter to partake of all its benefits. In the aftermath of World War II, however, feeling increasingly insecure and marginalized as a Jew in the dominant Western society, she began to embrace once again the minority Jewish culture that had steadily receded since her arrival in America in 1914. Her final question about Nietzsche suggests that, for her, there was no Jewish figure more fundamental than Moses. He had become the standard by which Western thinkers should be evaluated.

Acculturated Jews might be expected to inquire whether Jewish philosophers compare favorably with Western thinkers, but few would consider philosophers in the Jewish tradition such as Maimonides or Franz Rosenzweig as appropriate standards for judging, let us say, Kant or Heidegger. Yet Heine, Kafka, Freud, and Schoenberg—all marginal Jews who, for the most part and for most of their lives, strove for acceptance among the European intelligentsia—turned to the Mosaic tradition in texts that explored their own world and culture. Decades after his conversion to Christianity, Heine even called upon "Moses, our teacher, Moshe Rabenu [the Hebrew designation], noble opponent of servitude," to eradicate the servility of Germans.

As Jews in a period of flawed emancipation and troubled assimilation, these Jewish thinkers shared a common experience of prejudice and persecution; it is this experience that their writings about Moses reveal. All of these writers show a problematic concern with origins, which arose when their allegiance to dominant cultural values and practices were called into question and they were moved to seek alternatives in an often more tenuous personal alliance with Jewish tradition. As complex responses to adverse social and political conditions, the texts explored in this book articulate, within the discourse of the dominant culture, despair about the unfulfilled promises of equal social opportunity or, within the discourse of Jewish tradition, an alternative positive paradigm of freedom and identity. More often they articulate both: a continuing, albeit disillusioned, commitment to European culture *and* a return to Jewish heritage. The inscription of these texts about Moses, which are rooted in Jewish tradition, into the dominant as well as the minority culture secured their place among canonized German and Austrian cultural documents and thereby gained a forum for voices in opposition to social injustice and oppression; but it also recorded in the annals of Jewish history the difficult experience of life in the diaspora and, wittingly or not, revived and preserved the biblical story of national liberation.

Index

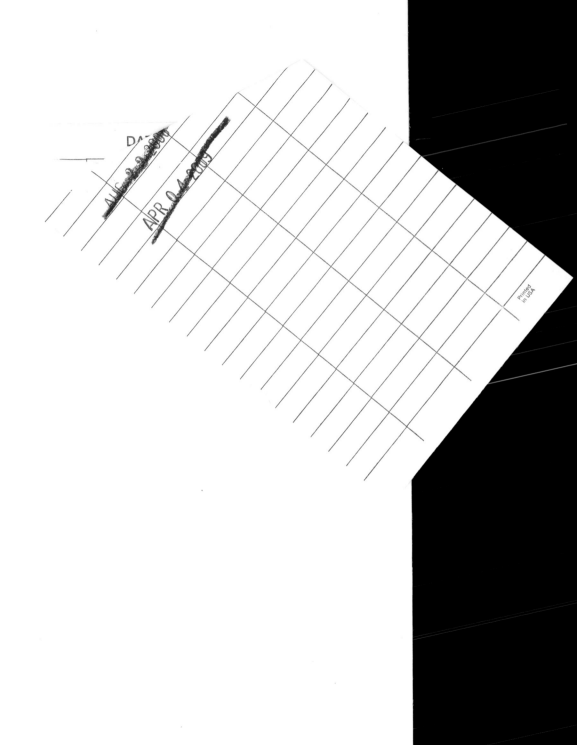

DATE

AUG 0 9 2000

APR 0 4 2003

Printed
in USA